THE Anatomy of Foodservice Design 2

CHARLES WOOD, P. E.
ELDOR A. KLUGE
PATRICIA D. ASMUSSEN, and SHERMAN ROBINSON
PHILIP GOLDEN
JOHN C. CINI and WILLIAM V. EATON

Jule Wilkinson, Editor

CBI PUBLISHING COMPANY, INC.
51 Sleeper Street, Boston, Massachusetts 02210

Acknowledgements

Collecting the material that is used to illustrate the various chapters in this book has taken a good deal of time and the cooperation of many people. Special appreciation goes to the many industry experts who have served as judges of the *Institutions/VF Magazine* Award Program entries over the years; to the several *Institutions/VF Magazine* editors who, under the direction of Jane Y. Wallace, editor, have been associated with these programs while this book has been underway, and to Russ Carpenter, editorial director, *Foodservice Equipment Dealer,* for the use of several of his analyses of foodservice design solutions, originally printed in that magazine, and for his invaluable assistance in the planning and editing of portions of this volume.

Jule Wilkinson, Editor

Library of Congress Cataloging in Publication Data   (Revised)
Main entry under title:

The Anatomy of foodservice design.

Includes bibliographical references and indexes.
1. Food service management.   I. Buchanan, Robert D.
II. Wilkinson, Jule.
TX943.A5   642'.5   75–5730
ISBN 0-8436-0569-3

ISBN 0-8436-2173-7
Printed in the United States of America

Contents

Text for all pictures, Jule Wilkinson

List of Figures

List of Tables

History of Institutions/VF Magazine Award Programs

The need in the foodservice/lodging industry for benchmarks to be used in evaluating foodservice and interior design was recognized many years ago. To answer the need INSTI-TUTIONS/VF Magazine launched two award programs: The Foodservice Award Program and The Interior Design Program.

The Foodservice Award Program was designed to honor operators who recognized that sound planning would increase productivity and that innovative solutions and flexibility were essential to continuing success in foodservice operation.

The Interior Design Award Program was initiated to honor the operations that complement their good food and service with exceptional surroundings.

Panels of highly qualified experts review entries individually. Each aspect of the material submitted is carefully scrutinized and evaluated. In Foodservice Award entries, judges check on such factors as the efficiency of the use of space, equipment, energy, and employee input; indications of good employee morale; marketing techniques that accurately profile patrons. In Interior Design Award entries, judges determine how well form and function relate; how the design selected enhances the operation; whether the elements combined in the interiors attract a predetermined clientele.

Not only does such careful critiquing honor individual operations, it offers an added value. Those ideas that are rated exceptional are disseminated to the entire industry through Institutions/VF Magazine, Restaurant Equipment Dealer, and through CBI Publishing Company.

Many of the floor plans and illustrations presented in this book come from operations that have participated in the Foodservice Award program in recent years. For many years, these entries have been an invaluable source of statistics and data which are then made available to qualified operators and designers seeking to solve problems in foodservice. The descriptive material that accompanies the plan and picture sections of this book is a further important use of Foodservice Award entries.

Operators of foodservice/lodging establishments interested in submitting entries can get full details on entering either of the programs—The Foodservice Award Program or The Interior Design Award Program—from the Awards Program Director, Institutions/VF Magazine, 5 S. Wabash, Chicago, 60603.

About the Authors

The author of each section of Anatomy of Foodservice Design, Volume 2, was selected for his/her special knowledge of the segment to be discussed. Each author has had extensive experience with a variety of operations in his/her assigned category and consequently can offer field-tested recommendations and solutions to the particular design problems that may be encountered. The authors are listed in the order in which their work appears in the book.

Foreword
    HARRY MULLIKIN, President, Western International Hotels
Specialty Restaurant
    CHARLES WOOD, P.E., Vice President, Group One, Inc.
Hospital
    ELDOR A. KLUGE, Matthei & Colin, Architect-Engineers
Day Care Center
    PATRICIA D. ASMUSSEN, R.D., M.S., Then Nutrition Director, Division of Maternal and Child Health, Indiana State
    Board of Health
    SHERMAN ROBINSON, Sherman Robinson, Inc.
Foodservice for the Elderly
    PHILIP GOLDEN, Consultants Collaborative, Inc.
Public Cafeteria
    JOHN C. CINI, ISFSC, FFCS and
    WILLIAM V. EATON, FFCS, both Cini Grissom Associates, Inc.
Hotel/Motel
    JULE WILKINSON, editor

FOREWORD
A Management View of Design

Harry Mullikin

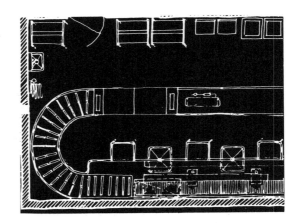

THE FOODSERVICE/LODGING industry—in its many guises—is perhaps one of the largest factors in the economic and social structure of any nation. It is an industry representing the investment of many billions of dollars in facilities and equipment. It is an industry affording employment to hundreds of thousands of men and women. Most important, it is an industry serving millions of people each day.

The foodservice industry also faces the challenge of change, the constant pressures of spiraling capital and operating costs, and the unceasing demand of the marketplace for quality and value.

From the viewpoint of the operator, the final assessment of foodservice design must be in terms of the design's contribution to employee productivity, to the quality of the product and, above all, to the satisfaction of the customer.

Profit is the lifeblood of any enterprise, and the foodservice/lodging industry is no exception. Profit is also a product of customer satisfaction, employee performance, and the maximum efficiencies achieved through competent facility design.

Those of us who are involved on a day-to-day basis in the preparation and serving of food are keenly aware of the ever-increasing capital demands for facilities and equipment. We are very much concerned with labor costs and the vital need to improve productivity at every work station. Finally, and most important, we are conscious of our obligation to the customers to provide the quality and value to which they are rightfully entitled.

Because so much of the result is dependent on the initial facility design and equipment specification, this two volume series addressing itself to the Anatomy of Foodservice Design is a milestone for our industry, a much needed and long awaited resource providing foodservice/lodging operations with a wealth of information and an exciting collection of new and innovative concepts of profit potential.

Volume 2 directs its attention to the management requirements of the lodging industry with its multi-billion dollar investment in foodservice facilities as well as covering other major foodservice concepts ranging from restaurants and cafeterias to hospitals, foodservice for the elderly, and day care centers.

Underscoring the significance of this volume is the expertise of its contributors, all of whom enjoy well-deserved recognition for their technical competence, their long experience, and their many contributions to a demanding profession.

Knowledge of design factors of particular importance to operating management has been revealed by all of the contributors in their efforts to provide design answers to management's concerns as to capital commitments and productivity factors. By the same token, a common thread is apparent in that designers, in setting forth their concepts, constantly reemphasize the need for management to commit time and involvement in the identification of facility and equipment criteria to assure that the designers are aware of all aspects of the desired operation.

Each designer has paid particular attention to innovative approaches that will stimulate employee productivity through improved working conditions, preparation flows that reduce physical effort, at-hand availability of equipment and utensils, and maximum utilization of work-saving devices. Yet each contributor has kept in mind the basic goal of design: satisfaction of the market's desire for quality of product.

Since it is an axiom of management that success is the result of proper planning, Volume 2 offers to foodservice operators many, many keys to improved facility planning, planning that will ultimately reflect itself in bottom-line contributions.

The time operators spend in carefully reading each of the chapters in this volume will pay dividends in the future. All of us are constantly involved in assessing new foodservice opportunities or in the improvement of existing facilities. Within these pages are hundreds of concepts which can readily be adapted to specific operating situations or can provide a new insight to operations concepts leading to wiser investment of capital funds and to the visible improvement of employee performance and morale with resulting customer satisfaction.

May I, on behalf of the thousands of men and women charged with management responsibilities in fooderservice, express our thanks to the publisher, the editor, and to the contributors for making available to our industry a most significant presentation.

From the pages of these two volumes the foodservice/lodging industry will reap the rewards of sound planning reflected in employee contribution, ever-improving levels of product quality, service and customer satisfaction, and expert help in achieving the ultimate goal: improved profitability.

Harry Mullikin, President
Western International Hotels

Specialty Restaurant

Charles Wood, P.E.

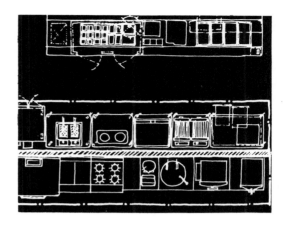

THE TERM "SPECIALTY RESTAURANT" has become part of the trade language of the mass feeding industry. Webster defines the word "special" this way:

(1.) *uncommon, noteworthy;* (2.) *individual, unique;* (3.) *particularly favored;* (4.) *extra, additional;* (5.) *confined to or designed for a definite field of action, purpose or occasion.*

These definitions or combination of definitions open infinite category possibilities for the commonly-used phrase, "Specialty Restaurants."

Ethnic restaurants, in a broad scope of international cuisines, represent the most popular category of Specialty Restaurants.

Specialty Restaurants in the ethnic mode are an American heritage. The variety of races that colonized the American continent made this a natural birthplace for specialized restaurant keepers. Immigrants of various nationalities and cultures were introduced to food and dining customs that added a pleasurable new dimension to their eating habits.

This transplanting process has continued through the twentieth century throughout most of the world. The major American hotel and restaurant chains have contributed to the development by introducing their own brand of specialty restaurants around the globe. For example, a charcoal-broiled steak restaurant, which is common in Chicago, has been proved by Hilton (Berlin Hilton) to be a special and unique concept in Germany.

American foodservice specialists, who have had the opportunity to develop, design, or manage a restaurant in a country foreign to them, discover very quickly that inventive ingenuity is not the exclusive product of any one country or continent. The development of foodservice methods and equipment, consequently, has become export as well as import commodities.

Other Types of Specialty

Specialty Restaurants are not confined only to the ethnic classification. A restaurant can be special because of a natural or a man-made environment. "Pier Four Restaurant" with its panoramic view of the harbor would lose one of its unique characteristics if it were located in downtown Boston.

Restaurants can become "special" because they attract celebrities, or are particularly favored by various business groups such as bankers, journalists, lawyers, and so on. These restaurants earn their recognition as special because they generally offer something additional which can range from a congenial atmosphere, to consistent food quality, to featuring king-size martinis.

The author wishes to credit and express appreciation for their assistance in the preparation of portions of the material in this chapter to: Charles Hamburg, Chairman of The Hotel/Motel Food Service Management Course, Bunker Hill Community College, Charlestown, Mass.; and Paul C. Bonanno, I.B.D., Vice President, Group One Inc., Boston.

FAMILY RESTAURANTS

Every community in this country and throughout the world is represented with restaurants that concentrate on the family market. The ongoing increase in leisure time and often income for many families should be an added incentive to family restaurant operators to further develop this very important market requirement.

But in spite of this enormous demand for quality family restaurants, the majority of restaurants throughout our cities and towns are merely surviving, rather than prospering. Yet, there is a market that is "starving" for better quality, service, atmosphere, and understanding.

Restaurants with the proper management technique and operating formula will eventually dominate this market because they are continually surveying their family group customers to determine who they are and what they want.

The results—whether from professional surveys or informal inquiries—indicate clearly that tasty, wholesome food and an appealing menu range are no longer enough to guarantee a restaurant's success. The difference between a "run of the mill" restaurant and a successful family restaurant cannot be defined in any singular operating detail.

The key, instead, is the development of a comprehensive formula, tailored to satisfy the needs of a specific market area. It is important to note that these needs may vary

Please take a moment to complete the questions below. Your replies will be a great help to us in providing food and service as you like it. Give your card to the hostess.

Fairfield Inn ☐   KING'S WHARF ☐
LA. PLAZA ☐   CAPRICCIO ☐
THE HANGAR ☐

Server's Name _____

My food was
☐ Excellent   ☐ Good   ☐ Fair   ☐ Poor

My drinks were
☐ Excellent   ☐ Good   ☐ Fair   ☐ Poor

Comments _____

Service was   ☐ Excellent   ☐ Prompt   ☐ Slow

The attitude was   ☐ Courteous   ☐ Unfriendly

Would you dine with us again?   ☐ Yes   ☐ No

Are you staying in the Hotel and/or attending a meeting?
☐ Yes   ☐ No

MAY WE HAVE YOUR NAME AND ADDRESS:

Name _____
Address _____
City _____
State _____ Zip Code _____
Date _____
THANK YOU VERY MUCH   718

FIG. 1—PATRON CRITERIA QUESTION-NAIRES

TO OUR GUESTS: In the interest of maintaining and improving our high standards of food and service, we would appreciate your comments and suggestions. Please fill in this card and mail it to us at your convenience. Thank you. *Howard B Johnson*

Restaurant Location: _____
Street or Highway   City   State

Date: _____ Time: _____ Johnson Girl's Name (or No.:) _____

	Excellent	Satisfactory	Unsatisfactory
Food Quality:	☐	☐	☐
Promptness of Service:	☐	☐	☐
Courtesy of Service:	☐	☐	☐
Restaurant Cleanliness:	☐	☐	☐
Rest Room Cleanliness:	☐	☐	☐

Additional Comments / Suggestions _____
_____
_____

If you wish you may sign your name:

Name: _____   Address: _____

dramatically from one community to another, depending on such factors as average family income, age, occupations, and social habits.

Patrons of family restaurants are usually willing to offer comments or suggestions, oral or written, if the operator is interested enough to ask any of the following questions:

"What did you think of our service?"

"Do you like our menu?"

"Do you have any questions concerning our operation?"

"Do you like the atmosphere?"

"Do you have any suggestions that we can apply to make your next visit more enjoyable?"

Two examples of a penetrating, yet diplomatic, technique for doing this are shown in Figure 1.

Many of the restaurant operators that I interviewed during the preparation of this text readily admit they learn something new about their business every day. Answers to the above questions might, for example, indicate the need for:

providing children's high chairs

developing a children's menu

designing a colorful dessert menu that would appeal to children

promoting bulk wine service

separating the bar/lounge from the main restaurant

featuring an open salad bar

engaging live lounge entertainment

making a vestibule for the doors leading to the kitchen

purchasing a dessert wagon

capitalizing on a Sunday morning brunch

improving or rearranging the parking facilities

improving air conditioning or heat control and distribution

establishing a direct mailing list promoting holiday menus

engaging an interior designer and decorator to upgrade, or to develop a concept and atmosphere in the public spaces

engaging a food facilities planner to improve the organization and implementation of the kitchen

The objective of a family restaurant operator should not be confined to the single task of satisfying an appetite. A more challenging and rewarding responsibility is to create a physical atmosphere and employee attitudes that simply make patrons and their families happy.

The Specialty Restaurant field represents a continuing challenge to a designer's ingenuity, not only to create new concepts but to make an intensive effort to overcome the inadequacies that take place in current food-service operation, planning, and design.

The following sections are concerned with defining some of the features that make restaurants special, and delineating the design disciplines that are common to all specialty restaurants.

DEVELOPMENT

Food Facilities Engineers specialize in planning mass feeding installations. They base their plans on factual operating and mechanical criteria information. Figure 2, (p. 4), illustrates a functional Operational Criteria Checklist and Figure 3, (p. 5), a Mechanical Criteria Checklist.

The information these Checklists help to develop is common to specialty restaurants and insures design conformity with the mechanical and operating characteristics of the project.

Specialty Restaurant designs, furthermore, require the development of a Concept Criteria to supplement the Operation and Mechanical Criteria information. There are no standard checklist forms that can be used to establish the concept criteria because innovative features that may apply to one design may be inconsistent with another.

There are basic research factors that are common to the development of any proposed Specialty Restaurant. Engaging professional accounting, architectural, engineering, interior design, decorating, landscaping, and food facility design firms should be considered an essential investment. The cost of professional counseling generally reflects a savings in the overall construction and operating costs.

Building a Specialty Restaurant (or any restaurant) has always been considered a high risk investment by the banking community. Loan agencies generally require that restaurant construction proposals be accompanied

FIG. 2—OPERATIONAL CRITERIA CHECKLIST FOR FOODSERVICE

OPERATIONAL CRITERIA CHECKLIST FOR FOOD SERVICE

Project _____ Date _____
_____ Job No. _____

Copy _____

Food and/or Beverage Rooms

type	no. seats service	menu information
A.		
B.		
C.		
D.		
E.		
F.		
G.		

1. Butcher Shop   yes ☐   no ☐
2. Bake Shop   yes ☐   no ☐
3. Pastry Shop   yes ☐   no ☐
4. Room Service   yes ☐   no ☐
5. Employee Cafeteria   yes ☐   no ☐
6. Need for Food Checker   yes ☐   no ☐
7. Kitchen Service Bar (liquor)   yes ☐   no ☐
8. Chef's Office   yes ☐   no ☐
9. Silver Burnishing   yes ☐   no ☐
10. Special Provisions ? (sea food)   yes ☐   no ☐
11. Dairy Products -- available   yes ☐   no ☐
12. Draft Beer Dispensing   yes ☐   no ☐
13. Wine Service   yes ☐   no ☐
14. Ice Cream   make ☐   buy ☐
15. Ice Capacities   cubes ____ # flakes ____ #
16. Attach Market Food Survey (if available)
17. Food Deliveries   good ☐   fair ☐   poor ☐
18. Any Special Liquor Restrictions   yes ☐   no ☐
    - Comment _____
19. Attach Info on Labor Market (if available)
20. Public Area Cooking/Prep.   yes ☐   no ☐
    - Specify Type _____
21. Convenience Foods - use -   yes ☐   no ☐
    - comment _____

Remarks:

GROUP ONE INCORPORATED
21 W. THIRD STREET, BOSTON, MASS. 02127
TEL. (617) 268-7000   CABLE: GROUPONE

Information Furnished
By _____
Date _____

FIG. 3—MECHANICAL CRITERIA CHECKLIST FOR FOODSERVICE

MECHANICAL CRITERIA CHECKLIST FOR FOOD SERVICE

Project _____ Date _____

_____ Job No. _____

_____

_____

Copy _____

No.	Item
1.	Prime Cooking Fuel Gas ☐ Electric ☐
2.	Electric ___ / ___ volts ___ phase ___ cycle ___
3.	Gas yes ☐ no ☐ type _____
4.	Steam yes ☐ no ☐ pressure _____
5.	Cooling Tower yes ☐ no ☐
6.	Refrigeration air cooled ☐ water cooled ☐
7.	Hot Water temperature ___ °F or ___ °C
8.	Comments on any unusual mechanical characteristics ___
9.	Fire Extng. Equip. CO_2 ☐ steam ☐ dry chemicals ☐
10.	Garbage Disposals yes ☐ no ☐
11.	Garbage Refrigerator yes ☐ no ☐
12.	Incinerator yes ☐ no ☐
13.	Compactor yes ☐ no ☐
14.	Bottles store ☐ crush ☐ dispose ☐
15.	Construction of walls ___ Clg. ___ Flr. ___
16.	Ceiling Ht. ___ feet ___ inches
17.	Elevator Size ___ wide ___ depth
18.	Approving local authorities ___
19.	Architect ___ Phone ___ Address ___
20.	Engineer ___ Phone ___ Address ___
21.	General Status of Project on Date of This Questionnaire ___

Remarks

Information Furnished
By ___
Date ___

GROUP ONE INCORPORATED
21 W. THIRD STREET, BOSTON, MASS. 02127
TEL. (617) 268-7000   CABLE: GROUPONE

by a feasibility report prepared by a professional accounting firm which specializes in preparing market surveys, site appraisals, estimated construction costs, operating costs, and a general forecasting of a proposed restaurant's success or failure.

The "technical task force" of architects, engineers, interior designers, decorators, and food facilities planners who specialize in restaurant planning all make a vital contribution to a Specialty Restaurant project. It is essential that their inputs be coordinated and a tight communication be established among the team of planners throughout the design and construction phases of the project.

The design and construction phases of a Specialty Restaurant should be used to good advantage by the operating management team. Long before a restaurant is scheduled to open, the operating managers should be developing an operating formula consisting of:

Menus and cost
Food and beverage cost and deliveries
Staff requirements, including job descriptions
Staff training
Payroll cost
Sanitation programs
Maintenance programs
Inventory requirements
Garbage and trash handling
Familiarization with local laws
Advertising and promotion
Utility rates
Control procedures
Hours of operation
Public relations
Laundry costs

The ingredients of good design should not be considered a guarantee of a Specialty Restaurant's success. The "success stories" of all Specialty Restaurants consistently depend on the excellence of management.

DESIGN

Human Senses

We obviously associate the sense of taste with restaurants. The designer of a specialty restaurant must implement his planning to satisfy all of the other human senses as well.

Let's consider some significant samples of how our other four senses (sound, sight, smell, and touch) affect the designer's planning details. Taken together, these constitute a partial checklist of general design criteria.

Sense of Sound

The noise level of any dining room is an important factor affecting guest comfort. If background music is used, special attention should be given to the installation of the background music sound system to insure the creation of a subtle sound rather than a noisy distraction.

Construction material and interior furnishings, such as ceilings, canopies, wall coverings, draperies, and carpeting, have a major bearing on achieving the proper sound level and should be selected on the basis of their acoustical as well as aesthetic value.

Something commonly overlooked is the noise and clatter generated from the kitchen and service areas. It is essential that service doors leading to kitchens be vestibuled to baffle the noise level emanating from the kitchen. To achieve the optimum in noise absorption, the vestibule should be constructed of a high density acoustic material.

There are many layout variations in designing kitchen service door vestibules. Some of the most commonly used are illustrated in figures 4 through 8.

Here are a number of recommendations and suggestions for the elimination or reduction of restaurant noises:

1. Mechanical equipment, such as furnaces, combustion units, pumps, air conditioners, and compressors, should be selected with consideration for their noise output.

2. Intake and exhaust fans should be specified on the basis of sound output and should be mounted on vibration isolators and connected to ductwork by canvas sleeves.

3. Ice machines should be selected for quiet operation.

4. Dishwasher noise may be minimized by regulating steam pressure and by using vibration isolators.

5. Water hammer can be eliminated by lowering operating pressures and/or by adding a small snubber.

FIG. 4—DOUBLE DOOR VESTIBULE

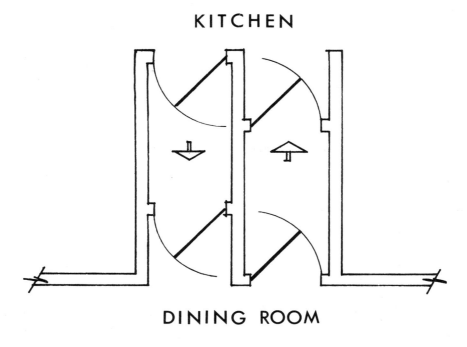

This illustrates a double door in each "in" and "out" door vestibule corridor. The double door design provides maximum sound baffling. This design application requires an area of approximately 80 sq. ft.

FIG. 5—SINGLE "IN"—"OUT" DOOR VESTIBULE

Illustrates a single door for each "in" and "out" door vestibule corridor. The single door design is less effective than the double door but is more commonly used because this design application consumes approximately 32 sq. ft. which represents a space savings of 48 sq. ft. over Figure 4.

6. Portable equipment noise can be reduced or eliminated by specifying proper casters and installing rubber bumpers.

7. Metal sinks, work tables, and dish-tables should be treated with an undercoating of a sound deadening mastic.

8. Cabinet doors and drawers should be equipped with silent closing devices.

9. Voice-paging equipment can be made less annoying through operational procedures, as adjusting sound levels and selective use.

10 Silencers should be specified for lavatories.

11. Kitchen walls adjacent to the dining room should be double partitioned or sound insulated.

FIG. 6—T-SHAPED VESTIBULE

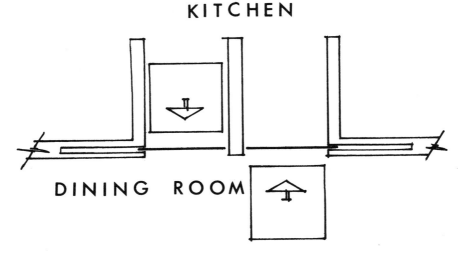

KITCHEN

DINING ROOM

Illustrates a "T"-shaped vestibule that baffles both light and sound from the kitchen. This layout regulates the directional flow of both the "in" and "out" traffic. It is essential that the kitchen layout be organized accordingly.

FIG. 7—VESTIBULE WITH AUTOMATIC DOORS

KITCHEN

DINING ROOM

Automatic doors, either sliding or hinged, are activated by floor walk-on pads (shown) or photo-electric cells. The additional cost of this application is worthy of consideration and allows the waiters, waitresses, or bus boys to concentrate all of their manual efforts on conveying both food and soiled bussing trays. The additional initial installation cost

is offset in the savings realized in breakage. Breakage is both costly and hazardous; a crashing tray may well be enough annoyance to discourage a guest from making a return visit.

The operating mechanisms of automatic doors must insure that they operate quietly with a minimum amount of maintenance attention.

FIG. 8—VESTIBULE WITH SERVICE STAND

KITCHEN

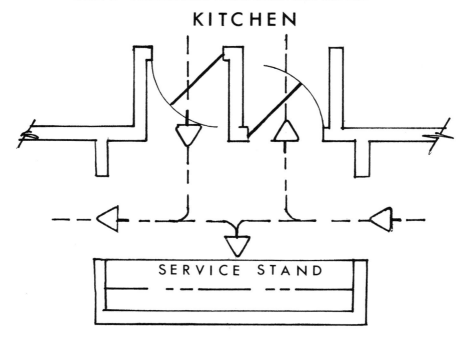

DINING ROOM

Illustrates a design application similar to Figures 5 and 6 except for the addition of a waitress service stand that can be implemented with waitress self-service items, such as beverage, rolls, desserts, etc. In some installations, the service stand can be designed into a checker's station.

The screening or wall at the service stand serves as an additional light and noise barrier. It is important that the service stand not include equipment that will create a distracting noise factor. Ice machines, refrigeration compressors, and other mechanical equipment should be specified for quiet operation.

Sense of Sight

The visual aspects of the public space areas of a specialty restaurant should establish a mood the moment the guest crosses the threshold. The interior designer's responsibility is to develop an atmosphere that has an immediately favorable visual impact.

Since the restaurant is "special," it should manifest a specific identity with design characteristics which will enhance the concept. Such an overall visual effect requires careful attention to well defined objectives and operating criteria. It is essential that the interior design be developed with close reference to certain key requirements. Here is a partial checklist:

Market description
Clientele anticipated
Menu and liquor service
Theme and/or name
Number of seats (with reference to local code)
Type of seating (flexibility of service)
Entertainment (type)
Breakfast—Lunch—Dinner service
Anticipated check average
Type of service
Service stand requirements
Hostess stand requirements
Cashier requirements/controls
Audio requirements/paging
Lighting (dimmers)
Budget considerations
Type of flooring
Type of ceiling
Take-out service
Merchandising (type)
Uniforms (style)
Furnishings (durability)

China, glass, silver patterns
Dining room service circulation
Wall treatments (durability)
Application of artifacts
Signage and logos
Split-levels and treatment
Interior window treatment
Acoustics
Climate
Mechanical interfacing, i.e., air conditioning
Maintenance (replacement)
Future expansion
Multi-purpose use
Lavatory requirements (handicapped requirements)
Fire Prevention Code requirements
Vestibule requirements at front entrance
Sun penetration at windows
Electrical outlets (carpet cleaning, etc.)
Telephone requirements
Vending machines
Coat room requirements
Office requirements
High chair requirements
Dining room storage (linen, etc.)
Emergency lighting
Waiting areas
Employees' facilities (lavatories, lockers, etc.)
Control locations (air conditioning, lighting, sound, etc.)

Interiors should be designed to present a specific theme or combination of themes with which guests can readily identify. Some might be authentic themes; others simulate and/or copy the authentic. Themes often capture or reflect the personality of the operator and/or a "special" menu item the restaurant prepares.

The concept that "form follows function" is one that should be followed in developing the interior design of a specialty restaurant. To succeed, the designer must have complete knowledge of the functional aspects of the proposed operation. The function of the design should have priority over the form, or aesthetic characteristics.

Selections of beautiful interior furnishings and fixtures are of little value to the investor if they do not have the lasting qualities to withstand the heavy usage and abuse that are typical of commercial foodservice installations.

Seating and furnishings should be planned with flexibility in mind. A rule of thumb formula—15 to 20 sq. ft. of floor space per guest—can prove incorrect if allowances are not made for guest circulation, service circulation, service stands, hostess stations, buffet equipment, entertainment, and similar factors. The only way to establish a realistic seating capacity is to make a scaled plan of the dining area that includes all of the space elements required to assure proper functioning of the dining room.

Sense of Smell

Controlling the odors that are inherently generated by any restaurant is essential. Air-conditioning, exhaust, and make-up air systems—the less visible parts of the design components—are too often looked upon as necessary design evils. While it is true that subtle cooking odors from a single food item may have a favorable patron reaction, remember that kitchens associated with most specialty restaurants are called upon to boil, fry, broil, roast and bake many different foods. The odor problem is compounded by the volume of food preparation and utensil washing that is taking place simultaneously. This situation creates an odor that, if not properly controlled, is distasteful to the patron, as well as the staff.

It is imperative that the kitchen exhaust and make-up air system be designed to create a slightly negative pressure in the kitchen; this insures that the natural air flow is from the dining room to the kitchen, rather than vice versa.

Most local health codes have minimum exhaust standards for restaurants. Successful specialty restaurant operators have learned to use the minimum standards as a baseline, and introduce higher standards of exhausting than building and pollution codes call for.

The design of any exhaust system should have a two-fold objective. First is to rid the interiors of smoke, fumes, and odors. The second is to insure that in that process the immediate exterior atmosphere does not become a pollution catch basin. A foul odor is just as distasteful to the patron in the parking lot as it is in the dining room.

Trash and garbage storage can also be a prime contributor to the odor problem.

The use of garbage refrigerators, garbage disposal units, compactors, and/or pollution-controlled incinerators should be considered as necessary items in foodservice design, not only to save refuse handling dollars but to control unpleasant odors.

Sense of Touch

The patrons' sense of touch should be given careful consideration in selecting utensils, supplies, and furnishings.

Silverware should be chosen not only for pattern and style, but also for its feel, weight, and balance, which are of equal importance.

Coffee cups and mugs should have comfortable handles and balanced handling qualities.

The general quality and feel of the china, glass, and silverware will enhance the diner's enjoyment of the food and beverage.

Glass and mug frosters have gained increasing popularity in Specialty Restaurants. (An example of such a unit is shown in Figure 9 (above). We can assume that frosting or chilling the glassware has little or no effect on the quality of the already iced or chilled beverage. Yet, this merchandising technique is a proved factor in increasing beverage profits by pampering the patrons' sense of touch.

Menu covers, cocktail stirrers, table linen, upholstery material, and other such items that are touched or handled by the patron are too often selected solely on their visual appeal from illustrated catalogs. The more prudent operators of specialty restaurants select such items only after seeing and handling an actual sample.

Probably the most expensive single investment in decorating a dining room is the carpeting. A 100-seat dining room will use a minimum of 200 sq. yd. of carpeting. Assuming a carpet cost of approximately $15 a yard installed, this becomes an investment of $3,000. Since carpeting has an important bearing on setting the visual mood of the room it should not, as many times happens, be selected on the basis of the color and pattern displayed on a 2 X 4 in. chip or a small swatch. Carpeting is one item the guest comes in direct contact with and it represents a major investment. Therefore, the

FIG. 9—MUG AND GLASS FROSTING UNIT

operator should put himself in the hands of a professional commercial decorator who has the ability both to make excellent selections of color and pattern and also to consider the important "walk-on quality" with regard to the patrons' sense of feel.

The placement of furniture in a specialty restaurant is an important element of the interior design. Both guest and service traffic must be considered. Tables and seating should be arranged to provide maximum flexibility for guest table settings. Guest party groupings of two's and four's are the most popular; however, combinations of tables should be available to accommodate larger numbers.

Booth, banquette, and table and chair arrangements represent the three basic choices in guest seating. While the table and chair plan offers the most flexibility, booths and banquettes ofttimes create privacy and un-regimented characteristics that add interest to a dining room.

The placement (and implementation) of service stands should be planned based on these considerations:

water and ice stations	glass and cup racks
roll warmers	coffee warmers
silver bins	storage for linen
	menus

FIG. 10—FURNITURE ARRANGEMENT

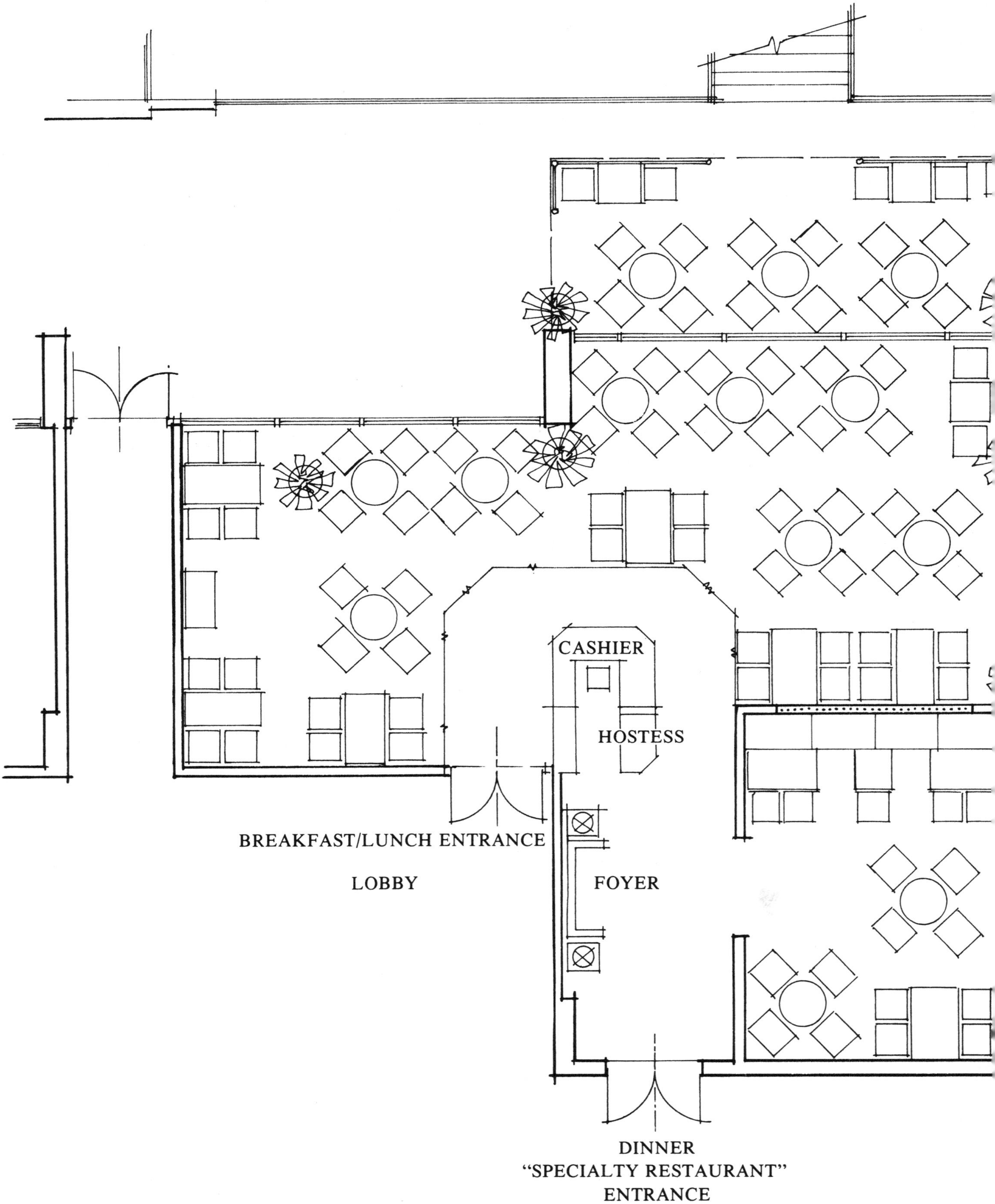

CASHIER

HOSTESS

BREAKFAST/LUNCH ENTRANCE

LOBBY

FOYER

DINNER
"SPECIALTY RESTAURANT"
ENTRANCE

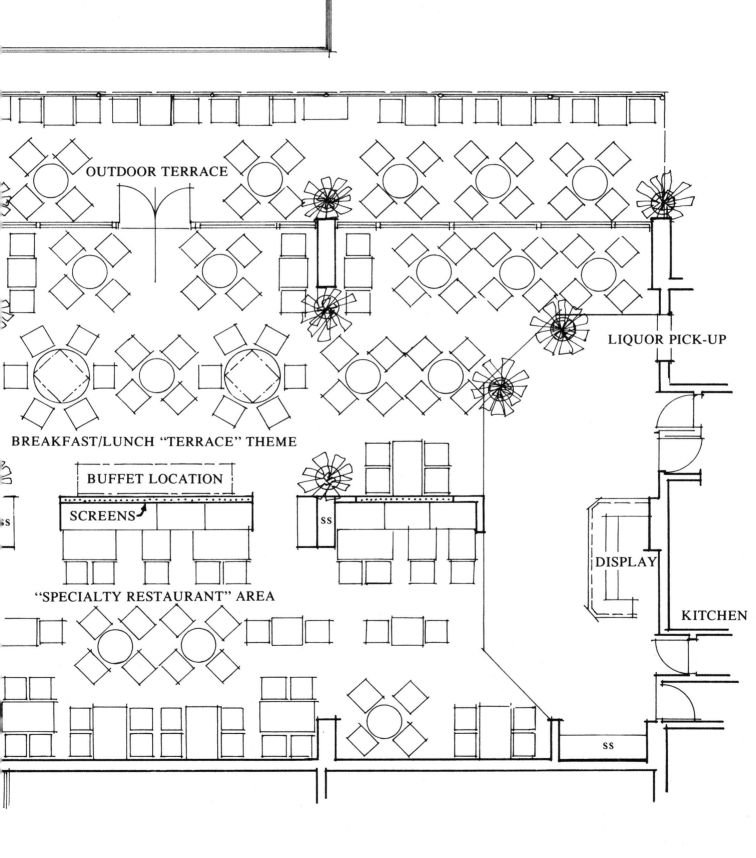

OUTDOOR TERRACE

BREAKFAST/LUNCH "TERRACE" THEME

LIQUOR PICK-UP

BUFFET LOCATION

SCREENS

ss

"SPECIALTY RESTAURANT" AREA

DISPLAY

KITCHEN

ss

A service stand should be designed to facilitate specific functions, and organized in a manner that does not create a negative distraction in the dining area.

The furnishing arrangement illustrated in Figure 10 (pp. 12 and 13) is an example of a multi-use specialty dining room. This type of room is a "work horse" space which must provide three meals to transient guests, as well as generate some support from local patrons. This task of providing more than one meal to the same guest is difficult to achieve successfully. The prospect of going to breakfast in a room where the previous night's meal was finished just hours earlier is not always appealing. Nor is the thought of dinner, with its higher check, in a breakfast atmosphere.

So a restaurant with multiple meal functions must somehow provide multiple atmospheres. Some of the simpler ways this can be achieved is by variable lighting, the addition of table linen, use of service plates, and the like to upgrade the room. This floor plan shows how the seating layout can aid in accomplishing the transition between meals.

The first noticeable feature is the dual entrance. This enables the room to have two related names and identities; for example, "The Hacienda" and "Garden Court." The area with the most daylight and view was selected as the breakfast and luncheon area to take advantage of this atmosphere. A cashier located at a control point allows patron checkout for those desiring quick service. The buffet area, accessible from the outdoor terrace, is located in this area. And, of course, the decorative theme is light and bright.

The second entrance, with its separate identity, opens to a foyer space which introduces the Specialty Restaurant area on a somewhat more formal note. A hostess desk is prominent as is some soft seating which implies a slower paced operation and experience to follow. A decorative theme with furnishings more suited to finer dining is used in this area. A focal point is provided at one end for some simple food display and preparation, such as roast beef carving, which adds interest since there is no outside view and service is slower paced.

The two spaces are separated by screen dividers since at times they may be required to flow into one another. Also, a glimpse into the "Specialty" area at breakfast or lunch may entice a customer to return at the dinner hour.

All of these features, with more in the areas of menus and service, are examples of the thinking that can make a dining room a three-meal success. Some compromise must be made, as is true with all multi-purpose areas, but with proper forethought, planning, and quality of operation no one should be disappointed because of an atmosphere that is not compatible with the meal being served.

Cash control and check handling are key functions in operating a specialty restaurant. Too often, as an afterthought, the cashier's station is poorly located in relation to the traffic patterns of the guests and/or service personnel.

An important design consideration affected by the type of restaurant being planned, is determining the location of the cash and check handling station. Where more leisurely dining is promoted, the kitchen is generally recommended as the place for the cashier's stand unless there is another area that will not create a guest distraction. In fast food operations, such distraction is of less importance.

Names of specialty restaurants are usually identified with graphics that become a trademark. This trademark serves as a valuable merchandising tool in advertising and promotion. Figures 11 through 15 (p. 15) illustrate logos that were created to capture the theme of specific specialty restaurant operations.

The general public is confronted with visual graphic communications in subways, public buildings, airline terminals, amusement parks, highways, and scores of other places. Specialty restaurant operators should take advantage of this visual language technique to help establish their own identity.

Requirements for Kitchen Layouts

Kitchen layouts designed to support the operation of specialty restaurants should encompass all of the criteria described in the development chapter.

FIG. 11–15–SPECIALTY RESTAURANT LOGOS

Snug
Harbour
Inn

FIG. 11

Pizza
Park

FIG. 12

Timothy's

FIG. 13

FIG. 14

Fatted Calf
Saloon
Eatery

FIG. 15

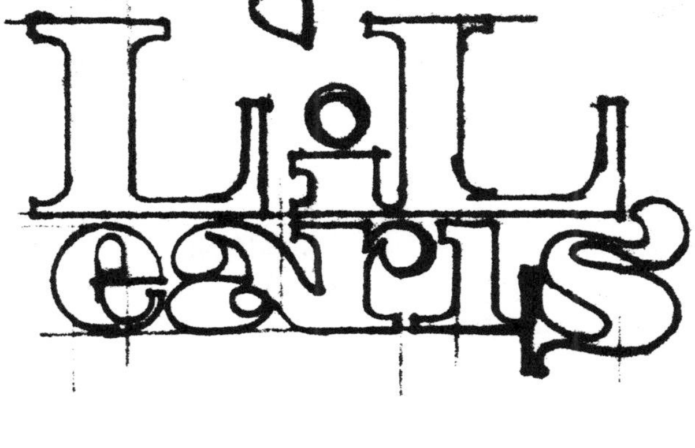

Li'L
EATS

SPACE ALLOCATION

Space is an important planning consideration, since every square foot of new construction costs approximately $35 to $40. What is the relationship of kitchen and dining room space allocation? This is a question that is commonly asked in the initial planning stage of a specialty restaurant.

There is not a formula to serve as a guideline, due to the inconsistencies of design criteria dictated by each specific operation.

Some of the specific variables affecting space allocations are:
   the menu
   storage requirements
   space allowance for seating
   space allowance for circulation
   convenience foods versus in-house production
   office space
   employees' facilities
   location of service stands
   beverage and liquor services
   physical relationship of the kitchen to the dining room

The seating capacity in a dining room varies as follows:
   12 sq. ft. per person is the code minimum
   15 sq. ft. per person is less congested
   18 sq. ft. per person is most common
   18 plus sq. ft. per person is classified as luxurious

The kitchen plan illustrated in drawing, p. 17 consumes 875 sq. ft. of space, exclusive of food storage and employees' locker areas. The dining room serviced by this kitchen is illustrated on pp. 18, and consumes 1260 sq. ft. The seating capacity is 105 and is based on 12 sq. ft. per person. In the summer months, the dining room is expanded into an open terrace that occupies an additional 1260 sq. ft., increasing the total seating to 210. The relationship of kitchen and dining area space allocation in this specific instance is shown at bottom of page.

This kitchen was designed to produce a limited menu selection based on quality rather than variety. The fact that the seasons vary the seating from 105 (winter) to 210 (summer) has little or no effect on the kitchen space allocation.

The explanation for the 1/3 to 2/3 spread in the comparison ratio is due to a careful selection of equipment which has a production range consistent with the high and low volumes dictated by the variable seat count.

For example, a three-compartment pot sink consuming approximately 22 sq. ft. of kitchen floor space, is a code requirement whether a restaurant services 105 or 210 seats. The same holds true of many items of foodservice equipment in terms of minimum and maximum production capabilities.

It is not good practice to use rule of thumb formulas for establishing kitchen areas based on dining space. The safe and sure method of determining the kitchen area is to develop a kitchen plan based on the operating criteria. This method of development will insure a balance in the proposed operation consistent with the facilities that support it.

If the spaces to be developed are existing, it is common practice to establish the ratio of dining room space and kitchen area in a preliminary plan that appears functional. The preliminary plan may then be used as a reference tool in establishing the operating criteria. The need for any compromises then becomes evident either in the plan itself or in the proposed method of operation, and adjustments can be adapted accordingly.

In summary, plans and operational development documents can be adjusted to suit the space available. This detail study and analysis should be made prior to the start of any construction. The key to the success of a specialty restaurant (or any business) rests heavily on good planning.

Figure 16 (p. 20) illustrates a kitchen equipment plan servicing a dining room with

SEASON	SEATING	DINING	KITCHEN	COMPARISON RATIO
Winter months	105	1260 S.F.	875 S.F.	approx. 2/3
Summer months	210	2520 S.F.	875 S.F.	approx. 1/3

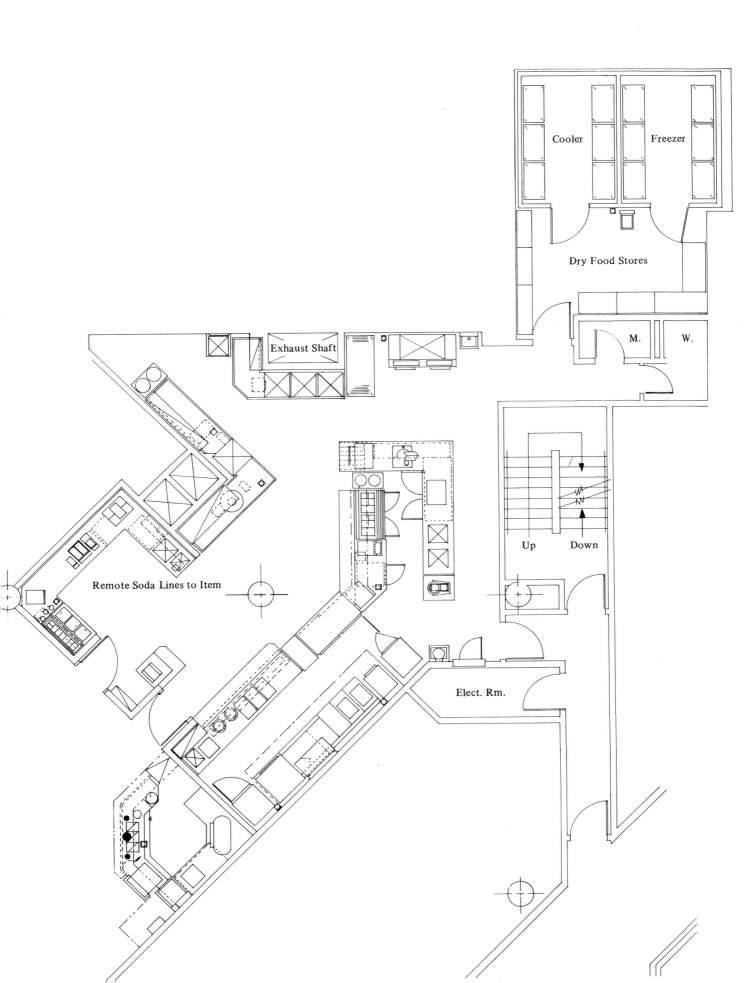

Cooler

Freezer

Dry Food Stores

M. W.

Exhaust Shaft

Up Down

Remote Soda Lines to Item

Elect. Rm.

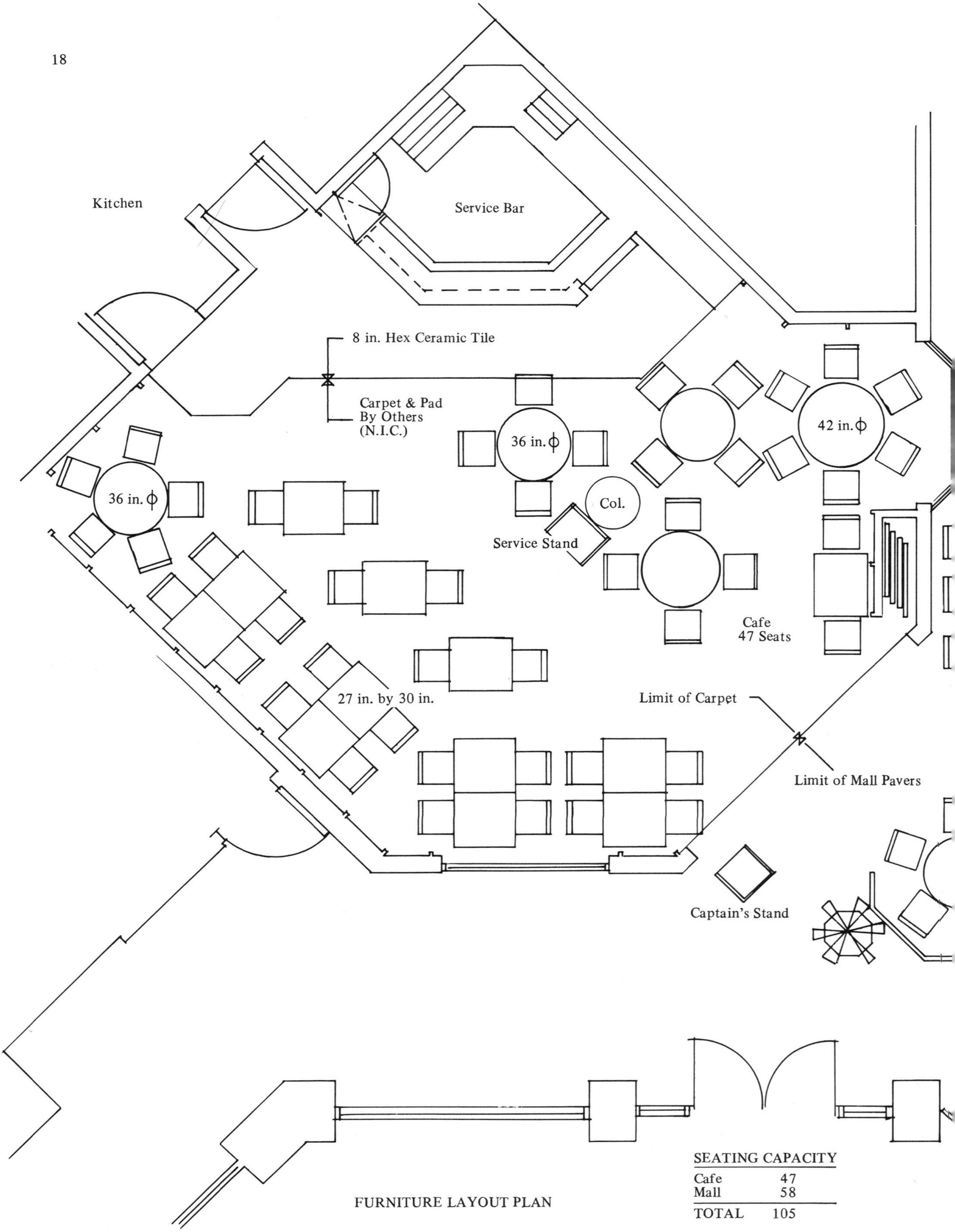

18

Kitchen

Service Bar

8 in. Hex Ceramic Tile

Carpet & Pad
By Others
(N.I.C.)

36 in. φ

36 in. φ

42 in. φ

Col.

Service Stand

Cafe
47 Seats

27 in. by 30 in.

Limit of Carpet

Limit of Mall Pavers

Captain's Stand

FURNITURE LAYOUT PLAN

SEATING CAPACITY	
Cafe	47
Mall	58
TOTAL	105

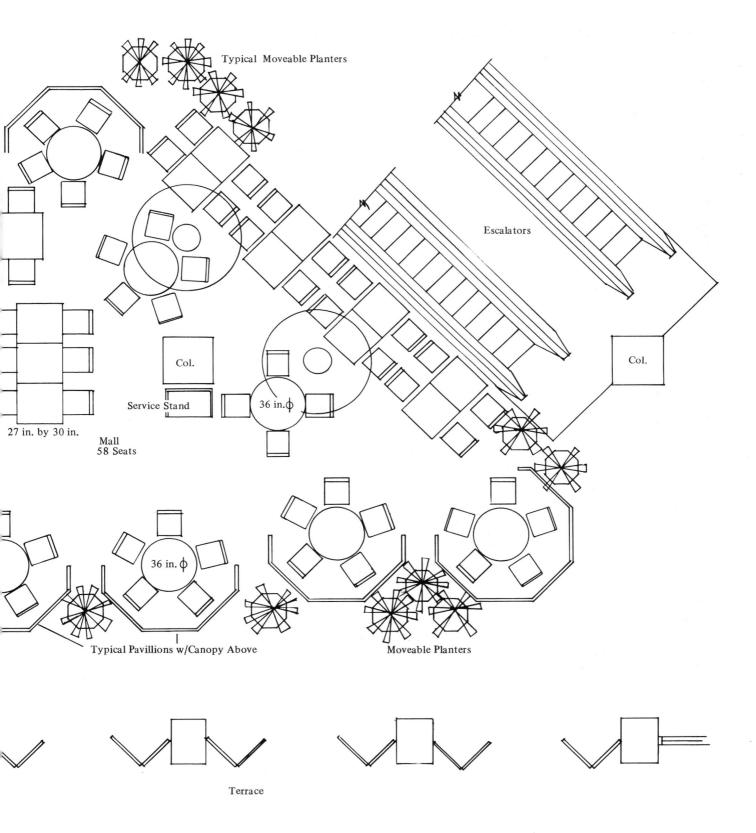

Typical Moveable Planters

Escalators

Col.

Col.

Service Stand

36 in. φ

27 in. by 30 in.

Mall
58 Seats

36 in. φ

Typical Pavillions w/Canopy Above

Moveable Planters

Terrace

FIG. 16—KITCHEN EQUIPMENT PLAN FOR DINING ROOM SEATING 200

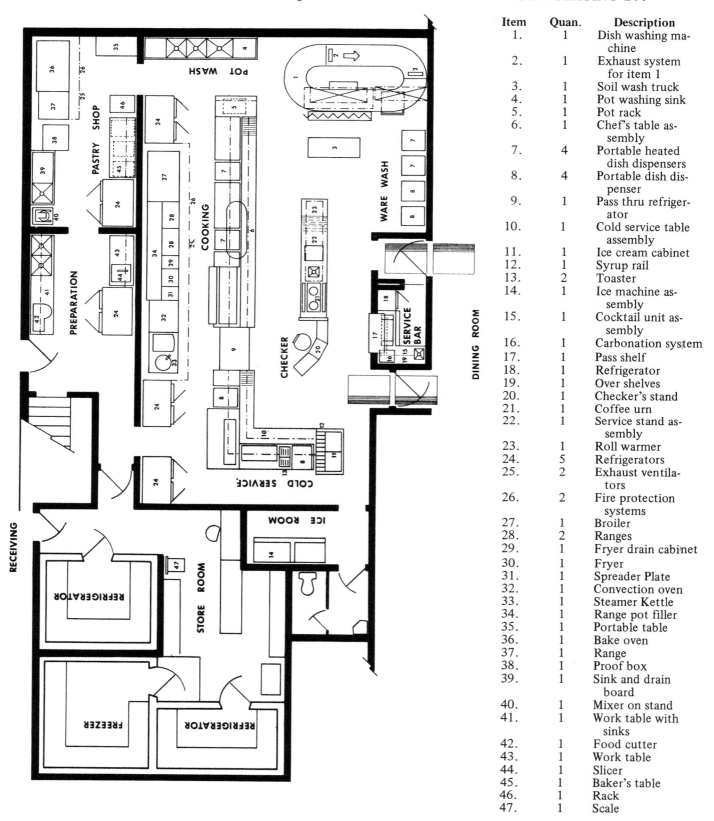

Item	Quan.	Description
1.	1	Dish washing machine
2.	1	Exhaust system for item 1
3.	1	Soil wash truck
4.	1	Pot washing sink
5.	1	Pot rack
6.	1	Chef's table assembly
7.	4	Portable heated dish dispensers
8.	4	Portable dish dispenser
9.	1	Pass thru refrigerator
10.	1	Cold service table assembly
11.	1	Ice cream cabinet
12.	1	Syrup rail
13.	2	Toaster
14.	1	Ice machine assembly
15.	1	Cocktail unit assembly
16.	1	Carbonation system
17.	1	Pass shelf
18.	1	Refrigerator
19.	1	Over shelves
20.	1	Checker's stand
21.	1	Coffee urn
22.	1	Service stand assembly
23.	1	Roll warmer
24.	5	Refrigerators
25.	2	Exhaust ventilators
26.	2	Fire protection systems
27.	1	Broiler
28.	2	Ranges
29.	1	Fryer drain cabinet
30.	1	Fryer
31.	1	Spreader Plate
32.	1	Convection oven
33.	1	Steamer Kettle
34.	1	Range pot filler
35.	1	Portable table
36.	1	Bake oven
37.	1	Range
38.	1	Proof box
39.	1	Sink and drain board
40.	1	Mixer on stand
41.	1	Work table with sinks
42.	1	Food cutter
43.	1	Work table
44.	1	Slicer
45.	1	Baker's table
46.	1	Rack
47.	1	Scale

a capacity of over 200 seats. This plan includes several design features:

1. An on-premise pastry shop, since the operation is recognized—and patronized—for its distinctive menu selection of pastry specialties.

2. A "mini" liquor service bar to assure prompt beverage service.

3. A "merry-go-round" warewashing system designed for direct conveyor loading by busboys. This design enables the dishwasher to do double duty by performing pot washing chores during off-peak hours.

4. All dishes stored in portable, self-leveling dish dispensers positioned in the serving line of the chef's table.

5. The "in" and "out" doors have vestibules and are automatically activated by walk-on floor pads.

6. A cashier's and food checker's station located in the circulation pattern of the out-bound door.

7. A service station positioned in an island arrangement to facilitate waitress self-service of coffee, soft drinks, rolls, water, etc.

8. A pass-thru refrigerator, positioned in the service line, has glass sliding doors to enable waitress pick-up of pre-plated cold entrees.

This plan was a winning entry in the 1972 *Institutions* Facilities Design Award Program.

Figure 17 (below) illustrates a bar equipment plan serving a 200-seat entertainment lounge and a 75-seat outdoor terrace. This three-station bar features:

1. Under-counter glass washing machine (the three-station sinks are a code require-ment used for soaking, washing, and sanitizing bar utensils).

2. Each bartender and waitress pick-up station is furnished with a carbonated drink console which is part of a post mix carbonation system. (The operator realizes appreciable savings by manufacturing his own carbonated drink products.)

3. Although not shown, each waitress station is furnished with glass storage, ice, and fruit jars that enable the cocktail waitress to provide her own set-ups. The bartender controls the liquor pour.

4. An ice machine located under the bar has a 200-lb. daily harvest capacity. A separate ice machine in a remote location supplements the requirements with an additional 500 lb. of cubes and 300 lb. of crushed ice.

5. Bottled beer coolers are provided, since no draft beer is dispensed from this bar.

6. All cocktail stations are furnished with bins for cube ice and for crushed ice, speed racks, towel rings, bottle openers, scrap chutes, and blenders.

7. The back bar serves to merchandise brand name liquors, as well as to provide a storage depot for both glass and supplementary under-counter refrigeration.

Figure 18 (pp. 22) illustrates a kitchen equipment plan that serves both a 180-seat specialty restaurant and a 220-seat coffee shop. This facility has a storeroom and pot washing facility in a remote location not shown on the plan. The layout features the following:

1. A service bar that assures prompt liquor service to the guests.

2. A walk-way behind the cooking battery to allow access for routine daily cleaning.

FIG. 17—BAR EQUIPMENT PLAN FOR 200-SEAT LOUNGE, 75-SEAT TERRACE

Item	Quan.	Description
1.	2	Beverage cooler
2.	1	Ice machine
3.	3	Cocktail stations
4.	1	Glass washing machine
5.	1	Hot water booster
6.	3	Carbonated beverage Disp. Bar-Tender
7.	2	Carbonated beverage Disp. Waitress

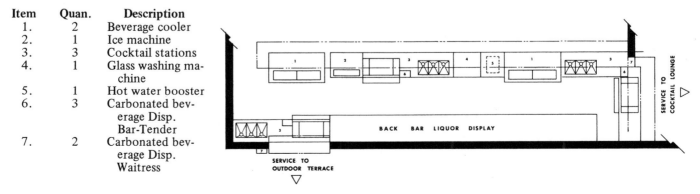

FIG. 18–KITCHEN EQUIPMENT PLAN FOR 180-SEAT SPECIALTY RESTAURANT AND 200-SEAT COFFEE SHOP

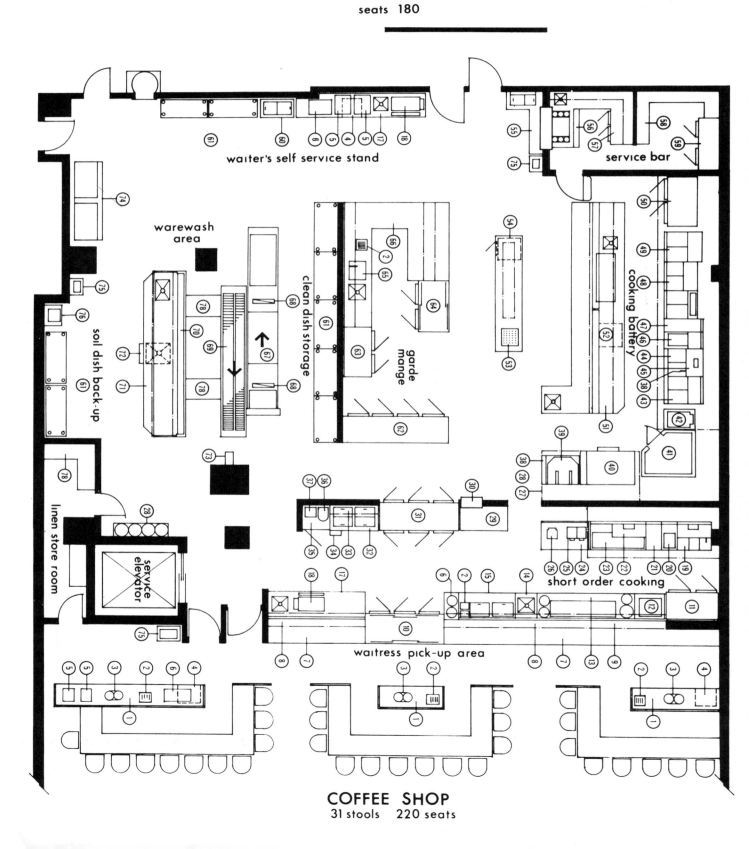

DINING ROOM
seats 180

COFFEE SHOP
31 stools   220 seats

EQUIPMENT LIST FACING KITCHEN EQUIPMENT PLAN

Item	Quan.	Description	Item	Quan.	Description	Item	Quan.	Description
1.	3	Waitress Serv. Std.	26.	1	Sandwich Press	53.	1	Make-Up Table
2.	4	Toasters	27.	4	Exhaust Ventila-	54.	1	Refrigerator
3.	3	Coffee Warmers			tors	55.	1	Waitress Liquor
4.	3	Roll Warmers	28.	1	Fire Protection			Make-Up
5.	4	Beverage Disp.			System	56.	1	Cocktail Station
6.	2	Milk Disp.	29.	1	Work Table	57.	1	Refrigerator
7.	2	Waitress Sto.	30.	1	Pass Shelf	58.	1	Storage Shelving
		Counters	31.	1	Pass Thru Refrig.	59.	1	Refrigerator
8.	2	Waitress Pass	32.	1	Ice Cream Cab.	60.	1	Ice Cart
		Shelves	33.	1	Syrup Rail	61.	12	Portable Trucks
9.	1	Heat Lamps	34.	1	Scoop Sink	62.	1	Refrigerator
10.	1	Pass Thru Refrig.	35.	1	Freezer	63.	1	Freezer
11.	1	Refrig.	36.	1	Frappe Mixer	64.	1	Pass Thru Refrig.
12.	1	Microwave Oven	37.	1	Hot Syrup Disp.	65.	1	Slicer
13.	1	Steam Table	38.	2	Water Filler	66.	1	Cold Serv. Disp.
14.	1	Sink	39.	1	Braising Pan			Ctr.
15.	1	Sandwich Unit	40.	1	Convection Oven	67.	1	Dishmachine
16.	4	Portable Self-	41.	1	Corner Refrig.	68.	1	Exhaust Ducts
		Leveling Dis-	42.	1	Steamer	69.	1	Feed Back Con-
		pensers	43.	1	Range			veyor
17.	2	Utility Counter	44.	1	Range	70.	1	Garbage Trough
18.	2	Coffee Urns	45.	2	Salamander Broilers	71.	1	Soiled Dish Table
19.	1	Range	46.	1	Fryer	72.	1	Silver Soak Sink
20.	1	Fryer	47.	1	Portable Spreader	73.	1	Hose Reel
21.	1	Portable Spreader	48.	2	Ranges	74.	1	Ice Machines
22.	1	Salamander Broiler	49.	1	Broiler	75.	3	Hand Sinks
23.	1	Griddle	50.	1	Refrigerator	76.	1	Janitor's Sink
24.	1	Work Table	51.	1	Chef's Table	77.	1	Shelving
25.	1	Waffle Maker	52.	1	Refrigerator	78.	2	Sliding Bridges

FIG. 19—INTERIOR DESIGNER'S RENDERING FOR NEW DINING ROOM ADDITION

GROUP ONE INCORPORATED

FIG. 20—DINING AREA WITH NAUTICAL THEME

The dining room of the Sheraton Motor Inn, Falmouth, Mass., features a nautical atmosphere. The high ceilings are accentuated with colorful sails. The use of room dividers provides intimate guest seating and eliminates the regimented look common to many restaurants.

FIG. 21—THEME PROMOTES WINE CELLAR

Authentic looking wine kegs at the Fernwood Restaurant, Revere, Mass., have proved to be effective in promoting wine sales. This design treatment is, in fact, an illusion constructed of false barrel ends.

3. A high-velocity exhaust system that reduces the cfm (cubic feet per minute) load (compared to a conventional canopy exhaust). The exhaust system is self-cleaning by means of built-in jets that automatically clean the sediment collection baffles.

4. A corner reach-in refrigerator is designed into the "L"-shaped cooking battery.

5. A separate short-order station is incorporated into the main cooking battery to service the menu from the coffee shop.

6. The coffee shop entrees (both hot and cold) are serviced over a pass shelf. A pass-thru refrigerator enables waitress pickup of pre-plated entrees.

7. One common conveyorized dishmachine handles the warewashing for both rooms. The dishtable is furnished with a two-way overhead rack shelf, undercounter silver soak sink (with chute), full length garbage trough, and sliding bridges connected to a feed back conveyor.

This plan was a winning entry in the 1975 *Institutions* Facilities Design Award Program.

Specialty restaurants are created to satisfy a specific market and field of action. Their theme and atmosphere concept should always be presented in the form of an illustrated rendering to insure that the developer has a visual understanding of what his investment dollars are buying. It is essential

that interior decorators have the design talent to create a "portrait" of their proposals. Elevations and perspective views are of importance to a floor plan.

A typical interior designer's rendering, shown in Figure 19 (p. 23), illustrates a concept presentation to a client for a new dining room addition to the Colonial Inn, Concord, Mass.

Figures 20 through 25 (pp. 24-26) are photographs of dining areas that illustrate an interesting cross section of themes and dining atmospheres.

FIG. 22—DESIGN FOR LEISURELY DINING

One of the dining areas at the Fernwood Restaurant, Revere, Mass., was designed with a wine cellar theme to encourage leisurely dining. The design characteristics of the furnishings and fixtures are in harmony with the interior. A relaxed and casual feeling is conveyed by the random layout arrangement and intimate lighting. The wine hutch provides additional interest.

FIG. 23—OPEN KITCHEN AS DINING ROOM FEATURE

The open kitchen at the Oak Hill Country Club, Fitchburg, Mass., becomes an interesting dining room feature. Open "Char Broil" kitchen designs, such as this, are popular concepts in the Specialty Restaurant field. In addition to the visual interest provided the guests, service is prompt, staffing is minimized, and the volume potential is high.

FIG. 24—DESIGN EFFECT OF MIRRORED BACKBAR

The mirrored backbar wall at Sheraton's Olympic Lounge in Washington, D.C., serves a dual purpose: the mirrors provide both a reflected view of an active pool deck area and a more spacious feeling for a compact area.

FIG. 25—WINDOW WALL DOMINATES DINING INTERIOR

The dining room of the New Seabury Country Club features a window wall to give guests the opportunity to view the lush golf courses and surrounding natural *beauty of Cape Cod, Mass. The interior furnishings were selected to complement the outdoor feeling but not distract from the view.*

FIG. 26—COLOR MAKES PLACE FOR COF-FEE MAKER IN DINING ROOM

Fully automatic coffee urns are available in a full range of colors. Because manufacturers are becoming conscious of the appearance of their products, many functional appliances are now suitable for dining room installations.

INNOVATION

Innovation in foodservice equipment, together with the design and planning of improved operating concepts, are generally conceived as a result of good communication between foodservice operators and foodservice engineers.

Engineers play a vital role in the research and development phase of the foodservice industry. This task force offering technical assistance is backed up by:

Independent foodservice consulting firms
Local foodservice dealer organizations
Foodservice equipment manufacturers
Chain operations' "in house" staff
Local, state, and national government experts
Military specialists
Educational institution committees

It would be impossible to list all of the innovations and improvements that have taken place in the past 20 years; however, the following partial list can serve as a checklist for restaurant operators in designing new restaurants or rehabilitating existing ones:

• Stainless steel and gray-painted finishes were, until recently, the only choice in foodservice equipment. Decorative colors and the application of laminates and vinyl finishes have added a new dimension to the designer's selection of equipment (see Figure 26 (bottom p. 26), a colored coffee urn, and Figure 27 (bottom p. 27), a vinyl-clad refrigerator).

• Functional equipment that is also decorative can serve as a means of increasing sales. Merchandising equipment is an excellent tool for increasing sales and profits. The bulk wine dispensers in Figure 28 (p. 28) and expresso coffee maker in Figure 29 (top p. 29) serve as examples of how basic equipment items can help convert a nondescript dining room atmosphere into something special.

• Kitchen areas generally are not exposed to guest view. A popular current design concept in specialty restaurants is to integrate the kitchen, or part of the kitchen, into the dining area. The open grille kitchen, shown in Figure 30 (bottom p. 29), is another example of designed merchandising. Open kitchens require continual attention on the part of the operator to insure a positive visual display. Maintaining sanitation standards is of vital importance. But an open kitchen, well maintained, can serve as an excellent merchandiser. More business can be generated if the public is given the visual assurance that the operator is proud to display his food preparation.

FIG. 27—DECORATIVE REFRIGERATORS FOR DISPLAY KITCHENS

Refrigerators are available in a full range of decorative colors and materials. The application of laminates and vinyls has proved to be a suitable substitute for stainless steel in many units. The introduction of color in equipment enhances the appearance of the display kitchens featured in many successful specialty restaurants.

FIG. 28—MERCHANDISER FOR BULK WINES ADDS TO DINING AREA DECOR

Wine service is featured in many specialty restaurants. This unit serves as a merchandiser to increase the sale of bulk wine. Serving temperatures are maintained with a self-contained refrigeration system.

Operators have learned that the excellent quality of American wines compliments all food entrees and contributes generously to the profit structure of the restaurant.

FIG. 29—ESPRESSO COFFEE MAKER
INCREASES DINING ROOM
SALES (left)

FIG. 30—OPEN GRILLE KITCHEN (below)
POINT OF PATRON ATTENTION

• The use of automatic liquor systems is far from universal in specialty restaurants. And yet these automated systems, besides adding a safeguard against pilferage, offer other advantages. Some of these are:

A consistency in beverage quality control

An accurate accounting of cost

Dispensing from less-expensive half-gallon bottles

A remote system that saves on storage in high-cost public space areas.

Many restaurant operators feel the push-button features of automatic liquor systems take away the showmanship displayed by some bartenders. This writer contends that a bartender should be more than a drink mixer. Automatic liquor dispensing systems allow him to be more productive and attentive to the guests.

• Refuse disposal is an important consideration and should not be overlooked in planning a restaurant. Garbage disposal units play an important role in disposing of animal and vegetable waste that has a 70 percent moisture content, but have limitations in handling bulk and solid waste. Consequently, many restaurants destroy the aesthetics of their building exteriors with piles of loose trash, refuse, and solid wastes.

Using a trash compactor reduces waste to approximately one-fifth of its bulk. Besides improving appearances and contributing to the community's improved ecology, other benefits follow:

Reduced space required for waste storage

Reduced fire hazards

Less frequent pick-up costs

Smaller bulk pick-up costs

Better control of pilferage

An investment in a compactor often pays for itself in a short period in the savings over the previously accepted standards in handling and disposing of bulk refuse.

• Specialty restaurants using table linens should carefully compare renting and/or commercial laundering costs against the investment of installing and operating their own in-house laundry. New synthetic fabrics with no-iron "wash and wear" characteristics have proved applicable not only for table cloths, but for napkins, uniforms, aprons, and wiping cloths as well.

A 200-seat restaurant considering an in-house laundry would have to make the following cost analysis:

Value of 120 sq. ft. of floor space (approximately 10 by 12 ft.)

Purchase of washer extractor (90 lb./hour capacity)

Purchase of dryer (71 lb./hour capacity)

Purchase of folding table

Installation and mechanical cost

Labor cost (one person for 40 hour week)

Cost of fabric inventory and replacement

Detergent cost

Utility cost

The foregoing costs amortized over a given period may well indicate a saving over the cost of linen renting and/or commercial laundering. The compact in-house laundry described has the following production capacity:

ITEM	HOURLY VOLUME
table cloths (54 by 54 in.)	150
napkins (20 by 20 in.)	650
uniforms	100
aprons	250
wiping cloths	800

• Until recently conventional exhaust hoods were designed and installed as custom equipment. Many manufacturers now offer a broad line of exhaust ventilators as standard items which can be selected directly from a catalog.

The prime function of any exhaust system is to remove the heated fumes through a grease extractor. The old formula for estimating exhaust loads was 100 cfm (cubic foot per minute) of air movement times the square footage of the hood surface. Newly-designed high velocity exhaust equipment allows reduction of up to 30 percent in the cfm load. This reduction in exhaust represents significant utility savings to the owner. The reason: there's no cost of heating or cooling the make-up air that's not now required. Other considerations in selecting exhaust equipment should include the following:

Automatic water wash (self-cleaning)

Methods of grease extraction

Types of fire protection

Lighting

Conformity with local and national codes
Future expansion flexibility
Interface with other related heating, ventilating, and air conditioning systems
Ease of washing filters
Equipment and installation cost
Operating and maintenance cost
Noise level

• Finally, specialty restaurants are subject to concept changes in menus and service. Portable rather than fixed foodservice equipment allows more flexibility to accommodate the operational changes required by new approaches.

Quick-disconnect manifold features can be applied to most items of equipment, including the components of the cooking battery. A typical new specialty restaurant design, for example, may be planned to include only one fryer and an expansion filler, allowing the operator the opportunity to add a fryer or other cooking appliance as the need may warrant.

The addition of portability and mobility to a kitchen design will contribute to easier food and utensil handling, as well as better sanitation and maintenance procedures.

MANAGEMENT

It is important that the managing operator of a specialty restaurant maintains a continual awareness of the unit's concept. He must train his staff according to disciplined operating rules to insure that the unique values of the concept are being maintained. Any changes in the details of the concept should be considered carefully.

Management must have, or develop, an instinct for second-guessing the public's reaction to any modification that may have an effect on the atmosphere, quality, and service. For example, the reaction of the dining public could prove negative to changes in such things as tableware, uniforms, and menus, even though the changes were motivated by a sincere desire to improve or upgrade the atmosphere. In this sense the manager of a specialty restaurant has the same responsibilities as a theatrical director in evaluating the details in the overall production.

It is important that management has, or develops, an understanding of the principles of design. One of the basic principles is that function should take precedence over form. Interior design and decorating objectives should always result in a design that is functional, yet in keeping with the concept and budget.

The design of the furnishings, fixtures, and equipment requires more than good taste. These elements should be evaluated in the context of such checklist considerations:
1. Cost within budget limitations
2. Delivery and warehousing time schedule.
3. Maintenance and service performance.
4. Replacement and parts inventory.
5. Fire code requirements.
6. Other safety and code requirements.
7. Durability.

Most specialty restaurant owners with previous exposure to design and development make it a policy to retain the services of professional designers and decorators to insure the fulfillment of their objectives and to protect their investment.

This text is not intended to imply that aesthetics and disciplined planning are guarantees that a specialty restaurant will succeed. The popularity of any foodservice establishment is dependent upon management. Managing a specialty restaurant successfully requires continuous effort to improve the menu concepts and service standards. It is important to be one step ahead of the expectations of the first-time patrons as well as the regular ones.

Training people is the single most essential requirement in managing a specialty restaurant. Some foodservice operators allege that the caliber of labor in the foodservice market is poor. More prudent operators contend that the help should not be criticized for poorly-executed foodservice; instead, responsibility for the success or failure of an operation should rest with the manager.

A prime group of employees in a restaurant will be motivated by training and will function more efficiently as they learn to understand their specific assignments, as well as the assignments of others.

It is essential that the kitchen staff be aware of the situations and problems that confront the dining room staff; for the same reasons, the service staff should be exposed to the responsibilities of preparation workers.

Job descriptions outlining each employee's tasks have proved to be a valuable management tool. Flexibility in assignments makes the employee's work more interesting and helps management get maximum return on labor costs. For instance, some operators assign dishwashing personnel additional scheduled work to be performed during off-peak hours; e.g., pot washing, refilling ice bins, cleaning, store room work, etc. As an employee becomes more familiar with the overall operation, he should become a candidate for advancement. Good management policy allows for promoting from within the ranks of the existing staff.

Many restaurants require that tips be pooled and distributed equally among all employees. Behind-the-scene workers are inclined to be more conscious of guests and service if they are sharing in such gratuity incentives.

Employee-management relations will be happier if the restaurant design includes well-planned employee facilities. Staff lavatories and locker areas are essential, as are separate eating and lounge areas. Restaurants should avoid the guest distraction that is caused when restaurant personnel take their coffee breaks and/or meals in the public areas and dining rooms.

It bears repeating: As important as aesthetics and disciplined planning are to the success of a specialty restaurant, the management of people is of equal or greater importance.

It is a matter of record that financial agencies consider new restaurant development a very high risk investment, due to the history of a high rate of casualties in the field.

Many new restaurants develop a very high turn-over in managers and ownership. Countless beautifully designed specialty restaurants have failed under the original developer's management. Yet the same restaurant, even bearing the stigma of a poor beginning has, in many instances, recouped under new leadership and new management. This fact—a restaurant's recovery from failure and achievement of success—proves that excellence in design is a wasted effort if it is not matched by the same degree of excellence in operational management.

Millions of sales dollars have been wasted by specialty restaurant managers who failed to understand and identify their operation. The promotion of a specialty restaurant must begin with an organized definition of the property, the market, and the competition.

There are three basic questions which should be answered in the development phase of any promotion:

1. Are the facilities being used in the best possible way?
2. What are the special features of the menu?
3. What are the special features of the facility?

Often these questions can be answered by inspecting and sampling other restaurants which may not duplicate your operation but may give you a "yardstick" for comparison. Your competition should serve as a constant reminder that you must improve and promote the services you feature.

When studying the market, go beyond the demographic areas of age, education, and income. Study your customers' personalities and life styles. Most people fall into categories when it comes to likes, desires, and needs.

Promotion for a specialty restaurant will take two forms—external and internal. External promotion consists of display advertising in magazines, newspapers, periodicals, and mailings. Radio and television should be considered if the commercials can be timed to capture the attention of your proposed market.

Advertising costs should be budgeted. Most operations use a formula of 1 to 2 percent of their gross sales for this investment.

There is no fool-proof method of successful media promotion. All areas of advertising should be tested and analyzed to determine which provide the best results. Some general rules for successful promotion are:

1. Develop your existing market, as well as new markets. It is just as essential to maintain existing patrons as it is to develop new ones.

2. Be specific in your message format.

3. Repeat promotional methods which have proved effective in the past.

4. Use language that is meaningful to the market you are promoting.

Sponsoring local Little League baseball or softball teams has proved to be an effective promotional tool for some operations. Gas stations and taxi companies are in constant touch with the public; some reciprocal promotion should be considered. Involving your facilities in social and civic activities with special rates will often generate good word-of-mouth promotion.

Internal promotion is equally important. It includes food presentation, merchandising displays, and special menu promotions such as table tents, but the most important of all internal promotions is making the guests feel that they are people of special importance to all of the personnel they encounter.

The moment a guest passes over the threshold of a specialty restaurant, internal promotion should be practiced. This is important in assuring that the guest feels he or she is getting full value, that he is of special importance and, therefore, leaves with favorable thoughts concerning a return visit.

An employee who is treated well by his management will, with few exceptions, reflect this treatment in his/her dealings with the customer. Reasonable incentives, proper employee training and direction by management are the basic ingredients that ensure internal promotion. The anatomy of a specialty restaurant consists of many elements, including a degree of excellence in food, atmosphere, and service. It is fitting to conclude that even a high degree of these elements cannot guarantee success unless based on the most essential element—good management.

Specialty Restaurant

All restaurants must be special in order to succeed; on that basis, the term Specialty Restaurant has been defined as encompassing unique restaurants of all kinds. In addition to the ethnic or theme restaurants, commonly classified as specialty restaurants, the author of this section would include every restaurant that demonstrates inventiveness in its surroundings, menu, preparation and service equipment, and management. The examples on these pages illustrate ways in which special qualities have been incorporated in restaurants of many types and in many parts of the country.

Imagination, creativity and a great respect for efficient design won an award of Special Distinction for Coy's, offspring of a landmark restaurant in Little Rock, Ark. An operation that cuts its own meat, bakes bread on-premise, and prepares its own fish for filleting also features an innovative cracker warmer. There is one installed at each waitress station and "warm crackers and butter beat shrimp cocktail in patron appeal," says its designer. Flair rests on a strong design foundation that assures smooth and organized traffic flow in the production of 2700 meals per week. Sales volume is $1½ million, with a check average of $11.30. The 352-seat restaurant is handled by 38 full-time and 50 part-time employees, testament to the high productivity that good planning provides.

Efficient kitchen traffic flow was achieved by (1) grouping food prep according to function with pass-thrus to eliminate unnecessary walking; (2) waitress stations that allow busboys and waitresses to perform duties without entering the kitchen since main waitress stations are in the hallway between the kitchen and dining room. As can be seen in plan at right, kitchen openings are purposely offset to screen all kitchen activity from diners.

Coy's Steak House

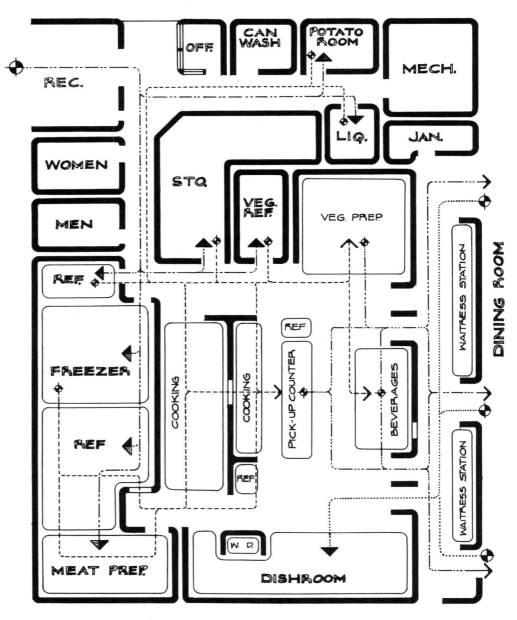

Designed by: Norman Ackerman,
The Fabricators, Dallas, Tex.

The 13th Floor

A top-of-the-tower operation, The 13th Floor Restaurant in Salt Lake City's Trave-Lodge Hotel, has a compact, efficient kitchen on the second of its four levels designed to handle final cook, set-up, and service of ingredients sent up from the first floor commissary. The restaurant's four levels give every patron a chance to enjoy the view through the large windows that are an integral part of the interior.

Merchandising, part of the specialty image of The 13th Floor, starts as guests are escorted to their tables. They pass an iced display of raw meat and seafood entrees. At the table they are offered a tureen of soup and a loaf of bread and invited to choose their favorite selections from a self-service salad bar.

Safety and comfort are other important aspects in patron areas which have stair and riser areas, with hand rails and ample lighting; use of textured, non-skid tile contrasts with carpeting. Heating and air conditioning for patrons is located in the ceiling for draft-free comfort.

Noise distraction has been minimized through use of automatic doors and baffle walls between kitchen and patron areas.

Food for The 13th Floor operation is received, processed, bulked, pre-cut, and portioned in the hotel's ground-floor commissary, then transported on portable equipment by an elevator that is used for this purpose during periods when patron use is infrequent. The elevator has a back door that opens directly to the 13th Floor kitchen's receiving area. Food is placed in dry, refrigerated, frozen, or heated storage. The kitchen was designed with an island cooking area that makes orders easy to prepare and set up for waitress handling.

Kitchen equipment was selected to meet menu needs, operate at maximum efficiency, and permit labor-saving location. A fast quartz combo griddle makes it unnecessary to turn products while cooking. An upright radiant broiler gives back-up during peak periods. Final cooking and set-up areas face the waitresses. A custom-fabricated, gas-radiant pass-thru handles heated plate supply, final glazing where needed, and ideal holding temperatures. The unit is separately fired and controlled on both sides, with control infinite from "off" to "broil" and variable from burner to burner.

Ninety employees (50 part-time) serve 4,000 meals a week in the 253-seat restaurant.

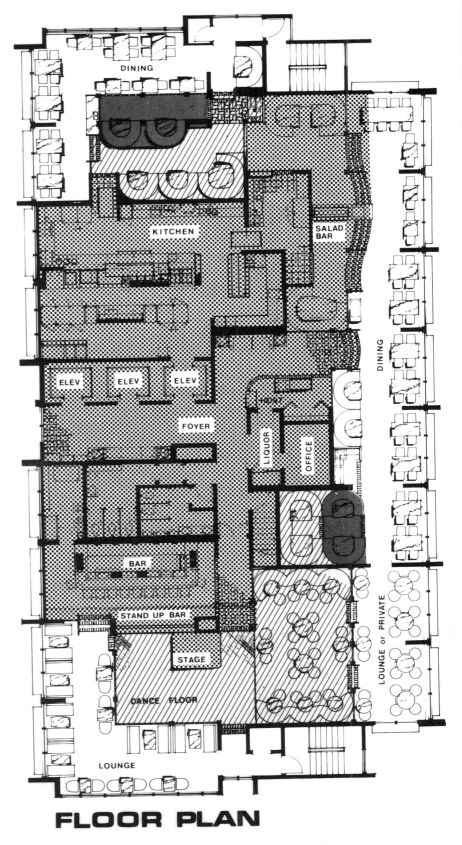

FLOOR PLAN

☐ LOW LEVEL   ▨ SECOND LEVEL

▥ FIRST LEVEL   ■ HIGH LEVEL

The Depot Restaurant

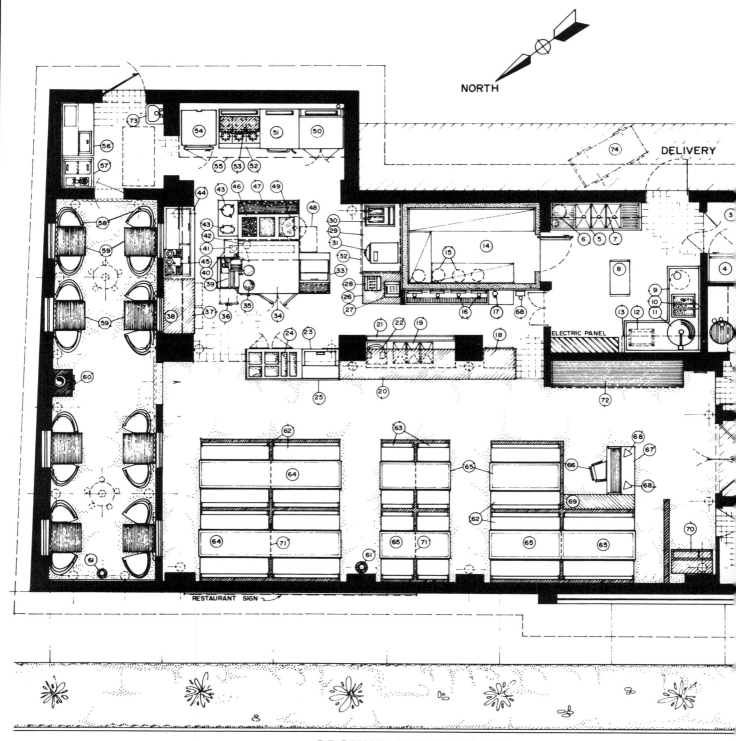

NORTH

DELIVERY

ELECTRIC PANEL

RESTAURANT SIGN

GROUND FLOOR PLAN

EQUIPMENT SCHEDULE

1. Dry Stores
2. Hot Water Boiler
3. Dry Stores
4. Reach-In Freezer
5. Pot Washing Sinks
6. Rinse Water Booster Heater
7. Overshelf and Pot Rack
8. Soiled Dish Rack
9. Soiled Dish Table
10. Pre-Rinse Sink
11. Dishwashing Machine
12. Silver Burnishing Machine
13. Clean Dish Overshelf
14. Walk-In Cooler
15. Wine and Beer Kegs
16. Wine and Beer Taps
17. Bar Mixer
18. Music Amplifier & Tape Deck
19. Under Bar Sink & Workboard
20. Bar Counter
21. Cocktail Mixing Station
22. Soda System & Flexible Hose Dispenser
23. Salad Dish Chiller
24. Refrigerated Salad Bain Marie
25. Glass Enclosure
26. Counter
27. Credit Card Register
28. Cash Register
29. Equipment Stand
30. Deep Fat Fryer
31. Steam Cooker
32. Copper Exhaust Hood
33. Refrigerated Appetizer Bain Marie
34. Lo-boy Refrigerator
35. Soup Warmer
36. Roll Warmer
37. Service Stand, Silver, Linen, Condiments . . .
38. Overshelf—Nut, Appetizer & Dessert Compotes
39. Slicing Machine
40. Serving Overshelves
41. Food Warmers
42. Roast Beef Heat Lamp
43. Heated Platter and Rarebit Dispenser
44. Wine & Beer Cooler
45. Coffee Maker
46. Hot Bain Marie
47. Hot Food Storage Cabinet with Work Board
48. Mobile Utility Table
49. Check Wheel
50. Convection Oven
51. Infra-Red Broiler
52. Open Burner Range with Oven
53. Salamander Broiler
54. Reach-In Refrigerator
55. Stainless Steel Exhaust Hood
56. Ice Cuber with Storage Bin
57. Water & Ice Station
58. Swivel Arm Chairs (16)
59. Tables with Acrylic Tops (8)
60. Pot Bellied Stove
61. Wine Coolers
62. 6-Seater Booths (7)
63. 2-Seater Booths (4)
64. 10 Foot Model Train Tables (2)
65. 5 Foot Model Train Tables (5)
66. Maitre'd Chair
67. Maitre'd Desk
68. Telephones
69. Model Train Control Console
70. Cigarettes Machine
71. Wrought Iron Ticket Windows (5)
72. Wine Storage and Display Racks
73. Hand Sink
74. R.R. Baggage Carts
75. Dry Stores
76. Walk-In Ageing Box
77. Walk-In Freezer

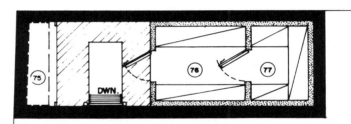

SECOND FLOOR PLAN
(STORAGE FACILITY)

Above: "America's Showcase Railroad Restaurant," The Depot located in South Miami, Fla., is the favorite stopping place of railroad buffs. The glass protector shield which incorporates a train etching over the salad bain marie in the display kitchen is typical of the imaginative use of railroad motifs.

Below: Depot food is as attention-getting as the decor. A popular menu offering is the skewered Prime Filet Flambé being prepared by the executive chef who wears the railroad man's traditional bandana around his neck, but he also wears the tall chef's hat, the traditional mark of the executive chef.

Pam Pam East

The impression is clear that caring for patrons is important to the management of this restaurant. Seating for waiting customers surrounds the entry and an additional waiting area occupies the center of the adjoining room. Showcase and cashier's stand (register is behind column) are at right.

Hogate's Spectacular Seafood Restaurant

The entrance sets the stage for an exciting evening in a restaurant that is an old favorite of Washingtonians that has been moved to new surroundings. With seats for 900 the restaurant requires adequate entry, lobby and checking space. The covered porte cochere makes entry pleasant in all weather.

A restaurant seating 900 to generate sales of $3 million a year was the challenge met by the designers of the new Hogate's Spectacular Seafood Restaurant. Actually, first year sales of $4.5 million indicate that the challenge was more than met. The menu in the new Hogate's is substantially the same as that of the old one. The foodservice facility design (right) accommodates the preparation procedures worked out over the years in the original Hogate's, as well as the carefully devised beverage service techniques and controls of the Marriott Corp., operators of the new restaurant.

There is a main production kitchen, warewashing department, and service bar. There are two service kitchens, located so that half the waitresses go to one, the other half to a duplicate. This, in effect, provides a short order and service kitchen for each half of the dining area, insuring prompt service to patrons and a dispersion of traffic in the kitchen. Designing a one-level operation diminished safety hazards, as does the use of a slight abrasive in the quarry tile floors in the kitchen.

A separate entrance for employees is apart from the food receiving entrance and the locker rooms and general offices are on the mezzanine level, both factors providing good security control. There is also a central cashier located in a well-protected area on the second floor to whom waitresses send the completed customer check together with cash or credit card via pneumatic tubes. Receipt and change are returned through the same tubes in a matter of seconds.

Hogate's is a seafood table service restaurant and cocktail lounge with entertainment. Effective design makes it possible for 307 employees to provide 12,000 meals per week.

Designed by: Fred Schmid Associates, Los Angeles; project coordinator, Carl Hansen FFCS; project designer, Zoni Kovacs.

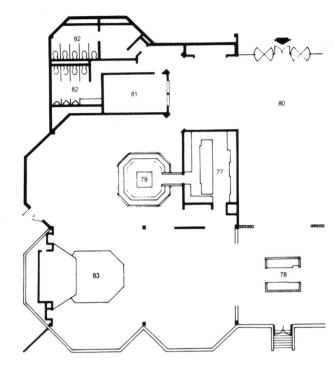

1   Enclosed can washer
2   Receiving table
3   Automatic scales
4   Fixed shelving
5   Mobile shelving
6   Mobile vegetable rack
7   Storage racks
8   Ice machine w/bin
9   Reach-in refrigerator
10   Salad sinks
11   Floor mixer
12   Open burner unit
13   Bench mixer
14   Ingredient bins
15   Salad work tables
16   Tilting kettles
17   Work table
18   Mobile food chopper
19   Dunnage rack
20   Vegetable peeler
21   Roll-in refrigerator
22   Vegetable sinks
23   Steamer

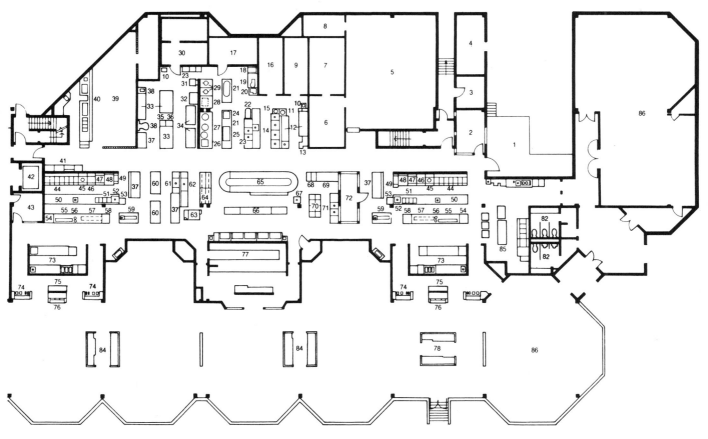

24	Food chopper	48	Refrigerator/Freezer	72	Tea urns
25	Utensil & pan racks	49	Pan racks	73	Water station & icer
26	Pass-thru refrigerator	50	Roll-in proof cabinet	74	Juice urns
27	Hand sink	51	Convection ovens	75	Coffee warmer
28	Pass-thru heated base	52	Bake ovens	76	Cup & saucer dispenser
29	Hot holding cabinet	53	Bench mixer	77	Cabinet
30	Mobile rack	54	Finished pastry rack	78	Beverage counter
31	Ovens	55	Utility storage rack	79	Coffee urn
32	Ranges	56	Hot pass-thru cabinet	80	High chairs
33	Tilting kettles	57	Pie cutting table	81	Bus carts
34	Meat hooks	58	Cut pie rack	82	Conveyor
35	Lug racks	59	Pastry racks	83	Warewashing machine
36	Lug carts	60	Tilt kettle w/mixer	84	Mobile silver sink
37	Meat chopper	61	Broken cooky rack	85	Silver wrapping table
38	Patty making machine	62	Pie shell machine	86	Mobile table
39	Scale	63	Dough roller	87	Disposer
40	Automatic slicer	64	Wrapped silver shelves	88	Pot washing unit
41	Meat block w/table	65	Dish carriers	89	Sink compartment heater
42	Open gas burner	66	Heat lamps	90	Carts
43	Ranges w/broiler	67	Refrigerated bases	91	Counters & shelves
44	Tilting fry pan	68	Milk carton dispenser	92	Display cases
45	Fryers	69	Rack dolly	93	Service stations
46	Accessory rack	70	Butter dispenser		
47	Dough divider	71	Glass dispenser		

Round Table Restaurant

HALLANDALE, FLA.

Dinners for 5000 patrons are served smoothly because of well planned layout in this 577-seat restaurant.

• Designed for speedy, tension-free service from central pick-up station to 4 separate, intimate dining areas; waitress entree pickup area provides 2 complete serving set-ups, each covering 2 dining areas.

• Open plan permits major circulation, yet layout keeps distance to be traveled by workers within areas to a minimum.

• Good flow from storage to preparation to cooking to entree pickup area.

• Service bar up front is open with no doors to slow waitress movement.

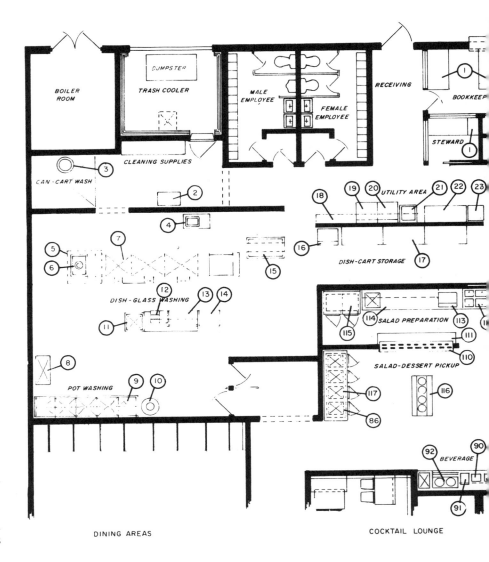

EQUIPMENT LIST

1. Office Equipment
2. Portable Detergent Spray Cleaner
3. Can Washer
4. Silver Burnisher
5. Overhead Sorting Shelf
6. Scrapping Table w/ Waste Disposer
7. Dishwasher
8. Clean Pot Cabinet
9. Pot Wash Sink & Tables
10. Pot Scrubber
11. Silver Soak Sink
12. Silver Washer-Dryer
13. Silver Sorting Table
14. Clean Silver Storage Shelving
15. Mobile Clean Dish Sorting Table

16. Vending Machine
17. Clean Dish Storage Cabinets
18. Overshelf
19. Clothing Washer
20. Clothing Dryer
21. Storage Shelving
22. Mop Sink
23. Platform Scale
24. Storage Freezer
25. Wood Storeroom Shelving
26. Ice Cuber Machines w/Storage Bins
27. Food Cutter
28. Work Table w/Sinks & Disposer
29. Overshelf
30. Floor Drainer
31. Vertical Cutter/ Mixer

32. Work Table w/Over-shelf
33. Exhaust Canopy
34. Braising Kettle
35. Mobile Salad Containers
36. Mobile Walk-In-Cooler Shelving
37. Walk-In-Coolers & Freezer
38. Meat Portioning Table w/Sinks
40. Bench Meat Saw
41. Work Table w/ Overshelf
42. Meat Chopper
43. Meat Processing Machine
44. Work Table w/ Overshelf
45. Hand Sink

46. Bakers Pan Sink
47. Bakers Walk-In-Cooler
48. Pan Racks
49. Bench Mixer
50. Bakers Table
51. Mixer
52. Mobile Flour Bins
53. Bakers Work Table
54. Roll-In-Proof Cabinet
55. Exhaust Canopy
56. Bake Oven
57. Rotary Bake/Roast Oven
58. Rotary Bake/Roast Oven
59. Bread Slicer
60. Bread Packaging Table
61. Water Cooler
62. Refrigerator

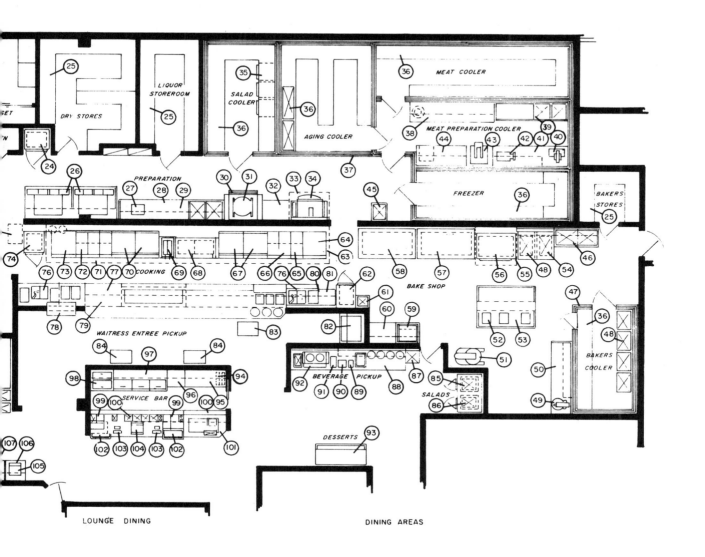

63. Exhaust Canopy	79. Overhead Plate Warmer	92. Coffee Urns	107. Beverage Counter
64. Broiler/Oven	80. Prime Rib Work Station	93. Refrigerated Dessert Case	108. Pan Racks
65. Spreader		94. Soda System Machinery	109. Refrigerated Dessert Case
66. Even Heat Top Range w/Oven	81. Overhead Plate Warmer	95. Back Counter	110. Pass Window
67. Charbroilers	82. Ice Flaker	96. Glass Washer	111. Work Table
68. Refrigerated Base	83. Serving Carts	97. Beverage Cooler	112. Ice Cream Cabinet
69. Fryer	84. Baked Potato Warmers	98. Ice Storage Bin	113. Milk Dispenser
70. Charbroilers		99. Cocktail Work Stations	114. Salad Preparation Table w/Sink and Overshelf
71. Even Heat Top Range w/Oven	85. Roll-In Salad Refrigerator	100. Underbar Sinks	
72. Spreader	86. Pan Racks	101. Service Bar	115. Salad Refrigerator
73. Broiler/Oven	87. Glass Rack Dolly	102. Service Bar Ice Stations	116. Salad Dressing Table
74. Refrigerator	88. Beverage Counter and Salad Dressing Station	103. Soda Dispensers	117. Roll-In-Salad Refrigerator
75. Prime Rib Warming Cabinet		104. Precheck Register	
76. Prime Rib Slicers	89. Ice Tea Maker	105. Digitmaster Control Register	
77. Cooks Table w/ Refrigerated Base	90. Refrigerated Cream Dispenser	106. Digitmaster Machinery Cabinet	
78. Prime Rib Heated Pass Shelves	91. Coffee Grinder		

Designed by Jerico Company, Stanley Tashman, George Bacher

Pumperniks of Lauderdale

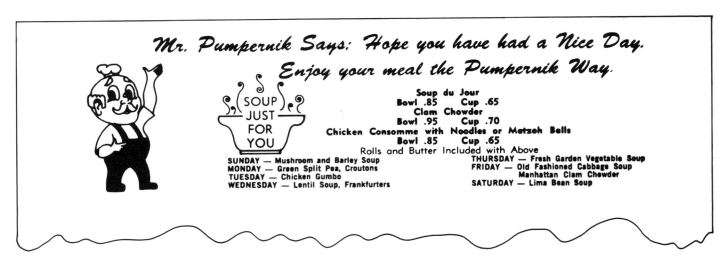

Mr. Pumpernik Says: Hope you have had a Nice Day.
Enjoy your meal the Pumpernik Way.

SOUP
JUST
FOR
YOU

Soup du Jour
Bowl .85   Cup .65
Clam Chowder
Bowl .95   Cup .70
Chicken Consomme with Noodles or Matzoh Balls
Bowl .85   Cup .65
Rolls and Butter Included with Above

SUNDAY — Mushroom and Barley Soup
MONDAY — Green Split Pea, Croutons
TUESDAY — Chicken Gumbo
WEDNESDAY — Lentil Soup, Frankfurters

THURSDAY — Fresh Garden Vegetable Soup
FRIDAY — Old Fashioned Cabbage Soup
          Manhattan Clam Chowder
SATURDAY — Lima Bean Soup

The menu at Pumpernik's starts with this warm message; the menu itself is a sizable collection of dishes with something to please everyone.

Pumpernik's of Lauderdale Lakes, Florida is located in a relatively expensive condominium area near Fort Lauderdale.

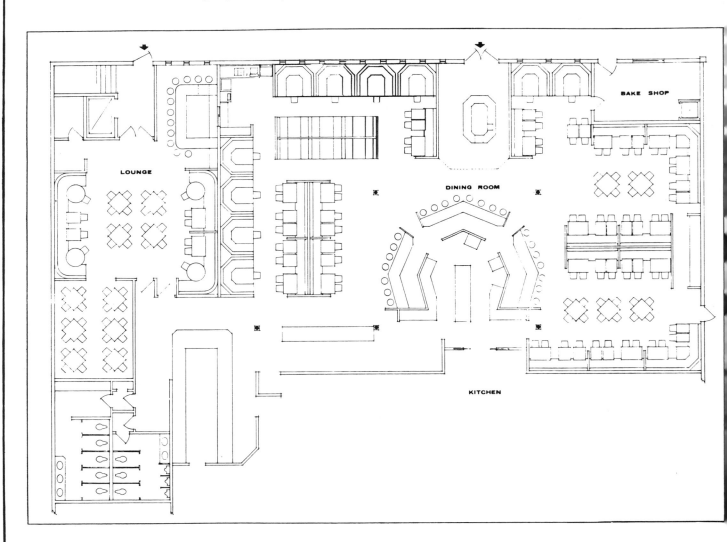

The restaurant's clientele is made up of seventy percent semi- or fully-retired, high income individuals; twenty percent upper middle class working people, and ten percent transients.

Seating is available for 650 patrons and they can be served from 7 a.m. to 1 a.m. on weekdays and 7 a.m. to 2 a.m. on weekends.

Pumpernik's restaurants have clung to the "old ways." In their newest operation, management has opted for a "return to basics"—wide variety, wholesome home cooking, and fresh, hot baked goods.

Patrons entering the restaurant are engulfed in the sweet aroma of fresh hot pastries, mingled with the heavy scent of hot delicatessen, and balanced with the tangy aroma of the complimentary relishes placed on the tables." The colors of the interior are warm; the hosts are friendly, and the seats are comfortable. There is a quiet sense of welcome which permeates the atmosphere.

While waiting for his meal, the patron entertained by background music as he samples the relishes on the table. Menu items emerge from the kitchen piping hot

or ice cold. Waiting time is kept to a bare minimum through small waitress stations and the effective expediting system in the kitchen.

Delicatessen is Pumpernik's primary product, and proper preparation and presentation are essential. To ensure proper care in the preparation of these popular items, the "Block" was created.

The Block (pictured below) is designed to handle all standard sandwiches and salads, along with orders for take-out. This area also functions as the retail bulk delicatessen counter.

Temperatures are an important facet of the presentation of fine delicatessen items. Separate warmers are used to maintain the corned beef, pastrami, and roast beef at proper temperatures. Separate slicers are used for each of these three primary products, so that tastes are not transferred. Plates are kept in heated plate dispensers to ensure proper temperature at serving. Gravies, potato chips, mashed potatoes, and other items normally served with these sandwiches are kept at the Block to save unnecessary trips to the main kitchen.

The opposite side of the Block is completely refrigerated. Salads, cold fish, and cheese are all stored in refrigerated dispensers and served on plates that have been refrigerated.

Control and convenience are added through the separate walk-in cooler assigned to the Block. Their high dollar items are kept in a locked cooler in close proximity to the Block.

The bake shop is a natural extension of this operation. Rolls, breads, and pastries are important elements of a quality delicatessen operation. Stale or poor quality packaging would destroy the finest of meat products.

To provide these high quality bakery items, an elaborate in-house bake shop was designed. Two large, revolving bake ovens were included in the operation. They provide piping hot rolls, breads and pastries throughout the serving periods.

Freshness and wholesomeness are the key words in preparing the goods for service. Rolls and pastries from one meal are never saved for use in the next serving. Management gives bags of left-over pastries to late night patrons.

The single department in their Lauderdale Lake installation considered the most innovative by Pumpernik's management is the warehandling system which occupies only a small area of the kitchen although handling ware for approximately 650 seats (picture below).

As the first step in the system, bus boys clear the patron areas. Tables are scrapped into small, two-compartment bus boxes. Glasses, dishes, and trash are placed in one compartment, while the stainless steel flatware is placed in the other.

Full bus boxes are placed on the conveyor in the dishwashing areas. As the dishwashers receive the bus boxes, they split the sorting procedure. The first dishwasher loads all plates and bowls into the long, flight-type dishwasher. As he does, he scraps the waste into a recirculating water scrap trough which feeds into a waste disposing system. (See picture facing page.)

The first dishwasher then slides the bus box to the second dishwasher. This man racks the cups and glasses in overhead racks, by type. All silverware is dumped into a soak sink, to be washed during slack periods. Full racks of glasses and cups are run through the smaller, flight-type dishwasher.

This second machine also functions as a back-up unit if anything should happen to the primary unit. Both machines are equipped with blow driers to fully dry the dishes.

The dishtable drain trough is equipped with a fail-safe system to reduce loss of stainless steel flatware. Heavy duty magnets are welded to the underside of the trough to prevent loss of flatware into the wash system.

The soak sink is equipped with a basket drain system to catch paper particles. In addition, a floating bridge is used on the top of the sink to make unloading the sink easier.

Flatware is randomly placed in multi-compartment silver washing racks. When the flatware comes out the clean end of the machine, an operator immediately takes the silver basket and dips it into a special sink. The sink is injected with live steam. When the flatware is removed, the utensils are dry and free of spots.

The flatware is then placed on a special silver-sorting table. An overhead rack was designed to permit sorting of the flatware into utensil containers. When these containers are full, they are placed in self-leveling mobile dispensers. The filled dispensers are then taken to the individual waitress stands. Each waitress stand is provided with a full day's supply of flatware to prevent problems in re-supplying during peak periods.

"The conveyor, unique scrapping table, waste system, and flatware system," says the management, "all combine to provide an efficient, low-labor intensive, efficient ware washing system."

Above: Food flows through Pumpernik's foodservice operation on a north to south flank movement. Raw products enter through the rear door at the north end of the facility. Items are either weighed, measured, or counted, then placed in dry or refrigerated storage. The first battery nearest the walk-in boxes (at rear of right line in picture) is for initial heavy preparation of food. It includes the steam-jacketed kettles, heavy braising pans, vegetable steamer, food cutters, and mixer. The trench and grate in front of the preparation line provide for better sanitation, ease of cleaning, and improved safety. Overflows and spills are quickly removed and cleaned up. Aisles were planned to be wide enough for unobstructed passage and worker activities.

Right: A unique design was created for the scrapping table. A maximum of two men work in this area, with a bare minimum of movements required. (See facing page for full description.)

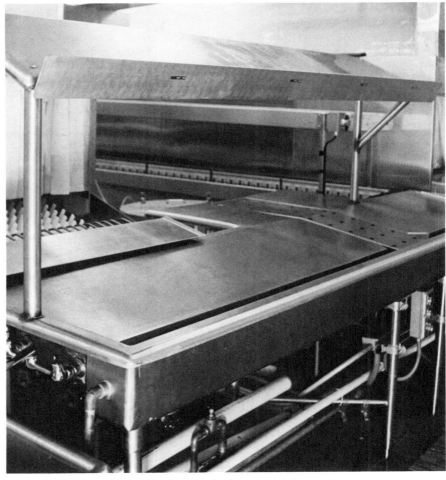

Pewter Pub

Design and menu above the normal level for department store foodservice facilities were dictated for the Pewter Pub by its location in a store, noted for quality merchandise, set in affluent surroundings in suburban Toledo, Ohio's Franklin Park Mall.

The criteria were met admirably with decor and furnishings in a Country French theme, unusual for a department store, and a menu broader than usual.

The preparation and storage areas (see plan below) are "tight" by conventional standards partly because of the menu and partly because some items are supplied by the commissary operated by J.L. Hudson Co. in their downtown Detroit store.

The service kitchen is equipped to provide everything from custom salads and cold sandwiches to charbroiled and casserole items.

The dining area seats 126 guests in Country French surroundings: timbered ceiling, low level lighting, carpeted floors, with pewter ware and other artifacts displayed to support the theme.

The pick-up counter is designed to provide an interesting view of the preparation function. Equipment, visible from the dining room, is constructed of specially treated woods with plastic laminate facings, which contribute to durability and ease of cleaning as well as aesthetic value.

The Pewter Pub serves about 2660 meals a week. Open 6 days a week, from 11 a.m. to 3 p.m. and from 4 p.m. to 8:30 p.m. There are 34 employees.

Does it work? "Economically," the designer reports, "this facility is producing a greater percentage of food volume than was originally anticipated."

1	Service stand	19	Refrigerator	36	Spreader
2	Tableware	20	Griddle counter	37	Steam-jacketed kettles
3	Water/Ice dispenser	21	Fryers	38	Range w/oven
4	Coffee warmer	22	Fries warmer	39	Work top
5	Pickup counter	23	Char-broiler	40	Sink-disposer unit
6	Hot food holding under	24	Open burner/griddle combination	41	Portable table
7	Hot food wells	25	Bun toaster	42	Portable equipment
8	Heat lamps	26	Freezer base under	43	Booster heaters
9	Garnish station	27	Steamer	44	Dishwashing machine
10	Hot dog grill	28	Butter dispenser	45	Disposer w/rinse spray
11	Storage under	29	Milk dispenser	46	Soak sink
12	Toasters	30	Hand sink	47	Clean dish table
13	Salad & sandwich station	31	Coffee maker	48	Soiled dish table
14	Dressing wells	32	Hot chocolate dispenser	49	Overhead sort shelf
15	Cold food wells	33	Iced tea dispenser	50	Conveyor belt
16	Microwave oven (on shelf)	34	Carbonated beverage station	51	Tool drawer
17	Plate/cup dispensers	35	Convection oven	52	Can opener
18	Ice cream cabinet			53	Mixer

Designed by: Fred Schmid Associates, Park Ridge, Ill.

Alexilion Restaurant

Murals reconstructed from fragments found in the Palace of Knossos, Crete, from the Minoan civilization of 1500 B.C., set the stage for fine dining at Alexilion Restaurant in Los Angeles. Operated in conjunction with the Parasol Coffee Shop, it was important to achieve a change of pace in the dining interiors. Plan for the kitchen which serves both is found in Vol. 1, p. 92. Restaurant serves 1600 MPW.

The waitress pick-up area has a built-in freezer for chilling salad plates and forks, perforated pans to hold salad greens, and dressings. Alongside the soup station are sliding drawers for the bowls. The refrigerated water station has an insulated ice bin and convenient glass storage. A hot beverage station with an instant hot water dispenser and a scrap well complete the set-up. (See picture below.)

54	*Food cutter*
55	*Slicer, portable*
56	*Utensil rack overhead*
57	*Ice cube maker*
58	*Hand ice crusher*
59	*Bar sinks*
60	*Blender*
61	*Cocktail station*
62	*Check register unit*
63	*Draft beer unit*
64	*Money changer*
65	*Ice cream vender*
66	*All-purpose vender*
67	*Condiment table*
68	*Coffee vender*
69	*Cold drink vender*
70	*Candy/pastry vender*
71	*Water fountain*

Designed by: Interstate Restaurant Supply, Los Angeles

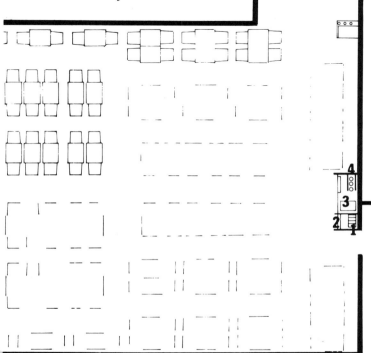

The Haberdashery Restaurant

Housed in a converted haberdashery shop on the Radisson Hotel's ground level in Minneapolis, The Haberdashery quickly demonstrated that foodservice can be simple, fun, and profitable. The kitchen was located most advantageously in a janitor's closet and stairwell off the lobby. Its size restricted the number of items on the menu and dictated selections of baskets rather than conventional tableware for service. Menu is easily changed; offerings, chalked on slates mounted in several strategic locations around the room, are merely rewritten.

Designed by: R. Johnston and S.E. Gully, Radisson Hotel; Joseph Palen, Joseph F. Palen Co.

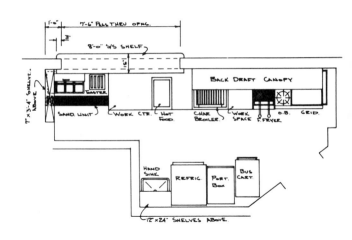

Holly's Steak & 4 Restaurant

A quality, low priced menu appealing to a broad segment of the market bridges the gap between the hamburger snack and the eight-course dinner in this Ann Arbor, Michigan restaurant. Preparation spaces are limited, requiring little set-up time. Low labor percentage dramatizes ease of operation for service personnel and patrons alike in this family-style restaurant which is both economical and soundly conceived.

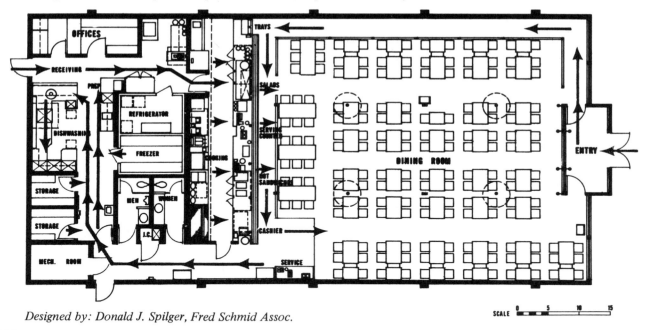

Designed by: Donald J. Spilger, Fred Schmid Assoc.

Page's Restaurant

This efficient, full-service restaurant in Woodland Hills, California was designed to follow the "time-proved Page's concept of operation."

The unit is basically a one-floor operation, except for mechanical equipment which is installed in a "well," formed by a modified mansard roof. All meats and vegetables go directly into the freezer or 38°F.

storage refrigerator. Other foods and supplies enter the storeroom or go directly to the point of use.

The preparation function is split over 2 areas. Since a number of menu items require initial basic preparation, a compact, efficient section called 'preparation and support cooking' is provided in the back of the house. (See plan, facing page.)

For those menu items that are cooked to order a "semi-exhibition cooking station" is centrally located.

Page's Woodland Hills Restaurant seats 156; serves breakfast, lunch and dinner, averaging 10,000 meals/customers per week. This is done with 48 employees. The operation is open seven days a week from 7 a.m. to midnight.

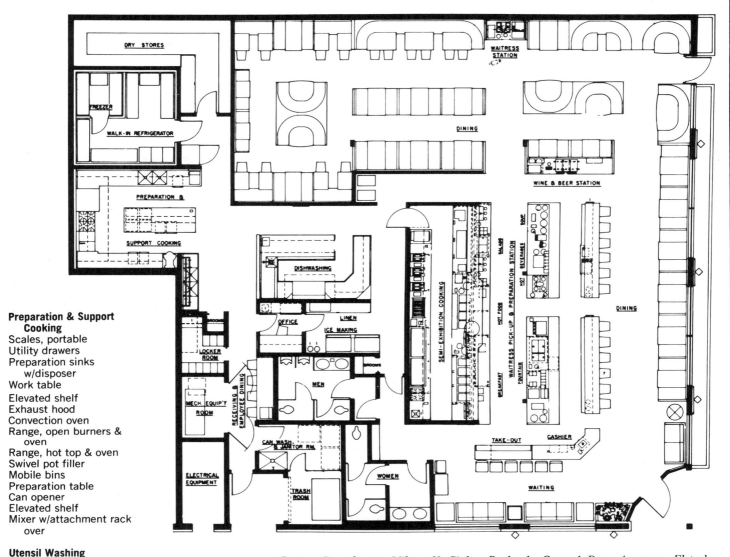

Labels within the floor plan:
DRY STORES · FREEZER · WALK-IN REFRIGERATOR · PREPARATION & · SUPPORT COOKING · DINING · WAITRESS STATION · WINE & BEER STATION · DISHWASHING · OFFICE · LINEN · ICE MAKING · BROOMS · LOCKER ROOM · MEN · MECH. EQUIP'T ROOM · RECEIVING & EMPLOYEE DINING · CAN WASH. & JANITOR RM. · WOMEN · ELECTRICAL EQUIPMENT · TRASH ROOM · SEMI-EXHIBITION COOKING · WAITRESS PICK-UP & PREPARATION STATION · HOT BEVERAGE · HOT FOOD · SOUP · FOUNTAIN · BREAKFAST · TAKE-OUT · CASHIER · WAITING · DINING

Design Consultants: Milton H. Sioles, Burbank, Ca. and Dave Aronson, Elster's

Preparation & Support Cooking
Scales, portable
Utility drawers
Preparation sinks
w/disposer
Work table
Elevated shelf
Exhaust hood
Convection oven
Range, open burners &
oven
Range, hot top & oven
Swivel pot filler
Mobile bins
Preparation table
Can opener
Elevated shelf
Mixer w/attachment rack
over

Utensil Washing
Drainboard
Sinks
Utensil rack

Dishwashing
Clean dishtable
Elevated rack shelf
Recess for flush-to-floor
comfort rack
Hood
Dishwasher
Scrapping trough
Pre-rinse
Sink w/disposer
Soiled dishtable
Silver soak sink
Busboy call panel
Bus carts

Semi-Exhibition Cooking
Sink
Scrap chute w/removable
receptacle
Built-in open burners
Refrigerated base
Built-in-griddles
Grease trough
Grease drain w/removable
receptacle
Insert for half pan
Built-in broiler
Insert for third pan
Built-in fryers

Exhaust hood
Equipment fixture, custom
Can opener
Steamer
Dish-up counter
Slicer
Food warmer
Steam freshener
Sink
Elevated garnish wells
Heated self-leveling plate
dispenser
Built-in food warmer
Built-in wet food table
Toasters
Refrigerated salad table

**Waitress Pick-up &
Preparation Station
(Salads)**
Refrigerated base
Refrigerated inserts,
dressings
Refrigerated bin, lettuce
Self-leveling underliner
dispenser
Refrigerated garnish wells
Built-in ice cream case,
plate & fork chiller

(Hot Food)
Steam freshener
Set-up counter, storage
under
Pick-up shelf
Order wheel
Under-counter storage

(Breakfast)
Steam freshener
Set-up counter, storage
under
Refrigerated base
Ice tea dispenser
Ice coffee dispenser
Under counter storage

(Soup)
Self-leveling soup bowl
dispenser
Self-leveling underliner
dispenser
Insert for crackers
Soup warmers
Scrap chute w/removable
receptacle
Hot water dipper well
Hot syrup dispenser
Hot chocolate dispenser

Work counter, storage
under
Hot water dispenser
Self-leveling saucer
dispenser
Elevated well for packaged
items
Self-leveling cup dispenser
Coffee maker
Scrap chute w/removable
receptacle
Dipper well
Refrigerated display case

(Fountain)
Stainless platform, storage
under
Milk dispenser w/4 mixers
Built-in ice cream case
Scrap chute w/removable
receptacle
Dipper well
Undercounter refrigerator
Fountain
Ice bin
Soft drink dispenser
Self-level glass dispenser
Orange juice dispenser
Hot wells

Refrigerated display cases
Dry display case

Wine & Beer Station
Set-up counter, storage
under
Decorative beer mug
holders
Display kegs for wine
dispensing
Beer dispenser
Glass chiller
Under counter refrigerator

Waitress Station
Self-leveling cup dispenser
Wall cabinet w/waitress
signal
Self-leveling saucer
dispenser
Scrap chute w/removable
receptacle
Coffee maker
Ice bin
Water dispenser
Self-leveling glass
dispenser
Remote controlled
television camera

The magic combination of superb Mexican food in classic Mexican surroundings has made an established success of the Red Onion Restaurant in Huntington Beach, California. Seating 252 patrons in four dining areas and a cocktail lounge/patio, the Red Onion offers a menu made up of such South-of-the-Border standbys as tortillas, burritos, enchiladas, tacos, and chili verde, as well as unusual specialties like Steak Verde, Steak Carne Ortega, and Steak Duisato. All of the food is prepared and served by 50 employees.

The Moorish style arch (pictured at right) is a true interpretation of the classic architecture found in the Mexican hacienda. This typical dining area affords guests spacious comfort in fully upholstered booth and table seating. Geometric Mexican tile patterns skillfully repeated in the red, gold, and black carpet provide a dramatic background for the entire area.

Vividly contrasting tones and textures are skillfully balanced and modern materials are given antique richness to enhance the total design, as illustrated in the picture on the facing page. Carpet colors provide a warm background for the natural, soft-toned adobe walls. Darkened beamed ceilings are finished to an aged richness. Lowered roofs covered in red Mexican tiles give an air of friendly intimacy to the four separate dining areas. Framed pictures of photographs depict scenes from the historical era of the 1910 Mexican revolution.

Walls glow with amber hue in the candlelight effect from the custom-made iron and wood hanging fixtures. Turned, high-backed chairs with natural woven seats are typical of Mexican farmhouses and provide comfort as well as authenticity.

Old World treasures are used to focus attention on the various areas of the interior. A traditional serape and sombrero emphasize the graceful arched entrance, with its massive raised panel doors, to the banquet dining area, shown at the rear of the picture on facing page.

The cocktail lounge, where food is also served, includes a shuttered patio overlooking a small lagoon. A colorfully striped awning provides protection, as do the shutters which can be opened and closed to suit weather conditions.

Right: The carts at the left in the waitress pick-up station are designed for appearance and function and are used to transfer the traditional hot dishes from the kitchen to the patrons' tables. When larger groups are served, a lazy-susan, used for dips and garnishes, is placed on top of the cart.

The cart's refrigerated base provides the necessary storage for garnishes. The refrigerated top inserts are for the "ready garnish." When these are depleted, full pans are transferred from the base section. Doors on all refrigerated bases are self-closing for efficiency and safety and are equipped with magnetic seals.

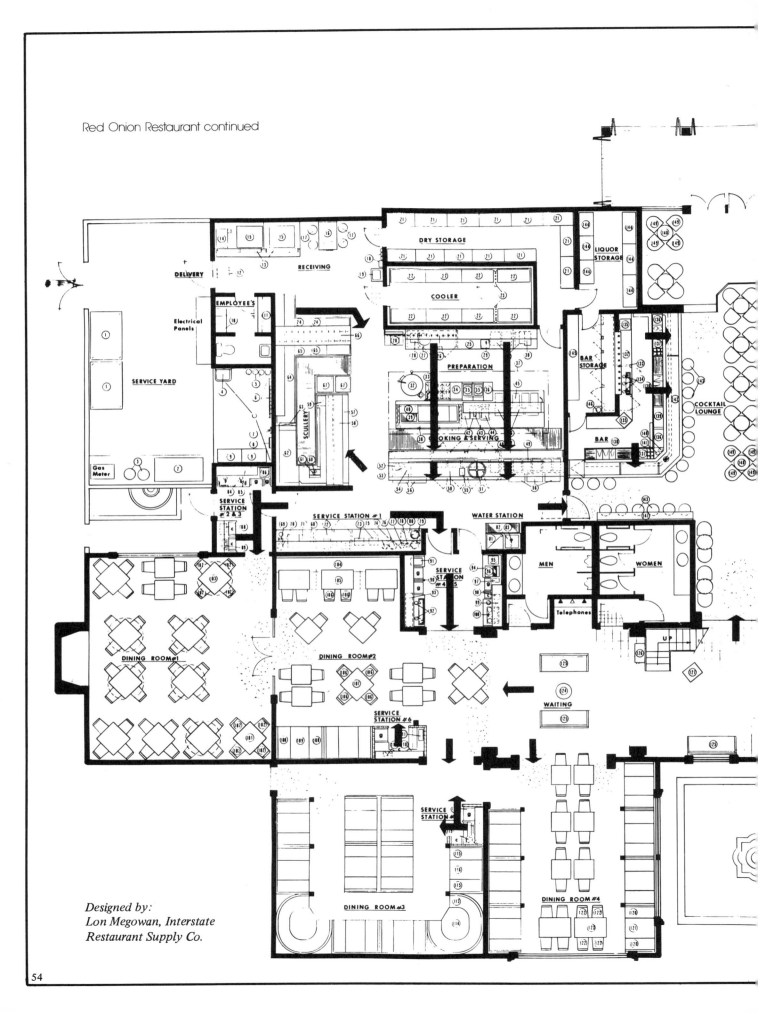

Designed by:
Lon Megowan, Interstate
Restaurant Supply Co.

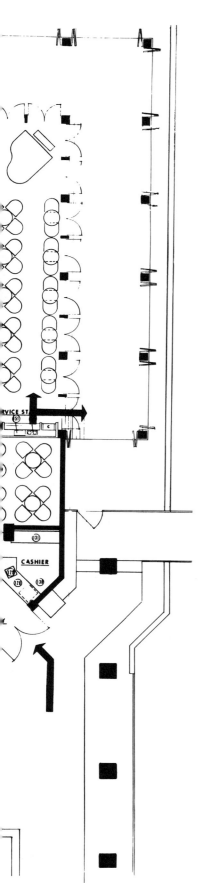

EQUIPMENT LIST

Service Yard
1. Trash Receptacle
2. Hot Water System
3. Water Softening System
4. Service Sink
5. CO_2 Tanks
6. Mop and Broom Rack
7. Hose Bibb
8. Hose Hanger
9. Metal Shelving

Employee's Dressing Area
10. Lockers
11. Clothes Pole and Shelf

Receiving Area
12. Fly Fan
13. Ice Storage Bins
14. Ice Maker—Flaker
15. Ice Maker—Cubers
16. Employee's Dining and Receiving Table
17. Stools
18. Time Clock & Card Rack
19. Hand Sink
20. Portable Receiving Scale

Store Room & Walk-In Cooler
21. Metal Shelving
22. Adjustable Metal Shelving
23. Security Fence

Preparation Area
24. Preparation Sinks
25. Preparation Table w/Elevated Shelf
26. Wall-Mounted Pot Rack
27. Self-Contained Freezer Base
28. Food Cutter
29. Can Opener
30. Slicer
31. Portable Bin

Preparation Cooking
32. Self-Contained Steam-Jacketed Kettle
33. Range—Open Burner
34. Table
35. Fryers
36. Table
37. Exhaust Hood

Cooking and Serving
38. Refrigerated Base
39. Grooved Griddle
40. Infra Red Broiler
41. Griddle
42. Hot Food Pans
43. Food Warmer
44. Fryer
45. Hot Food Table
46. Cheese Melters
47. Serving Fixture
48. Refrigerated Base
49. Hot Food Table
50. Pass Shelf w/Built-In Food Warmers & Check Holder
51. Check Wheel

52. Toaster
53. Mixer
54. Adding Machine
55. Time Clock
56. Serving Carts

Scullery
57. Soiled Dish Table
58. Elevated Rack Shelf
59. Silver Soak Sink
60. Pre-Rinse
61. Disposer
62. Dish Washer
63. Vent Stack
64. Clean Dish Table w/Elevated Shelf
65. Pot Sinks
66. Elevated Pot Rack and Shelf
67. Cup and Glass Storage Rack

Service Station No. 1
68. Service Station
69. Dipperwell
70. Dish Dispenser
71. Ice Cream Freezer
72. Salad Refrigerated Base
73. Fresh-O-Matics
74. Spoon Insert
75. Bowl Dispenser
76. Plate Dispenser
77. Saucer Dispenser
78. Cup Dispenser
79. Soup Warmers
80. Roll Warmer

Water Station
81. Water Station
82. Glass Dispenser

Service Station No. 2 & No. 3
83. Glass Filler
84. Beer Refrigerator w/Dispenser Towers
85. Ice Pan for Glasses
86. Milk Dispenser
87. Service Station w/Elevated Shelf
88. Silverware Box
89. Coffee Warmer

Service Station No. 4 & No. 5
90. Service Station w/Elevated Shelf
91. Silverware Box
92. Beer Refrigerator w/Dispensing Towers
93. Ice Pan for Glasses
94. Service Station w/Elevated Shelf
95. Milk Dispenser
96. Ice Sink and Drink Dispenser
97. Iced Tea Dispenser
98. Coffee Dispenser
99. Coffee Filter Rack
100. Coffee Maker

Dining Room No. 1
101. Table
102. Chair

103. Table w/Flips to Round

Dining Room No. 2
104. Settee
105. Table w/Flip
106. Chair
107. Table
108. Booth
109. Table

Service Station No. 6
110. Service Station w/Elevated Shelf
111. Silverware Box
112. Coffee Warmer

Dining Room No. 3
113. Circular Booth
114. Table
115. Booth
116. Table

Service Station No. 7
117. Service Station w/Elevated Shelf
118. Silverware Box
119. Coffee Warmer

Dining Room No. 4
120. Booth
121. Table
122. Chair
123. Table

Cashier and Waiting
124. Table
125. Bench
126. Cigarette Machine
127. Hostess Stand
128. Cashier Stand
129. Cash Register
130. Safe
131. Storage Cabinet

Bar
132. Back Bar
133. Beer and Wine Refrigerator (Pass-Thru)
134. Beer and Wine Dispensing Towers
135. Cash Register
136. Ice Pan Glasses
137. Jockey Station
138. Sinks
139. Ice Bin
140. Mixer
141. Blender
142. Bar
143. Stools

Liquor Store Room
144. Metal Shelving
145. Liquor Display Shelving
146. Red Wine Container

Cocktail Lounge
147. Singles Bar
148. Table
149. Chair.

Service Station No. 8
150. Service Station
151. Silverware Box
152. Coffee Warmer

Right: This view is of the heart of the production facilities of the Red Onion Restaurant—the very efficient entree cooking line. The cooking line-up consists of: built-in grooved griddle with an infrared overfired broiler mounted above the back half of the griddle. Combining these two appliances provides flexibility and speed in the production of steaks, and also provides one of the most direct solutions to the air pollution problems facing the foodservice industry. It is on this line that such specialties as Steak Verde, Steak Carne Ortega, and Steak Duisato are prepared. Built-in, thermostatically controlled smooth griddles are used to prepare tortillas, burritos, and similar dishes as well as those gringo favorites, bacon and eggs.

Refrigerated base is designed to hold enough back-up ingredients to carry through entire serving period. Removable, self-closing drawers are sized for modular pans. The No. 200 modular pan and its increments are used throughout the production and serving areas.

Below: There is ample table space alongside food cutter for placement of food pans. Spices and condiments are stored in air-tight containers. Slicer table was fabricated to provide safe, efficient working height. Removable can opener is installed on mounting plate attached underneath the table, with the sides of the square hole in the table top turned down to form a guide for the body extension of the can opener. A square hole is cut in a standard size board and the board is placed over the opening in the table top and the can opener then inserted through the opening. This prevents dangerous slipping of cans with subsequent damage to the cutter and marring of the stainless steel table top.

Above: This preparation station, planned for maximum flexibility and production in a relatively small area, accommodates four people. It is also used in training young people in food preparation and cooking skills.

Below: As a step toward maximum productivity, a stainless steel platform to hold containers alongside the fryers permits safe and efficient transfer. The same design principles were applied to the wet hot food table with its time-saving swivel faucet.

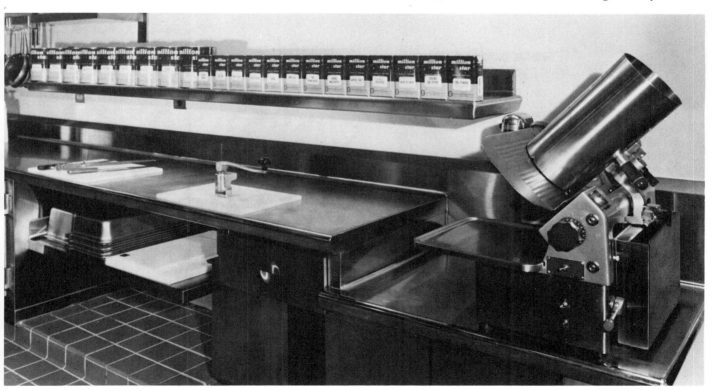

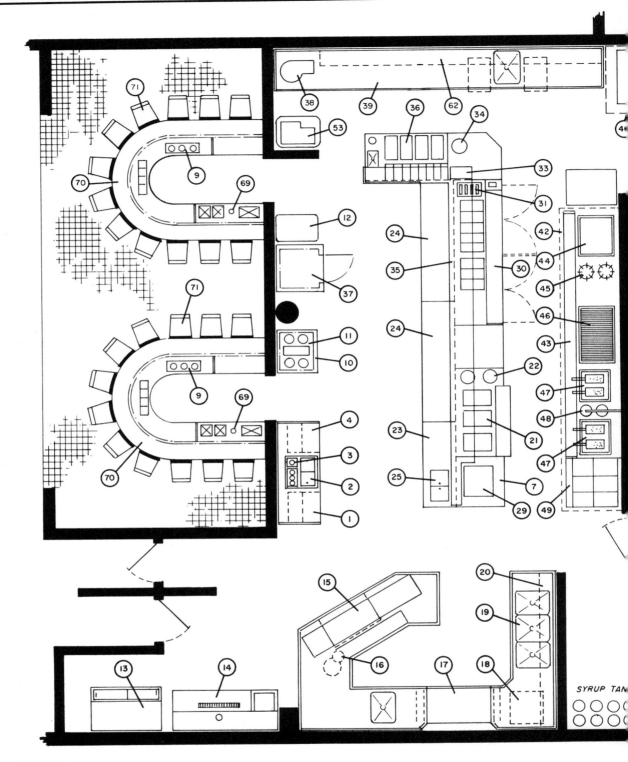

EQUIPMENT LIST

1. Dish Rack Unit
2. Drink Disp. w/carbinator
3. Iced Tea Disp.
4. Dish Rack Unit
5. Shelves
6. Service Stand
7. Utility Stand
8. Tables 24 in. x 30 in.
9. Coffee Warmers
10. Utility Stand
11. Coffee Maker
12. Port. Tray Cart
13. Ice Maker w/Bin
14. Beer Dispenser
15. Soiled Dish Table
16. Disposal
17. Dish Machine
18. Booster Heater
19. Clean Dish Table
20. Pot Rack and Shelving
21. Hot Food Table (3 wells)
22. Lowerators
23. Utility Stand
24. Utility Stand
25. Hot Food Well
26. Chairs
27. Booths (4 seaters)
28. Oval Tables 60 in. x 30 in.
29. Micro Wave Oven
30. Sandwich Unit
31. Toaster
32. Round Stools
33. Mixer
34. Fudge Warmer
35. Pass Shelf
36. Ice Cream Cabinet w/Syrup Rack

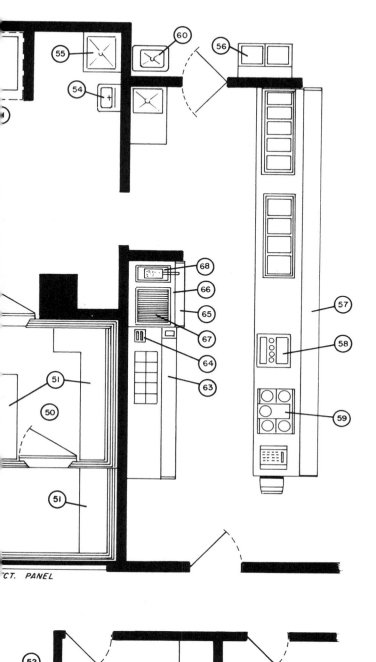

The Hearth Restaurant
HOLLYWOOD, FLA.

This dining-room coffee shop located in a shopping mall department store has 106 seats, serves 2640 meals per week.

• Designed for expansion, operation is based on pre-portioned and prepared foods; although menu offers various choices, dishes are simple variations on basic items.

• Use of prepared and pre-portioned foods curtails need for pot washing so facilities were built into dish machine.

• Cooking and storage core, centrally located between restaurant and 80-seat employee cafeteria is designed to provide each facility with access to any additional provisions needed without interference with the other's operation.

• Good back-up for counter service is assured by efficient location of dishes, beverage dispensers, salad refrigerator. Water, ice and sink unit and coffee warmers are placed in counters.

• Equipment for related tasks is just steps apart with fudge warmer alongside ice cream cabinets; salad center with slicer on mobile stand; food cutter near prep table and sink with overhead shelf for finished salads.

Designed by: Ronald Kruse, Donald Walsh, Federated Stores; H. Gordon Hooper, Edward Don Company

37.	Refrig. Salad Case	46.	Broiler	54.	Hand Sink	64.	Toaster
38.	Food Cutter	47.	Fryer	55.	Mop Sink	65.	Hood
39.	Salad Prep Table & Sink	48.	Dump Stand	56.	Tray Stand	66.	Utility Stand
40.	Hood	49.	Range w/Salamander	57.	Cafeteria Counter	67.	Griddle
41.	Convection Oven	50.	Walk-in Refrig. and freezer	58.	Drink Disp.	68.	Fryer
42.	Hood	51.	Shelves	59.	Coffee Maker	69.	Water, Ice & Sink Unit
43.	Utility Stand	52.	Scale	60.	Water Cooler	70.	Formica Counter
44.	Griddle	53.	Slicer w/Mobile Stand	61.	Round Table 72-in.	71.	Stools
45.	Range Hot Plates			62.	Shelf		
				63.	Sandwich Unit		

Bob Burns Restaurant

An intriguing blend of high style, yet functional and warm design, Bob Burns Restaurant in Woodland Hills, California is located in a $500 million master planned "downtown complex" for commercial, industrial, and residential uses.

The unit is a free-standing building, designed in the traditional Scottish style of a "main barn" or country manor with other rooms added later. The main part of the restaurant is also the entrance to the bar and hors d'oeuvres area. There are three dining areas and the But 'N Pub ("but" is Scottish for kitchen) for fast service at lunch, dinner, or for late night snacks.

At the But 'N Pub guests can order stand-up style and then dine at a nearby table or on The Loft, a balcony area overlooking the bar.

Basic design concept for the restaurant was that of quality, particularly reflected in decor, furniture, and furnishings, with a high level of service within the framework of "California Casual." The menu offers quality popular items as well as some Scottish specialties at a reasonable price since the area served is relatively affluent.

Throughout the restaurant there is a genuine Scottish aura, the product of gas lanterns, Queen Anne chairs, settle benches, pewterware, old prints, heraldic emblems, tankards, and antique silver objects. There are also working fireplaces; and fresh flowers are displayed on each table. Ceilings are high and cross-timbered, the whole providing the atmosphere of a large, yet cozy home with dining and reception areas as well as some very private nooks.

There are 225 seats and the operation is open seven days a week from 11 a.m. to 2 a.m. Service peaks are from 11:30 a.m. to 2 p.m., when an average of 225 persons are served, and 7 to 9:30 p.m. with 350.

There are eighty employees; these are divided into fourteen in preparation and cooking, thirty-seven in service activities, eighteen in cleaning, eight in dish and pot washing, and three supervisors, including the manager. The largest number on duty at one time—thirty-one—is at peak lunchtimes.

The plan at right illustrates the skillful relationship of production to dining areas. Pictures on the following pages detail some of the special facilities.

Designed by: Stan Abrams, Elster's, Inc.

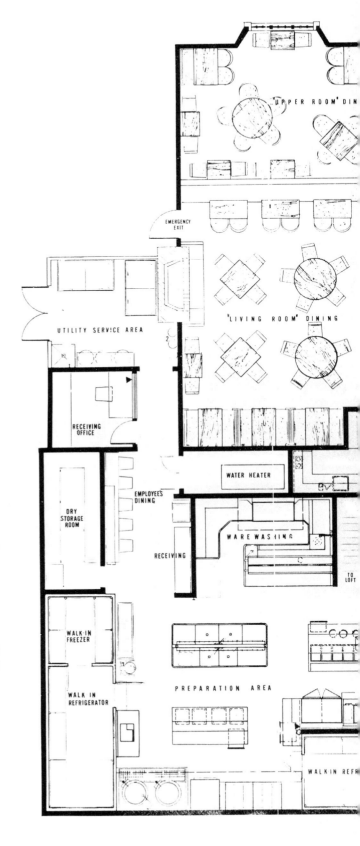

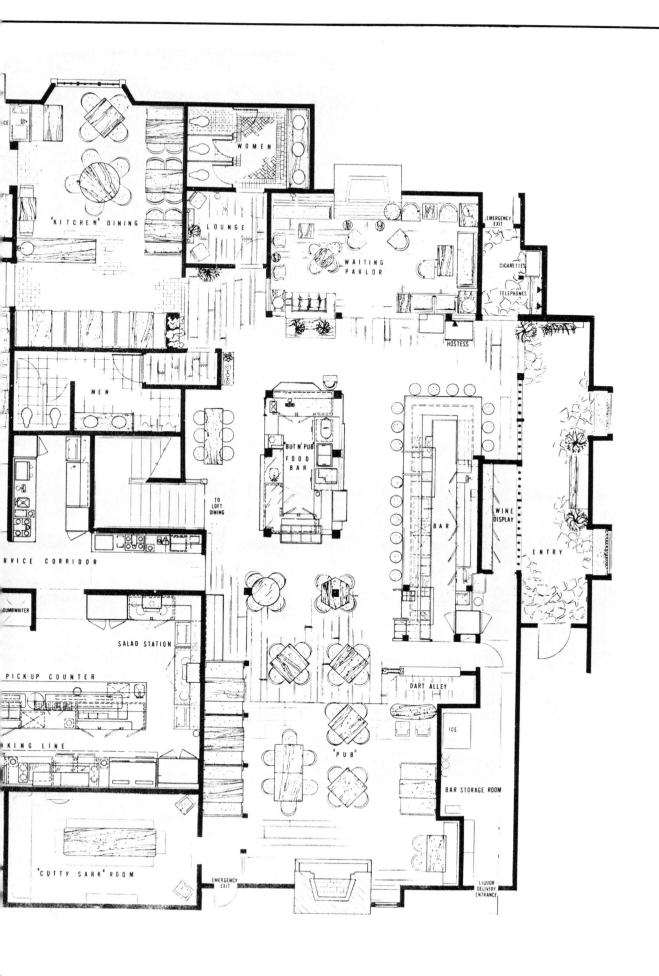

"KITCHEN" DINING

WOMEN

LOUNGE

WAITING PARLOR

EMERGENCY EXIT

CIGARETTES

TELEPHONES

HOSTESS

MEN

BUT N' PUB FOOD BAR

BAR

WINE DISPLAY

ENTRY

TO LOFT DINING

RVICE CORRIDOR

SALAD STATION

DART ALLEY

ICE

PICK-UP COUNTER

"PUB"

BAR STORAGE ROOM

DUMBWAITER

KING LINE

"CUTTY SARK" ROOM

EMERGENCY EXIT

LIQUOR DELIVERY ENTRANCE

Bob Burns Restaurant continued

Above: Excellent signage combines with interesting exterior design to attract patrons to Bob Burns Restaurant. Once inside, patrons find a pleasant waiting area from which they may proceed to their choice of several dining areas.

Right: This close-up view of a portion of the cooking line-up illustrates some of the excellent design details in this compact operation: (A) The support for microwave ovens has built-in slides accommodating 18- by 26-in. sheetpans making working storage of items not requiring refrigeration very convenient. (B) The stacked ovens are installed at optimum working height, fully accessible for cleaning and service. (C) The steam pressure cooker is close-coupled with its generator for proper operation; furthermore, the two are installed in an unusual manner designed to make service and cleaning easy. (D) The back and end splashes are coved and have been fabricated with a slanted return and sealed to the wall flashing to ensure maximum sanitation.

Above: The special emphasis placed at Bob Burns Restaurant on the dinner salad service is illustrated in this well-planned dual waitress service area. Two almost identical refrigerated bases have been provided for storage of back-up salads, salad dressing, and for chilling the bowls used in spinning the salads. Other special features: (A) Raised rim openings in the top of refrigerated bases accommodate drop-in containers of salad dressings and allow up to five waitresses to assemble salads at one time. (B) The portable freezer here and one out of view at right of picture dispense chilled salad plates. (C) Two wall-hung, refrigerated lettuce crispers, with unique cold wall refrigeration systems, store and dispense salad greens efficiently, ensuring crispness and coldness. Spare plastic containers of salad greens are readily available from a walk-in cooler. (D) Stainless wall shelf holds cocktail bowls and liners to be iced by waitresses and then filled. (E) Two-section reach-in refrigerator is fitted with removable angle slides to hold trays of portioned sauces and other service items needed by waitresses. (F) All porcelain enamel floor sinks installed flush with floor serve as condensate receptacles as well as area drains.

Left: A lift for employee morale is provided in their special dining area, furnished with comfortable chairs and covered with a wall material to which messages or bulletins are easily taped. First aid supplies are in full view here as well as in the Loft area.

Bagatelle Restaurant

EQUIPMENT LIST

1. Scale
2. Receiving Table
3. Under Counter Rack
4. Pot & Pan Sink
5. Disposal
6. Preparation Table
7. Mixer
8. Walk-In Cooler/Freezer
9. Salad Racks
10. Cooler Shelving
11. Freezer Shelving
12. Storage Shelving
13. Kettle
14. Oven
15. Portable Hot Top Range
16. Portable Hot Top Range
17. Pot Rack
18. Equipment Stand
19. Salamander Broiler
20. Hot Top Range
21. Grate Top Range
22. Fryers
23. Broiler
24. Fire Protection
25. Exhaust Hood
26. Fry Pan
27. Water Filler
28. Work Table
29. Food Cutter
30. Slicer
31. Toaster
32. Refrigerated Base
33. Pick-Up Counter
34. Refrigerator/Freezer
35. Hot Food Lamps—Over
36. Hot Food Lamps—Under
37. Order Wheel
38. Hot Food Lamps—Over
39. Microwave Oven
40. Pass Thru Refrigerator
41. Ice Cream Cabinet
42. Waitress Counter
43. Cup & Glass Dollies
44. Coffee Maker
45. Tea Dispenser
46. Ice Machine
47. Under Counter Freezer
48. Milk Dispenser
49. Cashier's Table
50. Rollwarmer
51. Buss Shelving
52. Plate Cart
53. Dishtables
54. Booster Heater
55. Dishwasher
56. Disposal
57. Coffee Warmer
58. Waitress Station

59. Waitress Station
60. Coffee Warmer
61. Under Counter Refrigerator
62. Waitress Station
63. Food Warming Drawers
64. Water Station
65. Tea Dispenser
66. Char-Broiler
67. Equipment Stand
68. Fryer
69. Grate Top Burners
70. Griddle-Broiler
71. Fire Protection
72. Exhaust Hood
73. Expresso Machine
74. Back Counter
75. Refrigerated Base
76. Wine Dispenser
77. Storage Cabinet
78. Drainboard with Sinks
79. Underbar Base
80. Glass Chiller

81. Cocktail Station
82. Soft Drink Dispenser
83. Cashier Counter
84. Ice Cream Cabinet
85. Food Warmers
86. Equipment Counter
87. Sandwich Unit
88. Toaster
89. Coffee Station
90. Coffee Grinder
91. Coffee Maker
92. Soft Drink Dispenser
93. Cocktail Station
94. Refrigerated Base
95. Bar Sink
96. Underbar Base
97. Front Bar Assembly
98. Back Bar Assembly
99. Linen Shelving
100. Liquor Shelving
101. Receiving Cart
102. Compactor

Designed by: Fabricators, Inc.

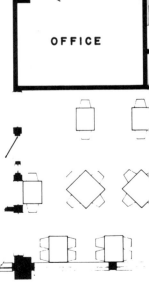

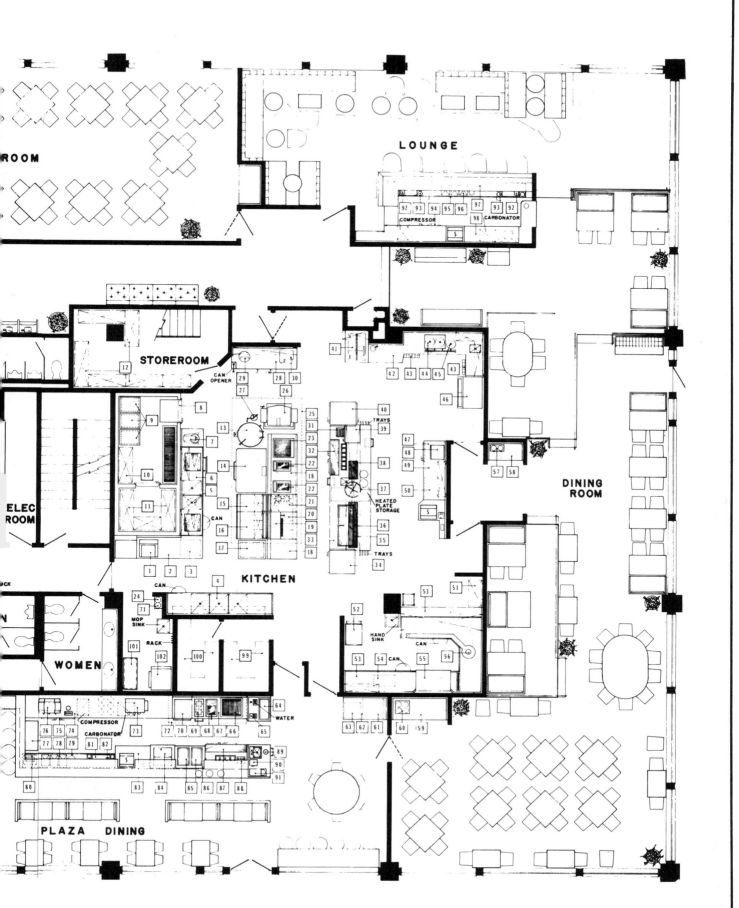

LOUNGE

92 93 94 95 96 97 93 92
COMPRESSOR 98 CARBONATOR
S

ROOM

STOREROOM

12

CAN OPENER

29 28 30
27 26

8

9

13

7

14

10

6
5

11

15
16

17

1 2 3

KITCHEN

4

CAN

24
71

MOP SINK

RACK

101

102 100 99

WOMEN

COMPRESSOR
76 75 74
CARBONATOR
77 78 79 81 82

73

72 70 69 68 67 66

64

WATER

65

S

89
90
91

80

83 84

85 86 87 88

PLAZA DINING

ELEC ROOM

41

42 43 44 45 43

46

25
31
23
32
22
22

21
20
19
33
18

40
TRAYS 39

38

37
HEATED PLATE STORAGE

36
35

34 TRAYS

47
48
49

50

S

57 58

DINING ROOM

52

HAND SINK

53 54 CAN

51

53

55 56

CAN

63 62 61

60 59

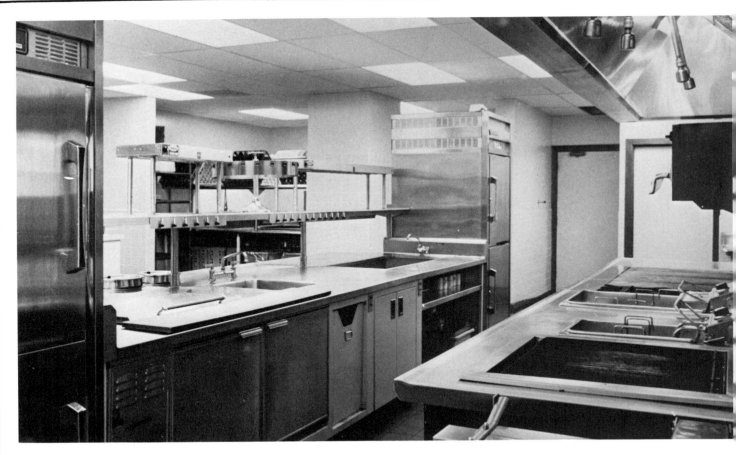

Bagatelle Restaurant continued

An affluent market surrounds the high-rise building where the Bagatelle Restaurant is located, and the continental cuisine of this Dallas operation has been attracting members of that market in ever-increasing numbers. The pleasant interior and the piquant veal specialties are important factors in the restaurant's success.

The successful operation is testimony also to the effective resolution of a difficult design challenge. The floor plan shown on the preceding pages grew out of the need to "put a restaurant in this space." The kitchen would have to supply food to three dining areas and overcome the problems of access unavoidable in high-rise foodservice. There could be no extension of space; all answers had to be worked out in the area assigned.

Above: Making space count on the chef's side of the serving counter was accomplished by locating working refrigerators at each end; building in standard manufacturer's refrigerated base for worktop use adjacent to sink; placing front trash can in base next to heated pass thru doors, and putting space for bain marie in top at right.

Right: View of checkers-cashier stand across from and out of the way of waitress pick-up counter. Aisles provide ample space for peak waitress and bus boy traffic.

Marie Callender Restaurant

Because his patrons began to indicate they could not live by pie alone, owner/operator Don Callender expanded his formula to provide a full-service dinner house complete with saloon, bakery, and take-out shop.

At the same time he has kept his pies showcased as the main attraction, since from opening day 1962 the public has never stopped buying Marie Callender pies to take home.

Of his fifty-five units, the smaller shops are being remodeled to 180 seats. All new units are retaining the country store-style to please both oldtimers and the new generation with its interest in nostalgia. The 225-seat complexes have kitchens large enough for on-premise pies production and for preparing the expanded list of menu items as well. The

Pies put Marie Callender Restaurants in the foodservice forefront, and their production is still a paramount activity. This rotary pie machine, can produce 500 pies per hour. Here it is being cleaned after use.

new San Bernardino, California unit built from the plan (p. 68–9) has 8,300 sq. ft., with 3,495 in the back of the house and the rest in a spacious front waiting area, lounge, retail pie sales area, dining rooms, and a salad bar.

Kitchen equipment includes such items as an 80-qt. mixer (that also grinds meat); a patty machine that turns out 1,200 an hour; a 60-gal. tilting kettle, and 2 5-gal. trunnion kettles that produce soups, chicken pie fillings, and chili, as well as custard and fruit pie fillings. By having the kitchen planned and equipped to handle both daily pie-making and general food preparation, Callender has his investment doing double duty.

Fruit pies are frozen in standard freezers (blast freezing is not necessary) and baked daily as needed. The crusts for custard pies are baked empty, then filled with pumpkin, pecan, and lemon custard. These are made fresh daily, not frozen but instead stored in racks in roll-in refrigerators. After they are filled, a sampling is placed on view so patrons can see the wide array of choices.

The refrigerated surfaces for custard pie service and cutting are sizable which makes it easy for waitresses to cut the 9-inch pies into five ample slices as orders are placed.

In the short-order cooking area, cooks turn out hamburgers (best seller is the Frisco Burger on sourdough bread with parmesan cheese), patty melts, beef stew, vegetable plates, and ginger chicken. Special ovens handle prime rib and ham hocks.

Cornbread, the unexpected accompaniment for every meal, underscores the operation's basic country flavor. It is prepared every morning from a dry mix of special corn flour. Baked in the revolving pie ovens, it is then held at room temperature. Pans of presliced cornbread are stored cold in drawers in the waitress pick-up area under the microwave ovens. Waitresses just pop their orders into the microwave when they are ready to serve them.

Putting other specialties with pie has kept Marie Callender Restaurants in the top position their products merit.

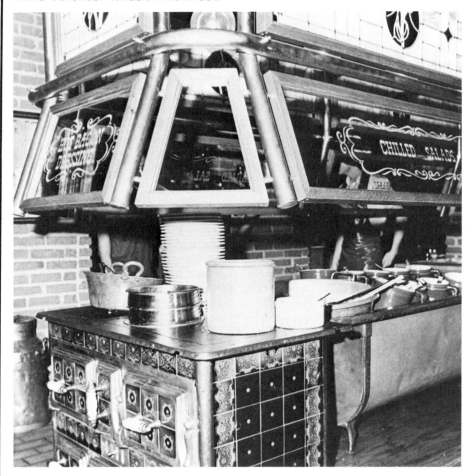

Left: The old-fashioned look featured in the new-style Marie Callender Restaurant has started the owner and his associates on antique hunts. An antique bathtub with a false bottom holds ice; an antique stove has a soup well in it to hold hot bacon dressing, and the plate chiller shown above is built into an antique ice box in the salad bar.

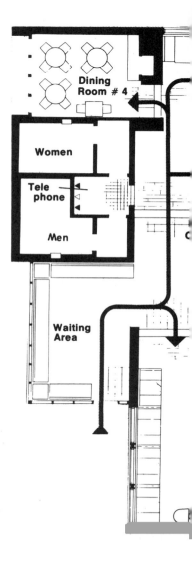

Left: A fringe benefit of making pie regularly is that the crust trimmings can be used for making chicken pot pies, and filling can be used for apple sauce, a popular accompaniment to many entrees. The special set up for making chicken pot pies is shown here.

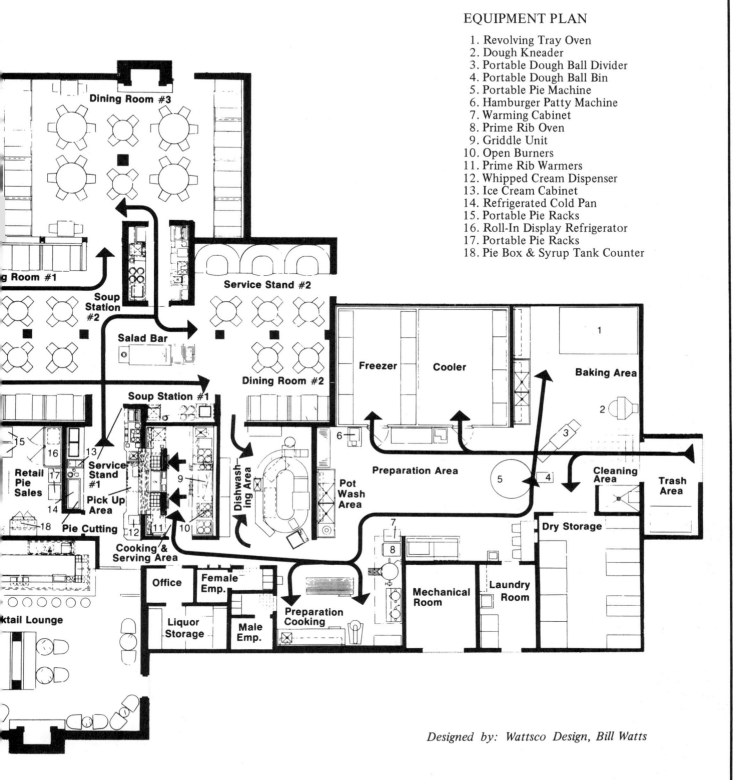

EQUIPMENT PLAN

1. Revolving Tray Oven
2. Dough Kneader
3. Portable Dough Ball Divider
4. Portable Dough Ball Bin
5. Portable Pie Machine
6. Hamburger Patty Machine
7. Warming Cabinet
8. Prime Rib Oven
9. Griddle Unit
10. Open Burners
11. Prime Rib Warmers
12. Whipped Cream Dispenser
13. Ice Cream Cabinet
14. Refrigerated Cold Pan
15. Portable Pie Racks
16. Roll-In Display Refrigerator
17. Portable Pie Racks
18. Pie Box & Syrup Tank Counter

Designed by: Wattsco Design, Bill Watts

Pie preparation is the product of excellent planning and equipment at Marie Callender Restaurant. The eighteen-pan revolving oven with six shelves at right can cook 150 pies at a time. Pies shown are called chilled pre-baked as crusts are pre-baked, then filled at point of service or order. Frozen pies in racks at left below will be baked the day following preparation. Each rack holds 80 pies. At right below is key equipment for preparation of pie fillings. The 60-gal. tilting kettle is used not only for pie fillings but for soup making. It has its own kettle filler. Two smaller tilting kettles are located adjacent to the larger unit. A hood above these steam kettles collects the condensate. Smooth flow speeds pie preparation and delivery to point of sale or service.

Hospital

Eldor A. Kluge

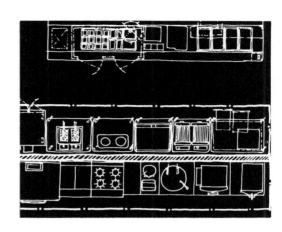

PROFESSIONALLY, THERE is perhaps a no more challenging or rewarding opportunity than participating in the planning and operation of a new—or remodelled—dietary facility in a hospital.

Dietary operations, more than any other foodservice facility, reflect the needs of the community they serve. Aside from the fact that the "patron" must participate at least three times a day (he is in no position to shop around), the level of therapeutic care for each individual, as well as his ethnic origins and environmental background, provide a unique challenge in recipe and menu formulations.

And, beyond that, the objectives of the community and governing boards, as they relate to service, quality, and therapeutic values, must be included in the programming and planning of any dietary operation whether it be under new construction or undergoing renovation.

There are, to be sure, numerous food and equipment systems developed in recent years to meet these requirements of quality, service, and economic controls. Still, the variables confronting dietary planners are tremendous, and these include the system resources for problem solving. However, there are some milestones in the decision-making process. These tend to accumulate the variables in groups, and so lead to orderly conclusions on the basic systems required to satisfy the needs of a given operation.

The Planning Team

Once an operation is authorized for planning, who will be the planners? Here is a list of those disciplines which should be involved and their roles or responsibilities.

1. *Architect/Engineer:* When the institution's board has determined that improvements or new facilities are necessary, a qualified Architectural/Engineering firm should be selected to develop the total project scope. This encompasses site survey, current and long range needs, community objectives, and cost forecasting—including potential growth and expansion requirements.

The A/E firm will be the focal organization for receiving and assimilating all data, resources, and input. For even what might seem a relatively unimportant renovation could prove a complicated mass of mechanical procedures and documents for the institution's planning or purchasing department if qualified A/E services are not employed.

2. *Foodservice Consultant:* Generally, after the Architectural/Engineering firm has been commissioned, consultants are employed for specialized operational areas including clinical laboratories, and mechanical, structural, and electrical engineering. It is also important that the foodservice consultant be brought on board in the very early stages of design development since his area of responsibility encompasses a significant portion of the planned area, and relates to space

allotment, traffic flow, and mechanical considerations. All of the project consultants, through the A/E firm, should counsel with the administration of the institution as the first step in programming the objectives of the hospital community.

Thus, the foodservice consultant should coordinate his work with the foodservice director and chief dietitian. (If these positions do not exist he should recommend they be established, even temporarily, for proper communication of therapeutic and operational needs.) The foodservice consultant should be responsible for the research and determination of all operational systems required to satisfy the operating plan.

3. *Foodservice Director:* This position is most often filled by the incumbent operator of the existing dietary department which is to be renovated or relocated. The foodservice director may be an employee of the institution, or of a contract caterer. In either case, his/her interest is in providing satisfactory foodservice to the patients and running the dietary department in the most efficient and economical way.

The foodservice director is usually familiar with the latest trends in operating systems and eager to lend advice in planning the new facility. Seldom are projects that are being planned without a foodservice director, but if this situation should exist, the consultant would need to assume this role.

4. *Dietitian:* The dietitian is a most important checkpoint in menu and operational planning, and can contribute much to the overall design development, from work station layout to personnel placement. The dietitian's concern is with the development of design as it applies to production areas, and the distribution of food to the patients. Sanitation, economics, and therapeutic values are of predominant concern in a dietitian's evaluation of a satisfactory plan.

The design plan for a new facility requires a projection of space and costs. There are several rules of thumb used to estimate broad parameters relative to space and cost. I, personally, do not accept all rules of thumb as they are more often proved wrong than correct. But, since they provide a starting point (and sometimes a finishing

point), they do provide some standards for estimating. They should, however, be very limited and general so as not to restrict thinking and creativity.

Space for a health care dietary operation will average out at approximately 20 sq. ft. per patient bed. This figure includes only functional and operational areas such as toilets and lockers, dry and cold storage, break-out and receiving, offices, hot and cold food production, tray assembly, cafeteria service area, ware washing, pot washing, cart breakdown, sanitizing, and storage. Cafeteria seating or private dining are not included in this, nor are coffee shop and floor galley operations. These latter items are variable, depending upon operational use, system, or concept.

The variables in space are affected by such questions as: How many times will the cafeteria seating area turn? Will there be a coffee shop, or will the cafeteria also assume this role? If there will be floor pantries or galleys, will they reheat foods, provide full beverages, etc.? (Frequently the floor pantry provides only ancillary service and is often omitted if the dietary department provides all services.)

Cost estimating is another hazard when it comes to rule-of-thumb estimating. In 1975 it cost approximately $1,000 per bed to equip just the operational areas described above, not including other areas such as seating, coffee shops, or floor galleys.

The Value of the Consultant

Since so many variables exist in determining space and budget, and no hard-and-fast rule-of-thumb is practical, a foodservice consultant should be employed as soon as possible to help evaluate the variables, and evaluate space and budget required for the project.

Thus far we have discussed the generalities of planning, and how each member of the planning team relates to the other. Dietary planning really begins with the variables in operational concept. The variations in operational choices can be paralyzing if no direction is provided by the operating staff as to experience, preference, and concept.

The difference between preference and concept is basically the difference between past experience and the planners' willingness to consider new concepts in the light of their experience.

Personnel of facilities that are to be remodeled can provide previous operational data which can help considerably in the planning. But perhaps this previous operation was affected by poor working habits, due to space and equipment limitations. The planners must then cope with additional challenges in developing a new and more advanced facility.

In an attempt to help us—though sometimes the result has been to befuddle us—the foodservice industry has, in the last several years, promoted many new-fangled ways and means to solve dietary planning problems. These foodservice industry innovators include both equipment manufacturers and food processors.

The 'Convenience Food' Question

Let me illustrate this point. A few years ago, I was involved with a "convenience food" program for a large caterer. We were convinced that we were not pursuing convenience foods as we should. As we got into the program, we found that convenience foods needed to be packaged differently and that more diverse cooking and reheating equipment would be necessary. We found that food processors and equipment manufacturers were willing to adjust to standards of size, product, and methodology, and to assist individual operations where future demand could justify the cost of development. I cite this illustration to point out that though the industry may present some "solutions," often these solutions create new problems.

One of the most important planning decisions is whether the dietary operation is to be a conventional, frozen, or chilled food type system. This question is critical in the early stages of planning and should be addressed as early as possible.

Why should one consider anything other than a conventional foodservice which has served, and will continue to serve dietary operations for some time to come? This question is particularly pertinent since there is some resistance to a strictly convenience food type operation which has been tried by many operators with varying degrees of success. The problem is that the words "convenience foods" need to be more carefully defined. The term is not a statement of inflexibility, but rather one of considerable flexibility, when convenience foods are defined to include the following:

Precut and portioned meats, poultry, and fish products

Canned goods

Packaged, dried, and kettle-ready products

Bottled items, such as sauces, dressings, etc.

Pre-cooked, or partially pre-cooked entree items, and

Pre-cleaned, shredded, or blended salad ingredients

As the list indicates, these commonplace products have been the heart of convenience foods for a long time. To talk about "going" to a convenience food program, one has to ask himself only, "How far?" You are already part way there.

Degree of "Convenience" Commitment

It was during the aforementioned study for an operating company that we realized that convenience foods were already a natural part of our operational life. The question then became: Did we want to commit to pre-cooked, frozen entrees 100 percent? After comparing their cost with our labor factors, we decided buying all pre-cooked entrees would be relatively expensive since we had to have skilled labor on board during all hours of operation and needed to use that talent in the best possible way.

Our studies revealed that a mixture, or blend, of convenience and conventional product made the most operational sense. From this study, a chilled food system evolved. As it became more apparent that certain applied labor was required, and could not be eliminated even using all pre-cooked entrees, we felt that a menu designed to supplement the convenience list would best serve the interests of the operation.

That led to a need for refrigeration equipment that could rapidly chill our prepared food products. This would achieve for them the basic advantage of frozen food. If you can bring food temperature down from 160°F. to about 34°F. as rapidly as happens in freezing, you can also achieve a longer shelf life and minimal bacterial content.

We came to the conclusion that chilled foods, in conjunction with frozen entrees, were our most economical format. That way we utilized residual labor and our natural institutional purchasing power for food. We were able to take advantage of buying food in advance of preparation, produce finished product, and store it in a food bank system.

Any decision to adopt a convenience food operation will depend greatly on whether food is transported long distances from the main dietary kitchen. Outlying units require independent staffing in that staff must be at their units at service times and so cannot be utilized within the main kitchen.

Based on my experience, I am most definitely in favor of some form of convenience foods operation, and recommend that chilled foods be most carefully considered as an integral part of nearly any dietary planning.

Kitchen Equipment and Systems

So much for food processing. What about kitchen equipment and systems? Most equipment manufacturers provide integrated systems in the major areas of:

Exhaust and ventilation
Dish and ware washing
Cooking batteries, including steam
Tray assembly
Walk-in coolers
Cafeteria equipment

Years ago, using modular equipment was considered costly and inflexible. Compared to custom equipment, it was. However, considering today's costs of installation and maintenance, and the stricter sanitation requirements now in force, modular equipment simplifies planning and eliminates many problems on location. Concerning the word "modular," frequently we see or assume portability. I am opposed to portable equipment if it cannot be moved with ease. Heavy production equipment is frequently installed on wheels, but never moved because of weight. Too often equipment on wheels is selected for sanitation but, in practice, only creates a more unsanitary situation.

Advantage in Limited Sources

I believe that working with a limited number of manufacturers provides many advantages. This belief in limiting sources is derived from experience with their capability to respond and provide service.

As mentioned, the many variables inherent in facility planning are sufficient in themselves without confronting dozens of alternate manufacturers offering their wares. Equipment suppliers must establish their service reputation to find themselves considered by planning committees.

The link between the operator (or specifier) and supplier is often referred to as loyalty. Once this line of understanding is established, good rapport between the parties will result in cooperation in accumulating experience and technical assistance in the development stages of planning. The only means by which to establish a workable rapport is through service; service on the drawing board, and service in the installation.

A hospital dietary operation cannot afford to be down because of equipment service failure. And while prudence should be used in selecting locally serviceable equipment, you should also insure that work areas within the kitchen are so designed that overlapping operations can be achieved with various pieces of equipment. It should be possible to switch production tasks from one piece of equipment to another. For instance, food that is normally reheated in a microwave oven usually can be reheated in a steamer. Properly planned work centers should flex with requirements in production needs.

Equipment and Space Utilization

In planning flexible production areas, space utilization should be optimized. Not only should similar work functions be grouped, but they should be contiguous for use and utilization. Further on in this chapter, there is a plan that illustrates equipment utilization. When equipment and space are utilized to greatest advantage, labor becomes an integral part of productive planning. After all, productivity cannot be accomplished without tight equipment planning and proper relationships for minimizing production or functional activities.

During the programming and planning procedures, remodeling and future growth or expansion must be considered. I always ask a client if he can project twenty years ahead. Usually what we think will happen in twenty years will happen a lot sooner.

Expansion is frequently a difficult item to build into a plan. Ideally, the kitchen should be located adjacent to an exterior wall so expansion is feasible through "knock-out" walls. Usually, though, the kitchen is locked into fixed spatial parameters. Still, much can often be done to provide for expansion. Though I tend to be conservative as a designer, considering today's cost of space and ongoing maintenance costs, the following can be planned with little increase in the budgeted project:

Dishroom. Consider a larger dishmachine. Space and cost for a larger unit are not excessive and will provide functional value almost immediately.

Cart Holding. Allow space for several additional carts. Room for these additional carts is often all you will need to service additional patient care units.

Food Production. Plan equipment for going "up." Up in capacity and expansion. Larger kettles require little more extra space than smaller kettles; plan for double decking ovens, etc.

Cold and Dry Storage. Again, going up is a good way to provide expansion. If possible, provide sufficient vertical space in coolers. Consider 21 in. wide shelving in lieu of 18 in., and so forth.

Tray Assembly. Provide for as much additional length as feasible. If possible, provide a longer conveyor than is needed initially. The additional cost will be negligible but gains in productivity are considerable.

Planning for expansion is necessary in dietary operations; while projected growth is difficult to assume, it is almost assured. Change must be anticipated as well; the change to ever-growing use of convenience foods. This change can be accommodated by specifying equipment that offers multiplicity of use. Convection ovens and high pressure steamers cook raw product or reheat frozen product with equal ease. Such increased capability in processing raw product is an advantage to be planned into the facility whether convenience foods are considered for use in the near future or not.

Disposable vs. Permanent Ware

The pros and cons of disposable *versus* permanent ware have been argued many times. I am a proponent of permanent ware. In my opinion, the use of permanent ware is the most economical in the long run. The availability of disposables, and their increasing cost make them questionable to me. At the risk of seeming old fashioned, I believe china service on a tray adds a margin of dignity to hospital foodservice.

To illustrate the variables inherent in hospital foodservice planning, there is perhaps no better way than to review the planning, and the alternate design considerations, in a typical example. We will use a facility that does not now exist, but is in the planning and conceptual stage.

This facility, designed for 500 beds, is being developed for the Candler General Hospital in Savannah, Georgia. (See plan, pp. 76–77.) Following is a description of the recommended and alternate solutions to specific design problems. The foodservice facilities offer flexibility in operational concepts and, interestingly, permit variable solutions or alternates within the planned area without disruption to major food handling flow patterns. Details as to specific equipment items or accessories are purposely omitted as they lend little significance to conceptual design and are generally worked out relative to specific operational preferences.

FOOD PROCESSING AND DISTRIBUTION ALTERNATES

Here are the design premises that have been derived from the operating program:

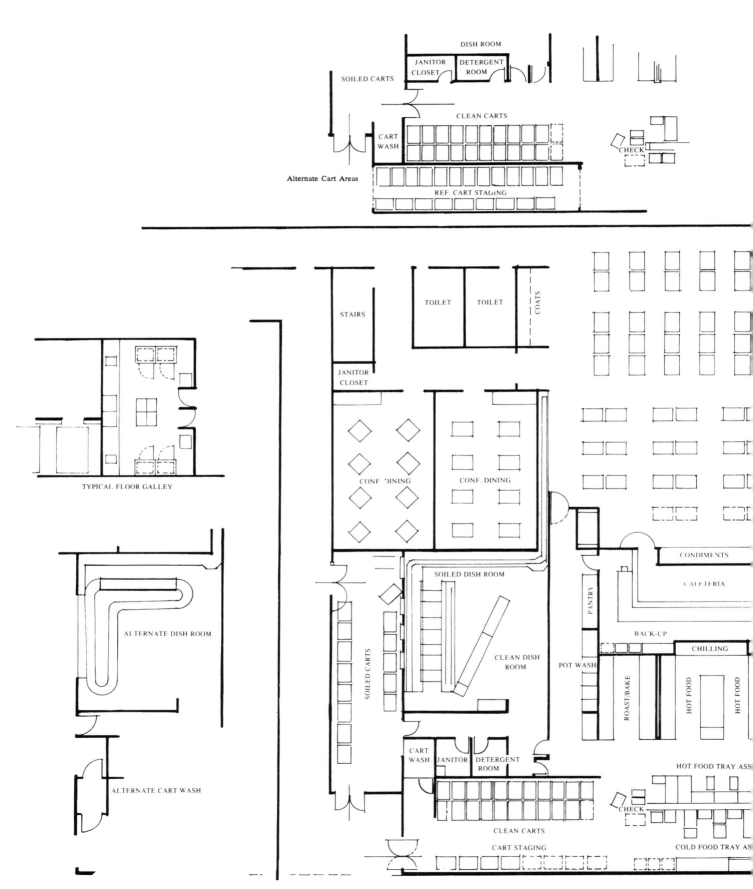

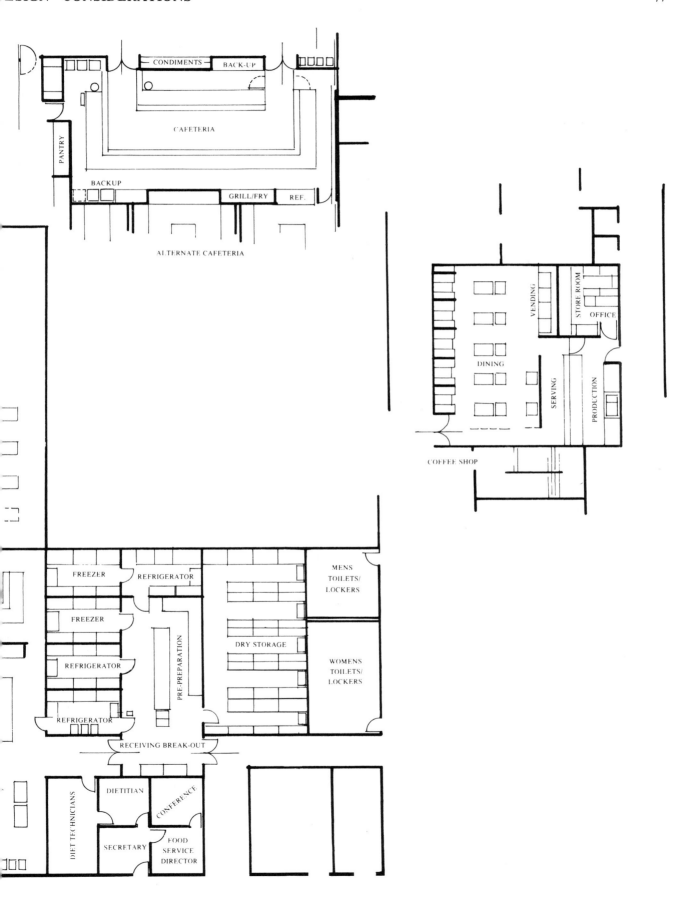

That the kitchen will operate conventionally, in that most products will be purchased raw (perishables), pre-portioned, and semi-prepared. Fully convenience products, such as canned soups, mixed items, fryer ready potatoes and fish, and other frozen and dried products will be used in the interest of portion control and elimination of waste and labor. This design features an environmentally-controlled (60° to 70° F.) pre-prep room allowing all final portioning, can opening, and rough prep (cabbages, lettuce, etc.; poultry, fish, and meat items) to be done in advance of final production, and in accordance with recipe formulas and menu cycles.

That all cooked foods, other than totally pre-prepared, will be produced at least one day ahead and chilled rapidly. (Freezing is not being considered due to complex equipment and operating costs, changes to recipe formulation, unnecessary shelf life, and undue reheating time.) The purpose of a chilled food operation is to provide reasonable shelf life, minimize overproduction, maximize labor productivity, and provide an ultimate in sanitation and nutritional controls.

That all patient meals will be portioned centrally in the kitchen, rather than delivered in bulk for galley portioning. The purpose is to centralize responsibility for quantity control, and to minimize labor.

That permanent ware will be used for satisfying presentation, lower operating costs, and higher sanitation.

The above design premises provide the backup for the following tray distribution systems being considered as adaptable to the current planning:

1. Integrated, pelletized dinner plate carriers and insulated side dishes (Finessa, Caddy, Dietary Products) distributing hot and cold foods directly from the line to the patient bed via enclosed carts. Galleys on floors would be used for beverages and nourishments. Distance of horizontal travel is less than 800 ft. to the furthest room from the kitchen cart staging area. Approximately half this distance of travel is on the patient floor. The combined horizontal and vertical travel time would be well within the food temperature keeping time of this relatively simple system.

  a. In conjunction with the above system, late trays would be sent up with all other trays and removed at the galley for microwave reheating as required.

  b. An alternate to the above system would be to hold late trays in the kitchen until required and microwave reheat them either there or in the galley.

2. Chilled food assembled from bulk pans (sized 12- by 20- by 2-in.) in the same manner as if the food were hot, placed on chilled plates. All entree and cold food items would be assembled on the same tray, loaded on open carts and stored in a holding roll-in refrigerator (see alternate) and delivered to floors well in advance of meal service to again be held in roll-in-refrigerators. The open carts would be enveloped with a disposable plastic shroud during transit. An alternate would be to use enclosed carts with doors on both sides that can be opened in the holding refrigerators to allow maximum air circulation. Entrees would be reheated by manually loading the dinner plates into counter-top microwave or convection ovens, depending on the needed volume demands, or speed of this operation. Late trays would be kept in the holding refrigerators on the floors until needed.

3. An alternate to the above system would be to use the Crimsco "Cybex 100" system or the Market Forge "Convectator" system, both of which are similar in design, use the principles outlined above, but have a "cassette" for storing the entrees on top of the tray cart. This cassette is inserted in a floor convection oven when required to reheat several entrees (14 to 42) at a time. Because of the high capacity of these systems, serving and scheduling would need to be coordinated more closely.

Generally, a simplified operational system that provides maximum sanitation, quality, and labor utilization is preferred. System number 1, described above with alternates, is one of the latest, uncomplicated, and universally utilized systems. But because of the numerous late tray requirements now experienced by the institution, we feel that system number 2 or number 3 should be considered, since these permit patient tray delivery as required, totally independent of kitchen scheduling.

The heart of all three is a bulk chilled food system. This separates hot food production from tray assembly scheduling, thus accomplishing maximum nutritional controls and labor utilization. This system permits inventorying both raw and finished product, and better purchasing and portioning controls. An important advantage is that the kitchen functions as a commissary producing all food to be served in the cafeteria, coffee shop, and special function rooms.

FOOD SERVICE OPERATIONAL SYSTEM

Dietary and Food Processing

This outline follows the general concept of a relatively conventional foodservice operation that utilizes a system of cooking and chilling food in advance of demand for all points of service, i.e., patient trays, cafeteria, coffee shop, and special functions. (See floor plan, pp. 80.)

The intent of the design is that all food products be received from the north (Receiving Dock) and checked into the area indicated on the plan as the Receiving/Break-Out Room. There all products are weighed and verified from the purchase orders. After the products have been checked, perishable products are stored in the west sectional coolers, and canned and other dry products stored in the Dry Storage Room. It is recommended that one individual on the Dietary Staff be designated as Controller, working with the Head Chef and Chief Dietitian in the process of receiving and distributing all incoming food supplies.

The Controller, working with recipe formulations and daily production data, would retrieve supplies from initial storage and supervise the breaking down and final pre-preparation of all ingredients in the area called Pre-Prep on the plan. These ingredients would include cleaned and portioned vegetables, and poultry and meat products, stored in convenient containers, and held in the east sectional coolers indicated.

Pre-preparation would be performed based on an established production run related to the cycle menu. This procedure will provide: maximum control of purchased products, as well as of products distributed to production; accountability, and reduction of waste in the preparation areas.

Offices in 'Management Core'

Adjacent to this operation, we have indicated the "Management Core" containing offices for the Dietitian, Diet Technicians, Foodservice Director and Secretarial staff. The location of the management core provides maximum supervision over the pre-preparation, receiving, food production, and tray assembly operations.

Hot and cold food preparation is shown on the plan directly between the tray assembly and the cafeteria areas. This location permits the direct flow of finished products to both of these operational areas. Each of these areas has hot and cold food holding equipment to support its functions.

It should be noted that three separate alcoves are indicated for food production. The first for cold food is closest to bulk refrigeration and convenient for serving both the cafeteria and tray assembly operations. The second, hot food preparation, is located directly opposite the hot food section on the tray assembly line and directly in back of the hot food section on the cafeteria line. The third is a roast and bake facility that separates these functions from general preparation and permits individuality to the baking operation, reflecting the ever-increasing popularity in on-premise baked goods. All three of these areas have direct access to a common pot washing area, which is also located near ware washing for better utilization of personnel.

An important feature of this plan is the alcove for hot food production. In the center of this is a 13-ft. section designated for chilling foods. This contains specialized equipment for chilling foods that have been panned and portioned directly from production. These chilled foods can then be stored in this location or in the walk-in or reach-in coolers for increased inventory.

FIG. 32–DIETARY PLAN FOR SYSTEM USING ADVANCE COOKING AND CHILLING FOR FOODS

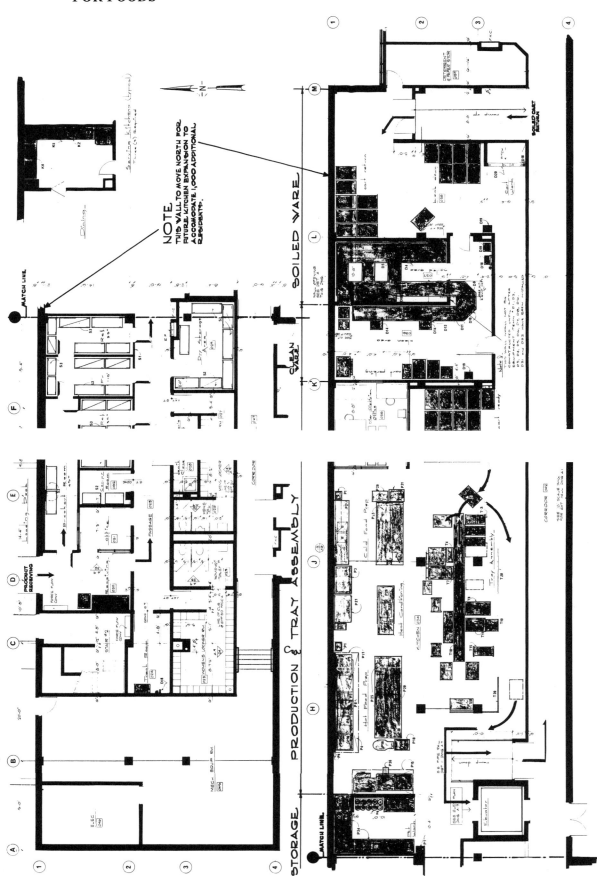

This chilling operation is the heart of the system described in "Food Processing and Distribution Alternates" where all hot food production is run at least one day in advance of serving. This method can confine daily labor to an 8-hour shift and, in the case of weekends, reduce back-up cooking labor by producing food during the week for service on Saturday, Sunday, and Monday. If desired, this advance inventory of prepared food can be extended to a week to ten days prior to service.

Tray Assembly Alternatives

The tray assembly area is designed to be flexible in accepting various forms of tray distribution as outlined in "Food Processing and Distribution Alternates," thus permitting the use of the latest means in delivering food-service to the patient floors. Three generally available systems are:

1. Caddy. This utilizes the Temp-Lock/ Finessa design which provides a heated base and an insulated cover for the entrees, and insulated side dishes for all other products. The trays are loaded into a conventional enclosed cart. The cart storage is as indicated on the main plan.

2. Market Forge. This system employs a cold dish-up process. The entrees are covered either with a disposable or a permanent cover, assembled on the same tray with the cold foods, and the tray is loaded on an open cart and stored in a refrigerated cart storage room. This cart storage configuration is indicated in the alternate layout shown in the upper left section of the plan.

3. Market Forge or Crimsco: These systems are similar in design, and are common to number 2, above, except that the entree plate is separated from the main tray and stored in a cassette. The carts with cassettes are stored in the refrigerated cart room.

You will note from the plan that entree make-up is directly across from hot food production and that cold food make-up is backed up by its own holding area. The tray assembly line provides for a grill station, and bread and toast for breakfast if required. The line also provides for assembling cups and

glasses. Most beverages are to be provided from the floor galleys.

The clean cart parking—and loaded cart staging—areas are shown as two alternates, as previously noted, to satisfy either hot or cold food distribution. However, note that the alternate plan could satisfy both types of operation and allow flexibility in decisions on food delivery concept, revision, or expansion at a future date.

Ware Washing Alternatives

The ware washing area, indicated on the plan as Soiled Dish Room and Clean Dish Room, is designed for maximum utilization of labor and simplification of traffic flow through the use of conveyors and carts. The layout in the main plan incorporates a system commonly called "the scrap and stack operation" where all trays coming from either the Cafeteria or the patient cart tray break-down arrive in the dish room by conveyor, moving past fixed scrapping stations.

The scrappers perform independent stripping procedures and accumulate ware by like kinds and sizes on connecting bridges and an accumulating conveyor. This process permits all hands to be utilized in the scrapping process and the dishmachine remains idle. When the soiled ware is scrapped and accumulated, personnel are transferred to the washing process. This type of operation has proved to reduce dish room labor by approximately 40 percent.

The alternate plan utilizes a continuous rack type machine which permits the cart breakdown people to scrap dishes and load the machine at the same time. While both systems require approximately the same amount of personnel, the alternate system may use the personnel over a longer period of time. The alternate scheme requires the use of racks for all dishware; the basic scheme requires racks for only cups and glasses. The decision on the type of system should be made after scheduling all patient and cafeteria service hours.

Cart washing is shown as two alternates. The scheme on the main plan is for manual cart washing using high pressure hot water mixed with detergent, and is a very acceptable method. The alternate scheme provides for an automatic cart washer, which has the additional advantage of washing trays, underliners, and plate covers on carts or racks. It thus relieves the load on the ware washing department, and works more favorably with the continuous rack ware washing system.

Separate toilet and locker rooms have been provided for Dietary personnel on the north end of the layout and are sized to reflect the approximate proportion of two-thirds female to one-third male employees.

Cafeteria

The serving area, as shown on both the main plan and the alternate plan, backs up directly to the hot and cold food production areas of the kitchen to provide convenient supply and replenishment. The Dish Room is adjacent for replenishment of glassware, silver and china.

The serving area on the main plan represents the minimum equipment required. If the full seating area, including the conference dining rooms, is now to be used, and if a potential growth in hospital facilities and staff is anticipated, the alternate serving area should be considered. The alternate serving area is a shopping center or scramble system configuration, permitting the separation of points of service, i.e., cold foods, entrees, short order, custom sandwiches, and beverage, and encouraging patrons to move freely about in the serving area.

The Cafeteria seating area, as shown, provides sufficient capacity for either plan, with the additional availability of 60 seats in the conference dining rooms. The dumbwaiter shown to the south of the Cafeteria serving area is to service the upper special functions area directly from the kitchen and, perhaps, utilize the Cafeteria serving area as a waitress pick-up station during off hours. Entree service is provided from the base menu using the chilled food system.

Coffee Shop

This operation has been designed to be self-sustaining in the sense that it could be provided with all chilled entrees and cold foods once a day and produce its own grilled and fried foods. The small work and storage areas are thus supplemental. A short counter handles patron self-service (or waitress service); however, most beverages and snack items are provided through vending machines. These machines would also allow snack and refreshment service after hours. The 54-seat dining area is a comfortable coffee shop environment that combines booths and loose seating.

Floor Galleys

These areas are an extension of Dietary Food Service and are equipped to handle the cold food distribution system with holding refrigerators and reheating ovens. If a more conventional system is used, these areas could be reduced. These galleys are planned not only to receive, reheat, and distribute trays to the patients, but to provide coffee, cold beverage, and ice.

The planning, as we have developed it, is inherently flexible, and provides alternate solutions for evaluating various operational systems and concepts. The purpose of the design program is to establish the fixed parameters of space and function, but permit variation in operational concepts.

All of the functions described and illustrated in this plan for a 500-bed hospital exist in plans for smaller or larger operations. Planning needs can be adjusted either up or down in spatial considerations. Alternate systems have been prescribed but are yet to be resolved. Still, any of the various systems will work well.

Much could be written about all the details to be considered in dietary planning. However, if the basic concept is thoughtfully planned, as illustrated by the enclosed schematic, the details will develop if worked in conjunction with the overall design criteria and manufacturer resources.

The layout Fig. 34 (pp. 84–85) of the Lutheran Home and Services for the Aged, in Arlington Heights, Illinois is an example of putting the programming and conceptual planning to work. The outline beginning on p. 86 was actually established for this operation. The pictures, too, are actual and illustrate the solutions to such important key factors as planning objectives, clientele type, site selection, basis for equipment decisions and relationships, utilization of space, mobility, labor utilization, effect of convenience foods, productivity, and planned accommodation for change and growth.

600 FT. ± —

KENNICOTT AVE.

1300 FT. ±

FIG. 33—PROPOSED HOSPITAL
MASTER SITE PLAN

⑧

⑦

VICE
O →

③

①

⑤

⑥

②

④

PROPOSED
MASTER SITE PLAN
1972
LUTHERAN HOME & SERVICE
FOR THE AGED

NORTH

OAKTON AVE.

KEY: 1·NEW MAIN DIETARY FACILITIES
2·EAST SATELLITE KITCHEN
3·FUTURE DIETARY EXPANSION
4·ORIGINAL BLDG.-220 BEDS
5·NEW WEST WING-126 BEDS
6·FUTURE SOUTH WING-126 BEDS
7·FUTURE APARTMENTS-500 RESIDENTS
8·FUTURE CONDO/COTTAGE COMPLEX-500 RES.

FIG. 34—EAST KITCH

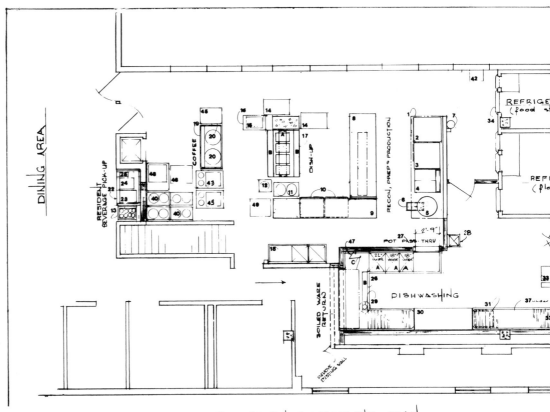

EAST KITCHEN REMODELING PLAN
SCALE 1/8 in. = 1 ft. 0 in.

EQUIPMENT SCHEDULE

NO.	DESCRIPTION	NO.	DESCRIPTION
1.	Exhaust Canopy	26.	Soiled Dishtable
2.	Broiler		A. Sinks
3.	Convection Oven		B. Scrapping Trough
4.	Hot Top Range		C. Overhead Rack Shelf
5.	Kettle—40 Gallon	27.	Pass-Thru Frame
6.	Floor Trough	28.	Hand Sink
7.	Fire Control System	29.	Disposer
8.	Work Table w/Cabinets	30.	Dishmachine
9.	Work Table	31.	Booster Heater
10.	Portable Hot Carts	32.	Clean Dishtable
11.	Platter Carts	33.	Sanitizing System/30 ft. Hose
12.	Bowl Carts	34.	Walk-In Refrigeration
13.	Glass Cart	35.	Freezer
14.	Utility Carts	36.	Storage Shelving
15.	Toaster	37.	Rack Carts
16.	Portable Stand	38.	Silver Truck
17.	Hot Food Server	39.	Bussing Carts (Not Shown)
	A. Overshelf	40.	Dinner Plate Cart
	B. Landing Shelves	41.	Delete
18.	Double Sink	42.	Hand Sink
19.	Urn Stand	43.	Cup and Saucer Carts
20.	Coffee Urns	44.	Silver Soak Sink
21.	Ice Maker	45.	Coffee Pot Truck
22.	Beverage Stand	46.	Dessert Dish Carts
23.	Ice Dispenser w/Water Disp.	47.	Pre-Rinse Spray
24.	Non-Carb Beverage Disp.	48.	Carton Milk Cart
25.	Iced Tea Dispenser	49.	Soup Bowl Dispenser

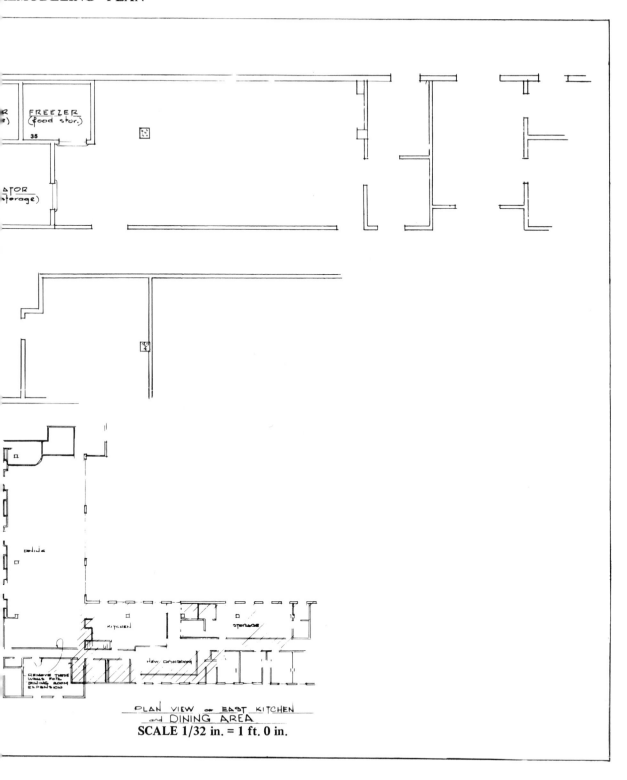

FREEZER
(Food stor.)

35

ATOR
storage)

KITCHEN

STORAGE

NEW DISH ROOM

REMOVE THESE
WALLS FOR
DINING ROOM
EXPANSION

PLAN VIEW OF EAST KITCHEN
and DINING AREA
SCALE 1/32 in. = 1 ft. 0 in.

Hospital Foodservice Design Outline

1. GENERAL PURPOSE

A. Create a new central food production and assembly facility capable of producing food for an existing 220 beds, plus the current addition of 126 beds, plus staff.

B. Central food production facility to be capable of serving the requirements of 126 bed addition in Phase B.

C. Existing east Dietary Department to be remodeled as a service kitchen, containing its own ware washing for the family style dining room in this area.

D. Provide a new central dietary facility capable of expanding in space and equipment (through architectural knock-out walls) to serve the long range plans of an additional 500 residents in a centrally served apartment complex, and 500 residents in efficiency bungalows, as a commissary service of the expanded Dietary Department.

2. GENERAL DESIGN CONSIDERATIONS

A. Originally a separate and more centrally located foodservice building was considered. However, due to the natural slope and configuration of the terrain, the new wing required a semi-subgrade area which would have represented considerable construction costs if unused. It was determined that the new Dietary could use this space and still provide adequate service to the institution. This location was better for receiving supplies, though its long, narrow shape posed a challenge.

B. Due to the considerable geographical space that the existing four-story structure now covered, and which would later include the two new bed wings and future apartment and condominium cottage complexes, the kitchen facility would be best located near easiest access to these complexes. This widespread dietary operation required an operational plan that could cope with distances, growth, and varying levels of care and menu:

(1) Population:
        220 Existing Building
        126 New West Wing, Phase A
        126 New South Wing, Phase B
        500 Apartments North (Future)
        500 Condo/Cottages Far North (Future)

    1,472 TOTAL ON-SITE

Of the above,
        310 Residents tray service
        162 Bulk panned portions
    1,000 Future commissary production

(2) The illustrated plan has been designed for Phases A & B expansion. Dietary has been planned for expansion to the north for future additional growth.

(3) *Most notably,* the foodservice system installed at this institution is quite unique as it is a prototype chilled food system allowing all entree production to be run two to three days in advance of the serving peaks. In effect, this system permits the Lutheran Home to create its own "convenience food" program and not be totally dependent upon outside purveyors. Though a primary determining factor for going to this system was logistics, other factors were a heavy preference for an ethnic menu, and better utilization of labor. It should be noted here that this facility is the first to use this simple, mechanically-operated system which had undergone two-and-a-half years of extensive development, laboratory, and bacteriological testing.

3. GENERAL RESPONSE

A. The new systems in food production, distribution and transportation have blended well into an integral system of providing a quality, nutritional foodservice under the strictest of sanitation and cost controls.

4. SELECTION OF EQUIPMENT

A. All equipment selection was based on quality and local service.

B. All operating systems consist of compatible units for design integrity and simplified service.
    (1) Dishroom Tables and Conveyors, Caddy
    (2) Tray Assembly Components, Caddy
    (3) Hot Food Production, Vulcan-Hart
    (4) Dishmachines, Vulcan-Hart
    (5) Portable Carts, etc., Caddy
    (6) Kitchen Machines, Hobart
    (7) Unit Refrigeration, Hobart
    (8) Ventilation/Fire Protection, Air Systems
    (9) Walk-in Refrigeration, Tafco

(10) Custom Fabrication, Illinois Range

(11) Sanitizing Systems, Sage Systems

C. All equipment was designed for ease of maintenance, operational efficiency, and conformance with NSF and local health codes.

5. LAYOUT, CENTRAL FACILITY

A. The general layout has been planned by operational zones:

(1) West Zone, Column Lines A to G, is planned for nonproduction or service areas. Note that delivery or trash removal personnel need not enter the production zone. A breakout room, under controlled environment, is provided for receiving perishables.

(2) Central Zone, Column Lines G to K, is planned to contain food production and tray assembly operations, and to be as free from contamination as possible, while making possible good working relationships between the various operational centers.

(3) East Zone, Column Lines K to M, is planned to contain ware washing and soiled tray receiving. It should be noted, however, that distinct soiled and clean ware areas have been provided.

B. The following features of spatial and operational relationships have been planned as shown:

(1) Receiving and trash removal at Column Line D, with breakout room for perishables, and Steward's office for control. No suppliers enter production area.

(2) Employee facilities in same area.

(3) Hot food production is a "work around" configuration encouraging convenience, communication, and teamwork. This work center feeds to the chilled foods unit, Item P21.

(4) The chilled food system feeds to the "Heat Conditioning" Center, Items P26, 27, 28, which in turn feed to the hot food stations on the tray make-up line.

(5) Cold food preparation is also in a "work around" configuration, and feeds to the holding unit Item P3 and P22, which in turn feed to the tray make-up line.

(a) Both hot and cold food preparation store food in portable units for distribution to the east wing.

(6) The tray assembly area has been designed for a maximum of 310 tray service residents (162 bulk panned portions are distributed as noted earlier).

(7) Management and Dietitian Office is located for optimum control and supervision (a Steward's Office is provided as indicated in 1 above).

(8) Ware handling posed a design challenge due to the narrow shape of the available space. Though a rackless conveyor machine would, space permitting, have been the solution, a folded rack and conveyor system resolved the operational problems, as well as those of space and labor utilization, and separate clean and soiled dish areas.

(a) The three tank dishmachine is supported on the soiled end by accumulating conveyors, tables, and bridges. Twenty-five feet of clean accumulating conveyors in the clean dish area provide maximum utilization of this rack machine, and adequate area for clean ware storage. (The east wing has its own dishwashing facilities.)

(9) Patient tray cart handling begins with an adequate area to receive soiled carts without "pressuring" the dish room. After the carts are sanitized and stored for reuse, all steps have been handled in cart recycling.

6. LAYOUT, EAST SATELLITE KITCHEN

A. This facility is the old kitchen remodelled to provide back-up, reheating, and distribution for the main dining room, staff dining rooms, and two serving pantries on floors above.

B. An interesting comparison can be made since this plan encompasses the spatial parameters of the old Dietary before the new facilities were completed.

C. It should be noted that the Lutheran Home operates its facilities in two distinct serving segments. As outlined, the central facility provides *all* production and tray service for two-thirds of the residents, and bulk food to the remaining third (ambulatory) residents.

D. Periodically through the year open house picnics are given on the east lawn, and this satellite kitchen serves as a production center for these functions.

7. SANITATION

A. The heart of the food service sanitizing system is provided by the Sage units located at strategic positions.

    (1) Master—in dish washing areas

    (2) Slave—at cart wash

    (3) Slave—in trash and dock area

B. Five hand sinks, with foot operated valves, are located in food and ware handling areas.

C. Floors are quarry tile, walls are glazed tile, and ceilings are non-absorbent acoustical. Floor drains or troughs are strategically located throughout.

D. Separate areas for janitors' and employees' trash have been provided.

E. All equipment meets or surpasses NSF standards; all that should be movable is on casters (including shelving), and all heavy duty equipment is on concrete bases, sealed to same and walls.

8. SAFETY

A. The kitchen is basically an open plan, minimizing doors, etc. Floors are non-slip and corners have resilient bumpers.

9. ECONOMIC SOUNDNESS

A. Simply stated, the chilled food system has held labor cost ratios in line even though the expanded facilities were considerably greater. Weekend back-up cooking labor was eliminated, and production over-runs and other over production has been virtually eliminated.

B. The increased productivity in preparation, plus the increased capacity of the cooking battery itself, has cut production labor costs. Both result from use of the chilled food system.

10. SPECIAL FEATURES AND INNOVATIONS

A. Perhaps the most significant innovation in this facility is the "chilled food" system, designed to chill approximately 400 lb. (or 600 to 800 portions) from cooking, to panning, to 38°F. in 3½ hours. The technique provides the same benefits as freezing, viz: bacterial and nutritional control, together with labor utilization, while permitting the use of existing recipes and conventional labor.

B. The above system permits the cycling of production equipment more frequently in a normal eight-hour shift, so increasing productivity.

C. The "work around" work centers provide more teamwork effort and improve employee morale.

D. The folded ware washing operation is unique, as it uses conveyors and space to the greatest advantage, making the best utilization of labor, space, and equipment.

11. SPECIAL FEATURES

A. All foodservice production areas have color on floors and walls to break up any traditional institutional appearance. Ceilings are acoustical but easily cleaned.

B. Dining rooms have a "homey" atmosphere for the residents who dine there; bedside or satellite service is maintained at a high level of quality so that there is no differentiation in dietary service to any level of care.

In summary, planning for a dietary operation is not deeply mysterious, but deeply profound. Address the problems and apply the alternates. But, above all, try to evolve a simple solution. Complex solutions to operational problems result in complex operations.

Serving community needs at the highest level possible in an installation designed to operate at the lowest cost feasible for that level of service is the challenge faced by hospital foodservice designers. Food to please a captive audience requires imaginative menu planning which must be backed up by a kitchen designed and equipped to produce the dishes chosen speedily, at whatever hour they are needed, and with minimum effort on the part of the staff.

Lutheran Home and Service for the Aged

Foodservice for convalescents in the Lutheran Home and Service for the Aged is provided in remodeled facilities devised by the process of conceptual planning outlined on the preceding pages. Plans had to be developed that would also accommodate the long range objective of adding beds that would ultimately take the total to nearly 1500.

Foodservice for the final projected group of 500 would use the existing dietary facility (through architectural knock-out walls) as a commissary service. The character of the dietary operation required a plan that could cope with distances, growth, and varying levels of care and the menus needed at each level.

A prototype chilled food system was selected, unique in allowing all entree production to be run 2 to 3 days in advance of serving peaks. It provides a tailored-to-the-operator convenience food system.

Above right: Hot food production area is a "work around" configuration that encourages convenience, communication, and teamwork. Foods prepared here go to the chilled foods unit.

Right: Foods to be readied for immediate service go to this Heat Conditioning Center which offers a choice of reconstitution equipment that meets all menu demands.

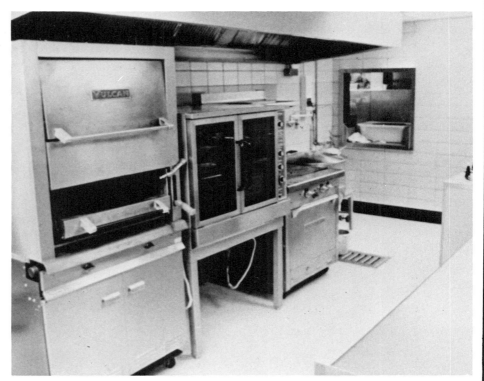

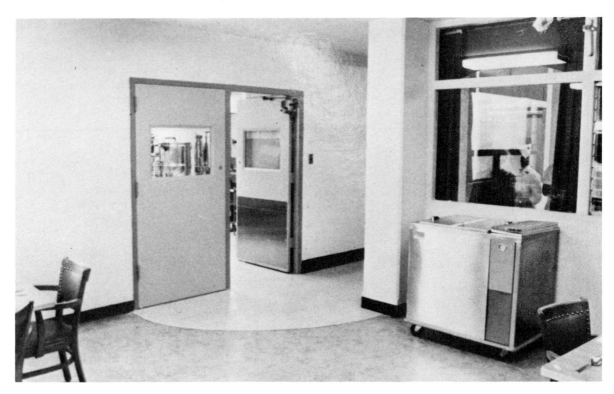

Above: Management offices are located at entry to kitchen and adjacent to administrative dining room. No suppliers are permitted to enter the production area. Separate area for receiving has steward's office as control.

Below: The design challenge posed by the narrow shape of the space available for ware handling was met by the installation of a folded rack and conveyor system. There are separate soiled and clean dish areas.

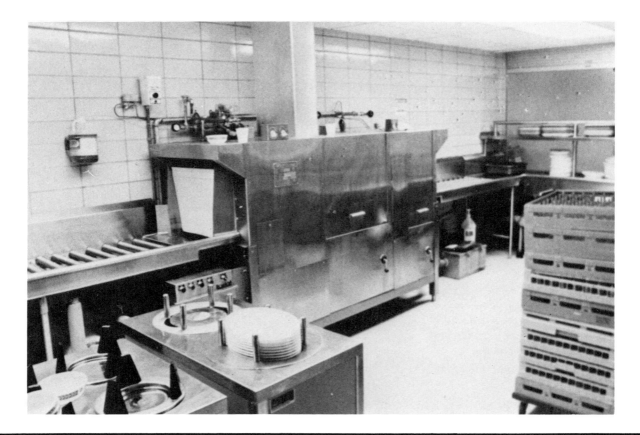

Methodist Hospital

A new layout coordinates the existing vertical conveyor system for patient trays with a new conveyor for cafeteria trays at Methodist Hospital, St. Louis Park, Minn. Conveyors push dish trays onto an open trough via skate wheels. Trough slopes to disposer in center area.

Paper waste drops directly into compactor or into waste cans to be emptied into compactor. Compactor is emptied at end of day when dolly wheels away one square plastic bag of paper waste.

Silverware drops into portable soak sink with slide chute and interior flat rack. When full, rack is placed on dishwasher conveyor belt. Silver is washed, then pulled off onto a portable table in clean dish area, sorted into racked silver cylinders, and sanitized in dishwasher.

Pots and pans are collected on a portable rack and wheeled to the scullery sink, where they are washed either by hand or with a swirl washer then placed on the dishwasher conveyor belt for sanitizing and placement on portable rack in clean dish area. A special clip mounted on the inside of the conveyor holds 18- by 26-in. bun pans at a 45° angle as they go through dishwasher.

Dishwasher conveyor belt is hinged on the inside so all sections can be lifted up to make counter cleaning easy. Placement of dishwasher doors on the outside with space between them and the wall gives cleaner easy access to the interior of the machines.

The soiled and clean areas as well as the scullery sink are completely separate. Workers can see each other but cannot work on the soiled and clean ends at the same time. Each area has its own hand-washing facility.

The soiled area has enough space to take tray carts from special areas and also to handle all cart delivery in case of a conveyor breakdown.

All dishes are scrapped next to tray they are delivered on (at any location in the breakdown area), then placed directly on the conveyor in a one-motion handling system. Water carries food waste down the round, sloped central trough to the disposer.

The flow of water is set by globe valves on each end (no flow control valve) and is started by the disposer switch. This system requires a disposer that can be started on a dry basis.

All cups, glasses and coffee pots are placed in racks directly above conveyor belt on a shelf which can be adjusted up and down as well as to the rear and front to suit the individual operator. Full racks go through the dishwasher on the conveyor belt and when clean are placed in self-leveling dispensers.

EQUIPMENT LIST

1. Pin Tray Conveyor
2. Vertical Up Conveyor
3. Transfer Conveyor
4. Vertical Down Conv.
5. Transfer Conveyors
6. Port. Waste Cans
7. Port. Sinks
8. Port. Tables
9. Waste Compactor
10. Skate Wheel Conveyor
11. Disposer
12. Scullery Counter
13. Wall Shelf
14. Overhead Shelves
15. Conveyor Counter
16. Exhaust Pentlegs
17. Detergent Dispenser
18. Dishwasher
19. Rinse Injector
20. Silver Cleaner
21. Overhead Spray
22. Hand Sinks
23. Swirl Washer

Designed by: Jan Van Hemert, Van Hemert Associates, Inc.

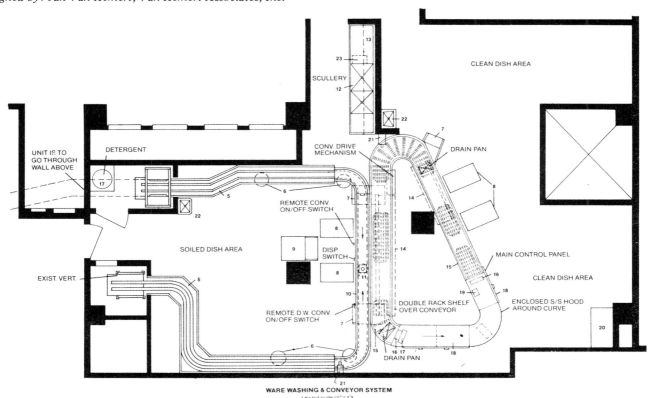

WARE WASHING & CONVEYOR SYSTEM
Lay-out scale (¼" = 1')

The Institute of Living

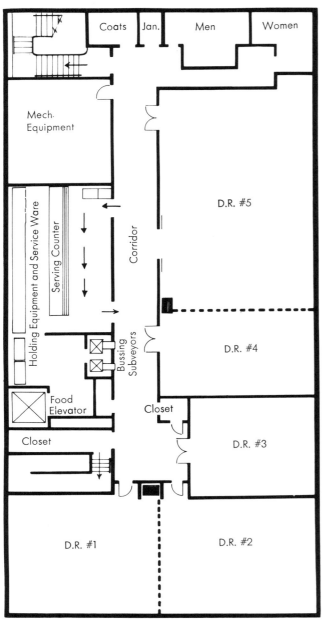

DOCTOR'S SUITE SECOND FLOOR

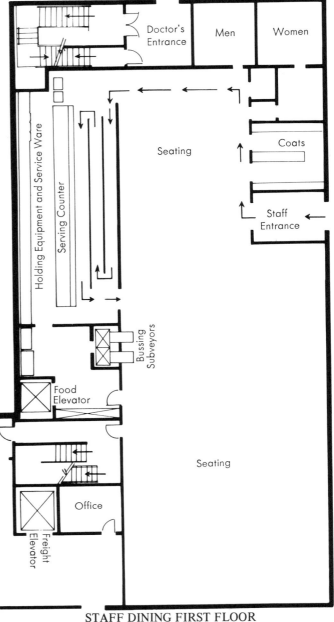

STAFF DINING FIRST FLOOR

The Institute of Living is a rather deluxe private, non-profit hospital dedicated to the relief of suffering and the treatment of emotional and mental illnesses.

Located on the outskirts of Hartford, Conn., it occupies about 34 acres, walled in around its perimeter. Around the outer boundaries of the property are some 12 buildings; the center area has a 9-hole golf course, lawns, trees and recreational areas.

The 12 buildings are required by the nature of services the hospital offers. In most instances, each of the buildings houses patients with similar requirements; i.e., a particular mental illness or emotional problem. In most cases the patients are restricted to their assigned building, and even to the floor they occupy.

Clearly, this presents a difficult set of problems for foodservice. All patient meals must be delivered to the patient houses and served under supervision.

The new central dietary building was conceived as handling all foodservice functions—receiving, storage, preparation, cart loading, and cleanup of soiled patient ware—as well as providing facilities for other-than-patient feeding. The Institute has 400 patient beds. Plans for expansion which would add another 50 beds were incorporated in the new foodservice.

The new dietary building is a 3-level operation utilizing two elevators. Receiving is done at grade level; material is taken down to the kitchen level in the basement. All storage, preparation, and clean-up facilities are in the basement. Loaded food carts for patients are transported by tunnel from this level.

The dietary department operates from 5 a.m. to 4 p.m. 7 days a week. There are a total of 37 full-time and 11 part-time employees.

The facility is largely self sufficient and adequate storage areas were provided. The foodservice produces about 15,000 meals (including about 750 snacks) weekly. Of these, about 8000 are for patients, the remainder for employees.

SELF-CONTAINED DIETARY BUILDING

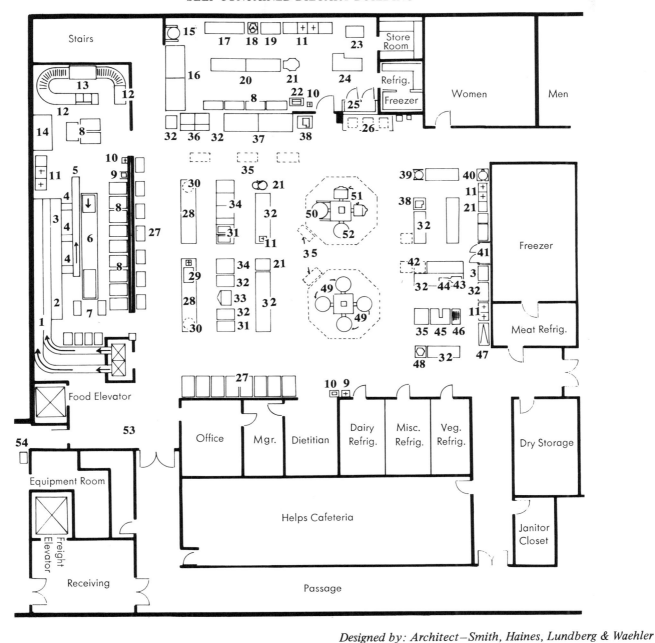

Designed by: Architect—Smith, Haines, Lundberg & Waehler
Foodservice Consultant—Vincent N. Antonell

EQUIPMENT LIST

1. Conveyor
2. Soiled Dish Table
3. Grinder
4. Bridges
5. Bussing-veyor
6. Dishwasher
7. Carts
8. Racks
9. Water Cooler
10. Hand Sink
11. Sink
12. Pot Table & Conveyor
13. Pot Washer
14. Cart Wash Trough
15. Tilting Kettle—40 Gals.
16. Bake Ovens w/racks
17. Table—marble top
18. Mixer—20 qt.
19. Mixer Parts Rack
20. Table—Baker's
21. Mixer
22. Crust Roller
23. Ice Cream Freezer Mixer
24. Tables
25. Freezer—Ice Cream
26. Refrigerator—Salad
27. Food Carts—Special
28. Table—Cook's
29. Bain Marie
30. Revolving Rack
31. Steam Cooker
32. Table
33. Fry Kettle
34. Range w/Spreader
35. Tables—Portable
36. Broilers
37. Roast Ovens w/racks
38. Slicer
39. Vegetable Cutter
40. Peeler
41. Refrigerator
42. Files—Mobile
43. Meat Chopper
44. Patty Maker
45. Meat Saw
46. Meat Block
47. Cooling Tank
48. Scale
49. Kettles—Steam Jacketed
50. Tilting Kettle—60 gal.
51. Steamers
52. Kettle—100 gal.
53. Ice Maker
54. Can Crusher
55. Can Washer

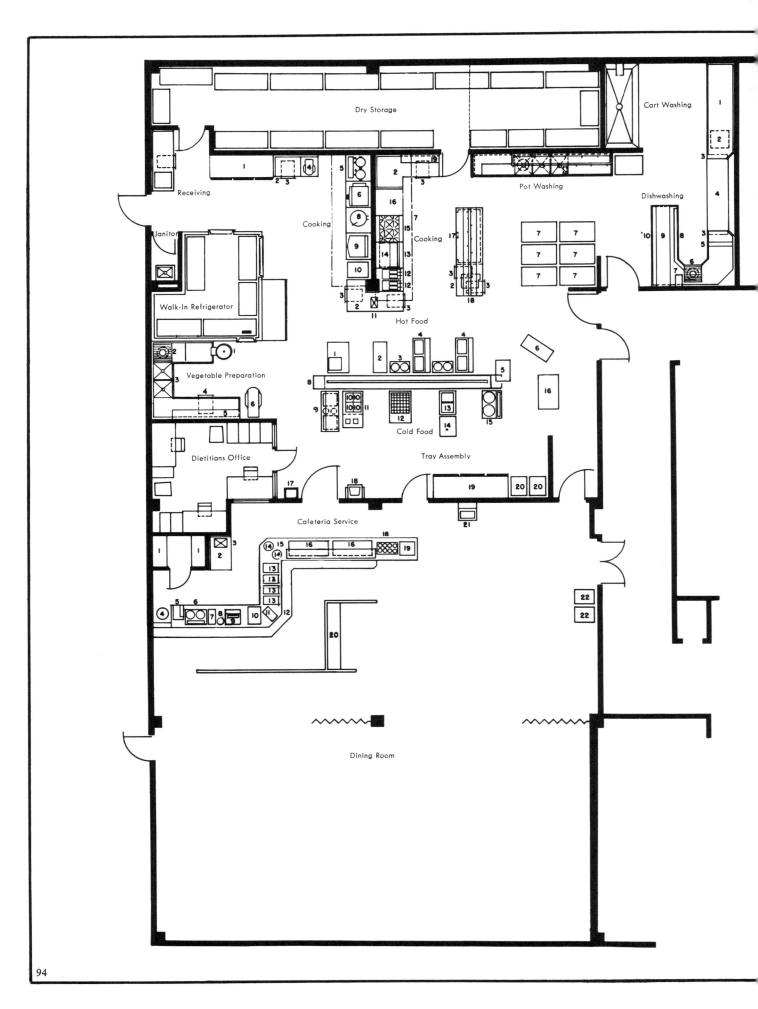

Dry Storage

Cart Washing

Receiving

Pot Washing

Dishwashing

Janitor

Cooking

Cooking

Hot Food

Walk-In Refrigerator

Vegetable Preparation

Cold Food

Tray Assembly

Dietitians Office

Cafeteria Service

Dining Room

West Adams Community Hospital

West Adams Community Hospital has the distinction of being unusual in concept. Not surprisingly, this generated unusual design criteria for the foodservice operation planners.

West Adams is a black ghetto in the Greater Los Angeles area. A few years back, two black doctors—Ludlow Creary and George Jackson—sensed a severe health crisis situation in the area and commissioned a survey.

Based on standards established by the California State Plan for Hospitals, the survey showed there to be less than one conforming bed per thousand people in the West Adams area. Meanwhile, the population of the area is increasing at a rate of about 10,000 per year, so it is evident the bed shortage will continue and become even more critical.

Determined to begin to rectify the situation, the two doctors organized a group for the purpose of obtaining financial support from other black doctors and community leaders. They were successful; a site was secured, plans drawn, and the hospital constructed.

The hospital was built with 196 conforming beds; in addition it meets other community needs; it has the only Pediatric Asthma Clinic, Cardio-Pulmonary Labo-

ratory, and Sickle Cell Testing Center in the area. There is a 24-hour emergency service for the community's half-million residents. Personnel are enlisted, where possible, from minority groups, and trained in hospital procedures. Overall, it represents one of the most significant construction projects ever undertaken in the U.S. with private black capital.

The present structure represents Phase I of the project. Phase II will consist of a towerlike structure immediately adjacent to the existing building. To the present 196 beds, the tower will add 254 beds, for a total of 450.

The plans for the Phase II structure include a main dietary department that will not only serve all the additional 254 beds, but provide most of the service for the present 196 beds. Thus the "convertibility" facet of the assignment as expressed to the facility designers pointed out in effect:

When the new dietary department is constructed, this existing kitchen will be used as a training center for dietary personnel, and will continue as a tray assembly center for the present 196 bed unit. This kitchen will also become an important facet of the Dietetic internship program that is planned as part of the

Phase II expansion. It will afford the interns a much needed opportunity to learn the practical approach to the use and care of modern institutional cooking equipment.

Besides this convertibility factor, the design project carried the twin problems of limited funds and limited allowable square footage (2,700 sq. ft.). In addition to patients, the kitchen also has to serve a staff cafeteria seating 150; this means that beyond the almost 600 meals served daily to patients, the cafeteria serves close to 500 meals to the staff daily. It is open from 7 a.m. to 3 a.m. daily. There are 32 fulltime and 5 part-time employees in food production and service.

While the basic thrust of the menu is, of course, toward balance and nutrition, every effort is made to include ethnic foods that appeal to the residents of the community.

In addition to the functional design concept of the dietary department, a warning-safety refrigerator and freezer system is employed. All refrigerated units throughout the hospital are keyed into a central security system where they are constantly monitored for deviation of temperature and mechanical malfunction.

EQUIPMENT LIST

Dishwashing
1. Clean Dish Table
2. Booster Water Heater
3. Pant Leg Hood
4. Dishwashing Machine
5. Quick Drain
6. Waste Disposer and Sink
7. Spray Rinse
8. Scrapping Trough
9. Elevated Dish Counter
10. Soiled Dish Counter

Vegetable Preparation
1. Peeler
2. Waste Disposer
3. Vegetable Prep Assembly
4. Drawer
5. Elevated Shelf
6. Floor Mixer

Tray Assembly
1. Pellet Heater w/Mobile Stand
2. Mobile Rack—Plate Bases
3. Mobile Heated Plate Dispenser

4. Mobile Hot Food Table
5. Mobile Rack—Plate Covers

Cooking
1. Reach-In Freezer
2. Work Table
3. Drawer
4. Bench Mixer
5. Tilting Kettles
6. Steam Cooker
7. Hood
8. Tilting Steam Kettle
9. Tilting Braising Pan
10. Mobile Food Warmer
11. Sink
12. Fryer
13. Griddle Top Range w/ Oven
14. Broiler (Salamander)
15. Open Top Range w/Oven
16. Convection Oven
17. Refrigerated Base Section
18. Elevated Shelf, Pot Rack
19. Elevated Shelf

Cold Food
7. Tray Cart Storage
8. Mobile Conveyor

9. Mobile Tray Makeup Cart
10. Toaster
11. Bread/Toaster Mobile Table
12. Mobile Milk Dispenser
13. Mobile Ice Cream Cabinet
14. Mobile Salad/Dessert Rack
15. Coffee Urn on Mobile Stand
16. Tray Cart—Loading Location
17. Drinking Fountain
18. Hand Sink
19. Roll-In Refrigerator
20. Utility Cart

Cafeteria Service
1. Shelving
2. Back-Up Table
3. Sink
4. Cashier's Chair
5. Cash Register
6. Coffee Urn
7. Cup Dispenser
8. Saucer Dispenser
9. Drink Dispenser

10. Ice Maker and Dispenser
11. Glass Dispenser
12. Tray Slide
13. Hot Food Well
14. Plate Dispenser
15. Serving Counter
16. Cold Food—Refrigerator Under
17. Elevated Display Shelves
18. Silverware Dispenser
19. Tray Dispenser
20. Condiment Stand
21. Ice Machine
22. Mobile Dish Bussing Cart

Designed by: Four Star Equipment and Design—Project Heads, Charles J. Rothkin and Faul Max

Doylestown Hospital

Opened only a year ago, the Doylestown Hospital, Doylestown, Pennsylvania, is a shining example of how attention to detail improves an operation.

Moving through the foodservice areas —from the rough prep, cooking, tray assembly, cafeteria, and dishroom—the attention to detail is obvious. Flow-through from one area to the next reduces steps and increases productivity.

The central preparation area is between the walk-in, dry storage, and cold food plating area, adjacent to the cooking battery. The prep sink has 2 compartments, with the area under the drainboard open for storage of a mobile refuse container and mobile bowl stand.

The preparation counter, 30 in. high to accommodate the women employees, has a food cutter, mixer, and slicer with attachments all on one long work table. Grater and shredder attachments are stored on a special frame between the table legs. Beaters, whips, and other attachments are stored on a special rack.

Positioned between the cold food plating area and the patient tray belt are 2 pass-thru refrigerators. Salads, desserts, and sandwiches prepared in advance are placed on 18- by 26-in. bun pans and loaded into the refrigerator. Special hold-open stops permit the doors to self-lock. When doors are opened to maximum, special stays engage; the doors stay open to permit 2-handed loading of the filled trays.

The cooking area is adjacent to the walk-in refrigerator/freezer (which at the employees' request has plexiglas doors), the patient tray belt, and close to the cafeteria hot food section, rough prep, and pot washing area.

The cooking area is electric and steam. Water taps were included near braising pans and oven areas so that the female employees would not have to carry containers of water across the kitchen area.

Above the cooking battery—ovens, broilers, steamers—is an automatic, self-cleaning ventilation system. As the last clean-up chore, an employee pushes a button, and detergent and hot water runs through every baffle. A rinse goes through, and a hot air blower dries the system for 2 hours. A similar ventilation system was installed above the cooking area in the cafeteria.

A steel stud lining built into the walls keeps dishroom noise to the minimum.

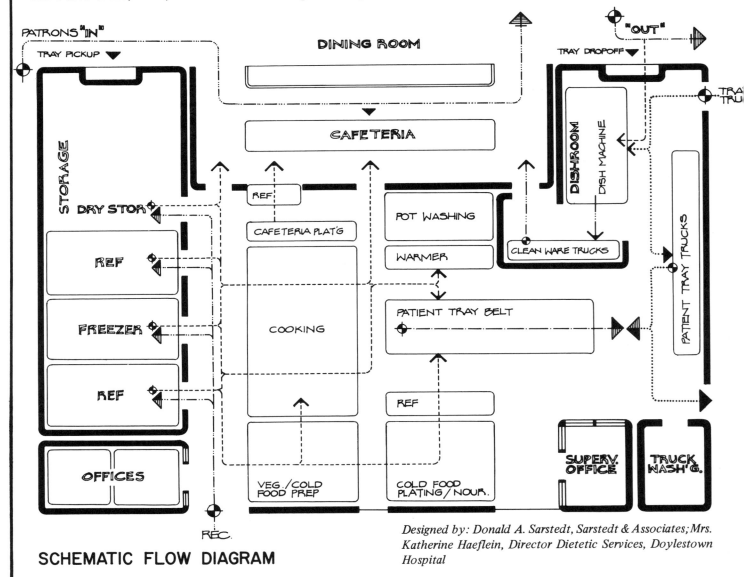

SCHEMATIC FLOW DIAGRAM

Designed by: Donald A. Sarstedt, Sarstedt & Associates; Mrs. Katherine Haeflein, Director Dietetic Services, Doylestown Hospital

Walter Reed Army Medical Center

Reaching beyond traditional kitchen design, the Army is building a food factory in its new Walter Reed facility in Washington, D.C. The sophisticated concepts incorporated have been tested and proved successful in Europe. Parts of the system have been adapted in other American hospitals.

Reaction in the U.S. has been mixed. It will probably be 1978 before sufficient data will be available to analyze the success of the operation. But the men involved—especially Major Ben Davis and Capt. David Stoehr—work with the confidence of true believers. Here is an outline of their plan:

Strategy for the new 1,280-bed facility at Walter Reed includes a semi-automated, innovative food production system. Major Ben Davis has searched the country—and the world—for equipment to maximize labor and space savings.

Initial decisions stressed semi-automation: a monorail system will carry food from receiving through production, on to storage, and finally to pantries on patient floors. A food processing system will be computer-controlled for quality checks; carts transporting patient meals will heat hot foods from chilled temperatures but keep cold foods chilled.

Major Davis has carefully researched carts, too. He favors an insulated cart that connects to wall-mounted refrigeration units. Since the cart does not need to carry heavy refrigerating elements, it is light and easy to keep clean.

Walter Reed will use the Gastronorm system of standardizing food handling. Dietary's storage racks will have shelves to accommodate 20- by 24-in. units. These will handle steamtable pans (10- by 12-in. or 12- by 20-in.) as well as patient meal trays (12- by 20-in.).

A major advantage of this system is that it saves space. And space is at a premium in hospitals costing $75 to $100 a sq. ft.

Walter Reed received special permission to purchase European equipment. Among the semi-automatic equipment specified: a continuous conveyor fryer grill, which permits one employee to load and unload from the same end (saving power as well as space and labor); pass-thru steamer; semi-automatic sauce and gravy maker.

In addition, approval has been requested from NSF for a self-basting oven for roasting meat. The roasts will be put in cradles moving in an oval pattern so that those above will baste the ones below. A pump will circulate the juices that collect in a pan in the bottom. Spray nozzles will recirculate the juices to baste the meats still rotating and cooking.

There is 40,000 sq. ft. of space for foodservice facilities in the new building. Less than 10 percent of the space—3,600 sq. ft., will be required for the hot food production area, preparing approx. 10,000 meals a day, five days a week. The rest of the area will house receiving, storage, serving, clean-up, and administration. In a system similar to that of a food factory, food will be individually portioned and stored in cassettes. During tray assembly, selected items will be loaded automatically.

WALTER REED ARMY MEDICAL CENTER — 3rd FLOOR

1. Employee Areas
2. Receiving
3. Non-Food Storage
4. Dry Storage
5. Freezer
6. Cryogenic Freezer
7. Refrigerator
8. Ingredient Room
9. Pot/Pan Wash
10. Test Facilities
11. Classrooms
12. Offices
13. Food Production
14. Patient Tray Assembly
15. Dishwash
16. Servery

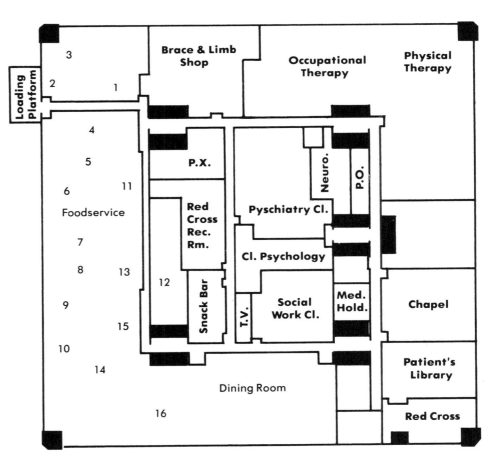

Ivinson Memorial Hospital

This totally new general hospital serves the Albany County area of Wyoming. The facility replaces a much smaller and greatly outmoded hospital which was located in an older structure near the center of town. The older facility, kitchen and hospital, was not capable of handling the patient load in the outdated structure that housed it. The new facility, from receiving to storage to preparation to distribution to patients and visitors, is working very well.

The people served by the hospital are ranchers, townspeople, and students attending the University of Wyoming which is located in Laramie. The educational level of the people served is mixed. The work force available to the facility is quite stable.

The fabrication of equipment is of top quality and was specified with health and dietary codes, maintenance, longevity, and function in mind. All tops of working surfaces, backsplashes, upper cabinets, upper shelves, hoods, portable conveyor counter, and tray slides are constructed of stainless steel. Undershelves of work counters are constructed of galvanized steel.

Buy-out equipment, such as carts, self-leveling dispensers, and similar items, are constructed of top quality materials. All portable equipment has non-marking wheels as well as wrap-around guards where applicable.

The patient foodservice system utilizes tray carts sent to the floors by a dumbwaiter. Visitors are served in a cafeteria with a line which is accessible for loading directly from the kitchen. Maximum use has been made of portable carts for dish storage and food distribution to serving lines.

The flow pattern for this foodservice is a direct flow from receiving to storage to preparation to cooking to distribution with no cross traffic, as is indicated on the flow pattern noted on the floor plan on the facing page.

The primary access to the kitchen is directly from the receiving area, and the dining room is accessible directly from the public areas and from a central exterior courtyard. This flow pattern has worked well, is efficient, and permits preparation and service to be fast and smooth during peak periods and to adapt well during slack periods.

Employees' lounge and locker space is not within the kitchen area but is directly across the adjacent service corridor with similar facilities used by all of the other hospital employees.

Among construction materials specified were: quarry tile floor in the kitchen areas and cafeteria serving area, structural glazed tile walls, and washable acoustical (removable) tile ceiling. The walk-in freezer and coolers have quarry tile floors and base and cement plaster walls and ceilings. The dining

EQUIPMENT LIST

1.	Hose & Rack	37.	Floor Pan
2.	Freezer	38.	Steamer
3.	Freezer	39.	Kettle Stand
4.	Shelving	40.	Table Tilt Kettle
5.	Pallets	41.	Exhaust Ventilators
6.	Spare No.	42.	Vegetable Cutter
7.	Disposal	43.	Slicer Table
8.	Dishtable	44.	Meat Slicer
9.	Upper Shelf	45.	Spare No.
10.	Dishwasher	46.	Cup & Glass Dispenser
11.	Pass Thru	47.	Fryer
12.	Cup & Saucer Dispenser	48.	Spreader
13.	Dish Carts	49.	Range
14.	Plate Dispenser	50.	Range
15.	Spare No.	51.	Broiler
16.	Potato Peeler	52.	Oven
17.	Disposal	53.	Pot Filler
18.	Work Counter	54.	Spare No.
19.	Pot Rack	55.	Refrigerator
20.	Pot Counter	56.	Work Counter
21.	Pot Washer	57.	Upper Cabinet
22.	Disposal	58.	Cart
23.	Work Counter	59.	Spare No.
24.	Refrigerator	60.	Starter Supply Unit
25.	Upper Cabinet	61.	Tray Dispenser
26.	Blender	62.	Pellet Oven
27.	Beverage Cabinet	63.	Oven Stand
28.	Urn Stand	64.	Milk Dispenser
29.	Coffee Urn	65.	Cold Food Unit
30.	Spare No.	66.	Spare No.
31.	Toaster Counter	67.	Hot Food Unit
32.	Toaster	68.	Conveyor
33.	Steam Cooker	69.	Tray Carts
34.	Work Counter	70.	Ice Cream Cabinet
35.	Spare No.	71.	Ice Maker
36.	Shelf	72.	Flour Bin

room has a carpeted floor, vinyl wall fabric walls, acoustical tile ceiling, and draperies.

Trash is placed in appropriate containers and then taken to an adjacent trash collecting area where it is placed in designated containers which a private collection truck removes. The containers are washed in the can wash room and returned clean to the kitchen.

The foodservice area is well-lighted, air-conditioned, and cooking odors are completely and quickly exhausted. There is a fire protection system within the hoods, the exhaust system, and within the kitchen. The kitchen area is separated from the dining area with an acoustical partition that goes to the ceiling so kitchen noises do not penetrate the dining room.

The prime function of this operation is to provide proper foodservice to the hospital patients in an atmosphere that will maintain high morale among patients, employees, and staff. Ivinson Memorial Hospital does that quite well in its effectively designed foodservice.

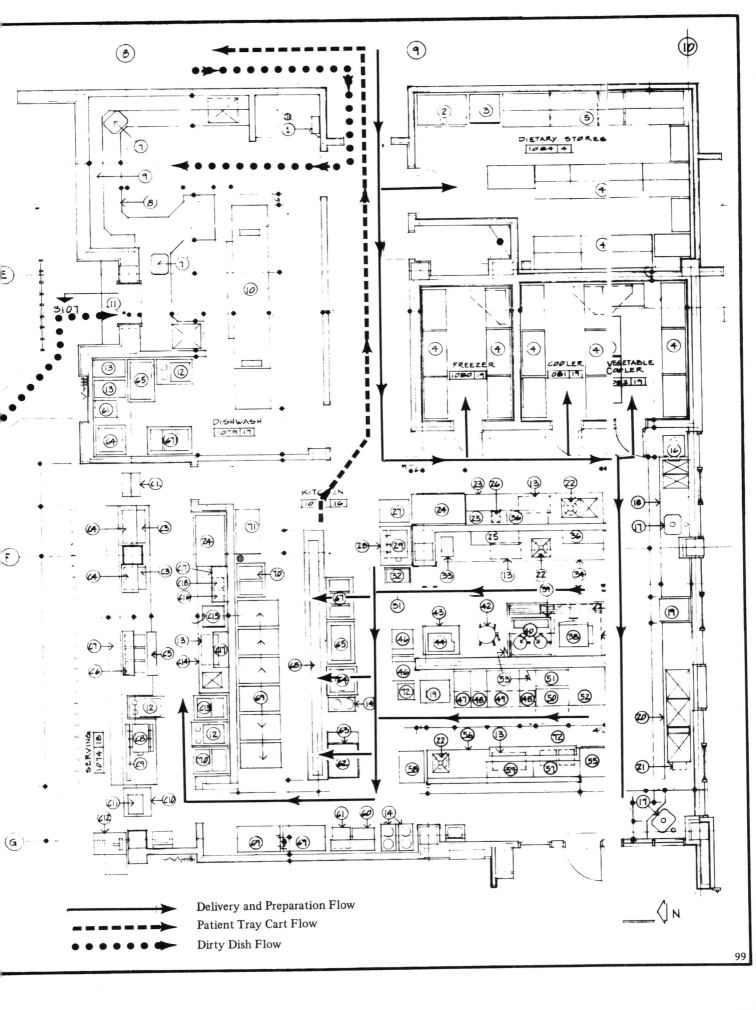

Delivery and Preparation Flow

Patient Tray Cart Flow

Dirty Dish Flow

Ivinson Memorial Hospital continued

Ivinson Memorial Hospital, Laramie, Wyo. serves 900 meals per day, the majority to patients, using a tray and cart system, the remainder to employees and visitors in the cafeteria. This is a new general hospital which serves the entire Albany County Area.

This is a view of the compact cafeteria serving line and the dining room in an area totally separated from the line. At the rear of the dining room is a vending area where there are also tables and chairs to make eating a relaxing time for personnel and visitors alike.

Above: View of the main cooking area showing the work counter on the right and the fryer, range, broiler, and convection oven on the left. Hood exhaust units are mounted above all of these cooking units.

Right: A menu selection form is prepared daily for patients to indicate their choice of items for each meal. Printed forms are filled in with each day's menu.

SELECTIVE MENU-IVINSON MEMORIAL HOSPITAL

BREAKFAST			DINNER			SUPPER		
ROOM _____ DAY _____ TUESDAY			ROOM _____ DAY _____ TUESDAY			ROOM _____ DAY _____ TUESDAY		
NAME _____			NAME _____			NAME _____		
Specify Serving: Small Medium Large			Specify Serving: Small Medium Large			Specify Serving: Small Medium Large		
PLEASE CIRCLE DESIRED ITEMS			PLEASE CIRCLE DESIRED ITEMS			PLEASE CIRCLE DESIRED ITEMS		
FROZ. ORANGE JUICE PEACH NECTAR			FRIED STEAK WEINER (2)			CR. OF CHICKEN SOUP		
MALT O'MEAL WHEATIES			MASHED POTATOES GRAVY			AMERICAN RAVIOLI BEEF PATTIE		
SCRAMBLED EGGS SOFT COOKED EGG LINK SAUSAGE			BT. SPINACH SAUERKRAUT			BAKED POTATOES & BUTTER PARMESAN CHEESE		
ENGLISH MUFFIN TOAST			RELISHES ON LETTUCE TOMATO JUICE			BT. CARROTS		
			RASPBERRY SUNDAE			COMBINATION SALAD WITH ITALIAN DRESSING PINEAPPLE JUICE		
						CND. W.P. APRICOTS		
WHITE TOAST W.W. TOAST BUTTER JELLY or JAM OLEO	SM. CREAM LG. CREAM MILK SKIM MILK BUTTERMILK CHOC. MILK	COFFEE TEA SANKA HOT CHOC.	WHITE BREAD W.W. BREAD MELBA TOAST CRACKERS BUTTER JELLY or JAM OLEO	MILK SKIM MILK BUTTERMILK CHOC. MILK ICE CREAM CREAM	HOT TEA ICE TEA LEMON COFFEE SANKA HOT CHOC.	WHITE BREAD W.W. BREAD MELBA TOAST CRACKERS BUTTER JELLY or JAM OLEO	MILK SKIM MILK BUTTERMILK CHOC. MILK ICE CREAM CREAM	HOT TEA ICE TEA LEMON COFFEE SANKA HOT CHOC.

University of Washington Hospital

Eye-catching signage at the University of Washington Hospital Cafeteria in Seattle quickly directs patrons to the full line cafeteria.

Right: To speed patron selection of menu items, lunch and dinner choices are listed with prices below Full Fare sign at the entrance to the cafeteria. Below: Cafeteria seating arrangements are flexible. There are vending machines with a dining area across from the machines at entrance to the cafeteria food line. A wheelchair aisle makes patronage possible for convalescent patients. Part of the cafeteria is designed to be closed off during weekend slow periods. There is also a private dining room for staff separated from the main cafeteria by its own hallway.

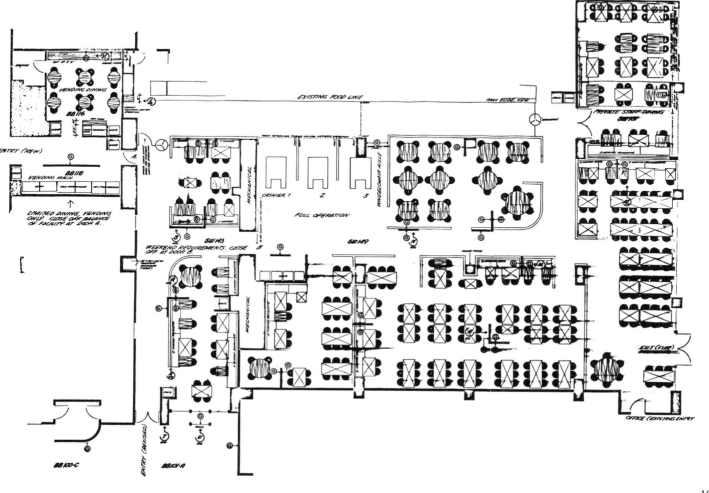

Harrisburg Hospital

For a most common reason—the need to enlarge the hospital, which also meant expanding the foodservice facilities—Harrisburg Hospital, in Harrisburg, Pennsylvania elected to choose a most uncommon solution.

Long uncomfortable with its existing, traditional operation, and fearful of the problems of rising labor costs, shortage of trained workers, and the increasing difficulty of staffing for a seven-day, two-shift operation, hospital management seized the need to rebuild kitchen facilities as an opportunity to make changes.

To investigate and implement a problem-solving program, the hospital administration engaged a foodservice design consultant and a contract food management company. The final proposal consolidated the changes into four areas.

(1) Convenience Foods: The use of convenience foods would allow the department to get along with fewer food preparation personnel. It would also assure greater consistency in meal quality. Products purchased prepared for service would increase the overall efficiency of the operation, as the need for less handling of foods would increase worker productivity.

Enough entrees, vegetables, salads, desserts, and other portioned items were available fully prepared for both regular and therapeutic menus to permit a 14-day menu cycle.

Although on first consideration they appear to be more costly, convenience foods as an integral part of an overall system will eventually be less expensive than the cost of operating a conventional system.

(2) Multiple Meal Program: There is a trend in major medical institutions across the country toward a 4- or 5-meal-a-day program for patients. Research indicated a 4-meal plan would be advantageous in a hospital of the Harrisburg type.

Not only does this plan have advantages for the patient, it is also considered by staff physicians to have great therapeutic value. Meal service hours for patients are as follows:

Continental Brunch—7:00 a.m. to 7:30 a.m.; Brunch—10:30 a.m. to 11:30 a.m.; Dinner—3:30 p.m. to 4:30 p.m.; Snack—7:30 p.m. to 8:30 p.m.

This schedule allows the patient complete privacy for meals as it falls outside visiting hours. It allows full help in patient feeding by the hospital staff, as foodservice for employees is at later hours and does not conflict. Moreover, the four-meal plan follows today's trend toward eating lighter meals, but eating more often.

Because most medical tests are done in the morning, patients have generally had to miss breakfast. They now have the opportunity to make up for this at Brunch.

The plan has distinct advantages for the foodservice department since two of the four meals can be assembled prior to actual distribution, thus allowing maximum use of employee working time.

(3) Microwave Ovens: This method of heating patient food is an integral part of the overall system. Its prime value is to provide the patient with the hottest meal possible.

A second value is that it allows the food to be assembled in a thawed state in the main kitchen, then held refrigerated in the appropriate wards until meal time. The assembly and plating while thawed allows maximum use of the assembly belt and personnel in the main kitchen.

This aspect of the program did create one new problem however. In order to properly reheat the hot foods, all of the items on a plate must be of a consistent density. While it has been demonstrated that it is possible to write diet menus taking this factor into account, it does not make the job easier.

(4) Single Use Ware: The exclusive use of disposable service has important ramifications in the overall system. It eliminates the need for a two-way dish system. It reduces the number of employees required overall, so lessening the possibility of cross infection among patients and employees.

It reduces the ambient noise level, particularly important in this hospital, since reheating "kitchens" are located in every patient area throughout the hospital.

Because the new foodservice facilities were to be located on the site of the existing kitchen, it was necessary to use the basement as a 6-month temporary facility. The switch from on premise preparation occurred with that move. The four principal equipment components of the new foodservice system are refrigerators, assembly conveyor, mobile refrigerated carts, and microwave ovens.

Refrigerated storage, both low-temperature (freezers) and normal temperature, encompasses considerable square footage. The low temperature units are used to hold the purchased frozen items until needed. The normal temperature units hold those items bought refrigerated, as well as serve to temper the frozen items for plating.

The mechanical conveyor rubber link belt is 32 ft. long, and it requires eight employees to staff it for a major meal assembly. Mobile refrigerated carts were specially fabricated to hold specified numbers of trays. Each cart has a freezer unit on top that can hold 2 gal. of ice cream.

One microwave oven is allocated for each 30 patient beds; at this time there are 25 microwave ovens located throughout the hospital.

The operation now serves about 24,000 patient and employee meals daily, using the full-time equivalent of 59.6 workers, a figure expected to decline. The hospital has 680 beds presently, with long range plans to add another 200.

There are three small cafeterias handling non-patient feeding. Convection ovens are used to heat the frozen prepared food served in these areas.

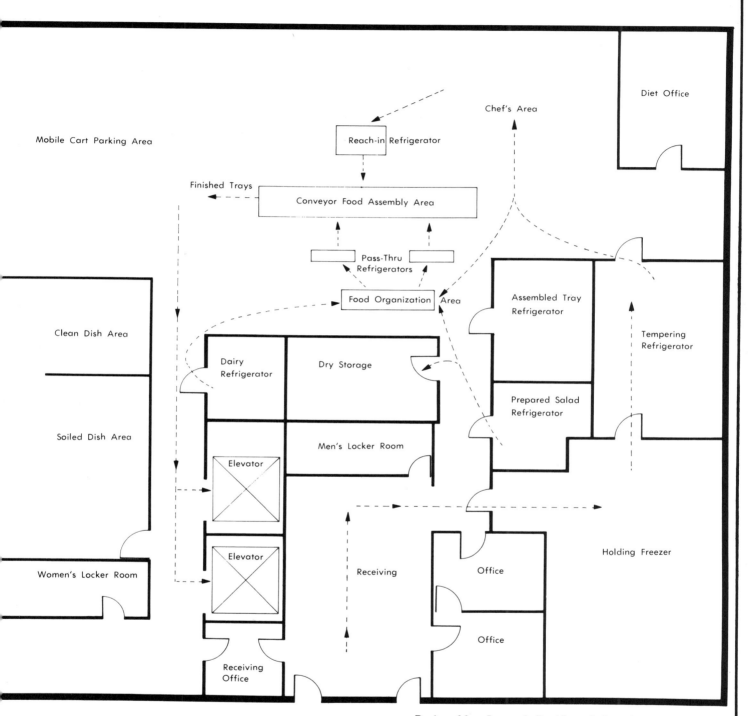

Diet Office

Mobile Cart Parking Area

Chef's Area

Reach-in Refrigerator

Finished Trays

Conveyor Food Assembly Area

Pass-Thru Refrigerators

Clean Dish Area

Food Organization Area

Assembled Tray Refrigerator

Tempering Refrigerator

Dairy Refrigerator

Dry Storage

Soiled Dish Area

Prepared Salad Refrigerator

Men's Locker Room

Elevator

Elevator

Holding Freezer

Women's Locker Room

Receiving

Office

Office

Receiving Office

Designed by: James A. Davidson & Associates

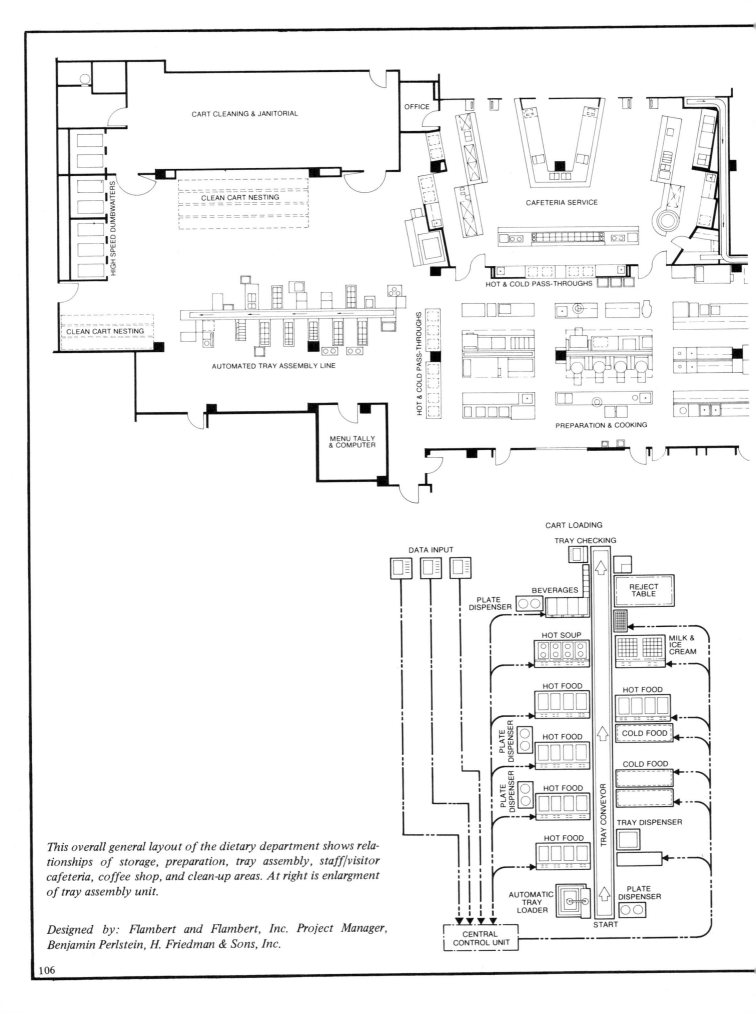

CART CLEANING & JANITORIAL

OFFICE

CLEAN CART NESTING

HIGH SPEED DUMBWAITERS

CAFETERIA SERVICE

CLEAN CART NESTING

HOT & COLD PASS-THROUGHS

HOT & COLD PASS-THROUGHS

AUTOMATED TRAY ASSEMBLY LINE

PREPARATION & COOKING

MENU TALLY & COMPUTER

CART LOADING

TRAY CHECKING

DATA INPUT

REJECT TABLE

BEVERAGES

PLATE DISPENSER

MILK & ICE CREAM

HOT SOUP

HOT FOOD

HOT FOOD

HOT FOOD

COLD FOOD

PLATE DISPENSER

COLD FOOD

PLATE DISPENSER

HOT FOOD

TRAY DISPENSER

HOT FOOD

TRAY CONVEYOR

PLATE DISPENSER

AUTOMATIC TRAY LOADER

START

CENTRAL CONTROL UNIT

This overall general layout of the dietary department shows relationships of storage, preparation, tray assembly, staff/visitor cafeteria, coffee shop, and clean-up areas. At right is enlargment of tray assembly unit.

Designed by: Flambert and Flambert, Inc. Project Manager, Benjamin Perlstein, H. Friedman & Sons, Inc.

Memorial Sloan-Kettering Hospital

SCULLERY

DISHROOM

COFFEE SHOP

Automation as a concept has been put to use in an actual operation and it is functioning. It does what automation is supposed to do: achieve increased productivity with reduced labor.

The site of this installation is Memorial Sloan-Kettering Cancer Center, New York City. It is a 611-bed facility.

The mechanics of the system include a 38-ft. high-speed, automated tray assembly belt, with a checking station that uses auxiliary electronic data processing equipment and processes eight trays per minute.

This unit, in conjunction with custom-designed tray carts and a high-speed vertical dumbwaiter sys-

tem, assures that any patient in the 21-story building is served within 10 minutes of the time his meal is portioned.

The set-up was arrived at through a systems analysis of the tray assembly and distribution function. This consisted of five steps: (1) consideration of the new hospital's design (before construction); (2) examination of the foodservice department's objectives; (3) investigation and observation of equipment available (in this country and Europe); (4) development and testing of models of various tray assembly alternatives, and (5) evaluation of the results of the tests.

Architecturally, the hospital is 21 stories high, with patient rooms on floors 4 through 19. A central core on each floor accommodates all services, including a high-speed, vertical transportation system with seven floor-loading dumbwaiters, five for clean products and two for soiled. Because the dumbwaiters are used for medications and supplies as well as foodservice, their use by the department is limited to no more than 1-¼ hours per meal.

Equipment investigation began with the design constant: the floor-loading, high-speed dumbwaiters. Loaded carts are positioned at the door. In a building-wide average of 50 seconds, the door opens, the cart is pulled on, the door closes, the dumbwaiter ascends to the pre-set floor, and the cart is ejected. To take advantage of this speed requires that eight complete patient trays be assembled per minute.

To achieve this an automated system of tray assembly was chosen. The Voss Optacon unit in use is European designed. It includes an automatic tray loader, a light bank at each menu category station to indicate which item(s)— and portion size—should go on the tray then passing.

As it now operates, the meal selections patients circle on daily printed menus are transferred to punch cards. These cards are then sorted according to floor delivery sequence and patient location so

that trays come off the line in the order in which they are to be served. The card reader sends the data to a memory bank—or data collector. (Shortly a more sophisticated electronic process will be substituted.)

The control unit establishes the time intervals at which trays are released by an automatic tray dispenser. As the tray passes the card reader, a card falls on the belt in front of the tray to identify the patient who is to receive it. Because the card falls flat on the belt, employees cannot read any information from it, and must rely solely on the signal lights at their individual stations.

Having released the tray, the control unit programs the item/portion light signals at the proper station. The lights glow for six seconds when each tray reaches the appropriate point on the belt.

Delivery is accomplished by two teams of four employees each. One team begins serving the 19th floor, the second the 10th floor. After serving these, each team moves to the floor directly beneath, and continues until all patients are served.

Modifications made in the system include the addition of a hot beverage station; a small, insulated carafe is used for coffee, hot water and hot milk (for cereal). To match line speed two employees are assigned here; one to fill the carafes, the other to load the tray.

A color-coded card system distinguishes meals for isolation patients who are served on disposable dishes.

Salads, desserts and other cold items are pre-wrapped, and pre-plated to speed service. To permit greater menu flexibility, hot and cold stations on the line are interchangeable.

Among the systems back-up provisions is a manual card reader integrated into the system to process last-minute patient menu changes. It can also provide backup if the mechanical card reader should fail.

Day Care Center

Sherman Robinson
and
Patricia D. Asmussen

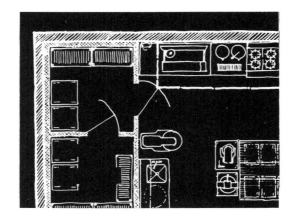

A DAY CARE CENTER may be defined as any institution operated for the purpose of providing care and maintenance for children separated from their parents or guardians during part of a 24-hour day, excepting a *bona fide* educational institution.

Day care centers, also known as day nursery or child care centers, have been in limited existence for over a century. But the last decade has brought about a phenomenal growth in these facilities that reflects economic and social changes in our society. And increasingly, a greater number of women in the childbearing age are working outside the home and so require the service of competent child care in a safe, healthful, and happy environment. Therefore, growth in the number of day care centers designed for the specific purpose of providing an ideal environment for the care of very young children—from six weeks to six years old —should be even more dramatic in the future.

The U.S. Dept. of Health, Education, and Welfare, under Title XX, allocates monies for the purchase of child care from a licensed center. For parents with larger incomes the cost of child care is an authorized federal income tax deduction. So it would seem logical to assume these two types of subsidy will generate the same kind of growth spiral that Medicare and Medicaid did for the nursing home industry.

One of the most common problems that plagues day care organizations is a lack of adequate information and planning about the market they wish to serve. Before any attempt is initiated to start a day care operation, it must first be determined whether the area or community to be served can support such an operation, even though there is an indicated need for such a service.

Good business sense calls for a survey to determine if there is enough financial strength in the market to support an organization of the type projected.

Elements of Design

The foremost planning objective for day care centers should be a facility that provides an appropriate physical atmosphere for the health and safety of young children. To determine criteria for the planning process, the rules and regulations governing the construction and licensing of day care centers in the specific state within which it is to operate should be obtained.

The State Departments of Public Welfare or Social Services are the usual licensing agency and they, of course, must be contacted. Still other agencies at the state level may have input or regulatory control. These might include the Department of Health, the Administrative Building Council or its counterpart, and the Fire Marshall's office.

Regulatory agencies in the city and/or county where the center is to be located should be advised of the intent of building and operation, since approval from local zoning authorities will be necessary. The city and/or county government may have ordinances that are more stringent than those regulating day care centers at the state level, so it is also necessary to contact the local Welfare Department, Health Department, Fire Department, and building authority.

Non-Profit Centers

Day care centers can be divided into two basic groups: non-profit and for-profit. We can sub-divide the non-profit group into church-sponsored and philanthropic groups. Let us first explore the church-sponsored center and its problems.

A church-sponsored center exemplifies the basic philosophy of a non-profit organization. Its main objective is to provide low cost child care for the people in its community. It relies on its congregation, grants, donations, and governmental organizations for some or all of its financial support.

The number of church-sponsored centers is growing rapidly because churches typically feel a need to provide more service to their communities. Moreover, their congregations frequently desire greater use of the facilities because of their large economic investments in site and building.

Many existing churches are adapting present areas or remodeling to meet day care licensing requirements. Existing kitchens usually must be updated to provide separate service and storage areas for the day care center to eliminate conflict of use with other church organizations.

In many new church construction programs, areas are designed specifically for day care. Since these facilities will be a focal point in the community, good design must reflect an emphasis on efficient and economical use of space since the operational budget may be supplemented by the congregation.

Philanthropic agency-sponsored day care centers have been historically the leaders in providing competent care. Beyond that, they have contributed expertise in developing licensing standards, and in design development of building structures that carry out program objectives for good child care.

Centers sponsored by a philanthropic agency usually receive greater public notice and community support than other types. They are thus charged with the responsibility and accountability of being a leader in community child care and, therefore, desire a physical environment that provides the ideal in services. These centers usually operate on a non-profit basis, with charges for child care to the parents based on a sliding scale, determined by ability to pay. Additional operating costs are provided by the sponsoring agency or agencies, with a Board of Directors responsible for management and budget policies.

A real hurdle facing any non-profit day care center is securing financial backing. Probably this is the most difficult of all the problems to master. In today's money market, few lending organizations are willing to provide financial backing to non-profit day care centers—or even to profit-oriented groups for that matter. This reluctance is due mainly to the poor financial track record of day care centers overall.

Volunteer Help

One problem the non-profit day care center can avoid, however, is volunteer help. While volunteer help sounds good, it is imperative that professional paid help be obtained.

The use of volunteer help can be costly. A volunteer helper, like a paid employee, must have a yearly physical examination to assure freedom from communicable disease and that immunization shots are updated. In most instances it is the day care center which picks up the bill for the exams required for volunteers.

Nor should volunteer helpers be counted on for the day-to-day staffing operation, since the ratio of staff to children required by license regulations must be maintained. The volunteer helper is best utilized as an additional hand for special functions: helping with a trip to the zoo, providing a puppet show for the children during a quiet period, and similar activities.

The Fee

The fee determination for each child must incorporate not only the cost of food and its preparation, but must also reflect other costs: building and equipment maintenance; equipment replacement; salaries; insurance; and so on. Only by careful analysis and planning of the fee structure, will the non-profit organization survive, even with the help of grants, donations, and reimbursements from governmental agencies. It is imperative that day care centers, especially those that are non-profit, be business-like in operation at all times, since they will come under the scrutiny of many fiscal audits.

For-Profit Day Care Centers

Privately owned and operated for-profit day care centers are generally small, providing for under 40 children. The owner is usually the director of the center, and has a more limited operating budget, and a greater need for profit, being engaged in a proprietary operation.

The privately owned center usually rents or purchases an existing building, and remodels to meet license requirements. Minimum expenditure is the usual rule, until such time as growth and profit allow for building a new facility designed specifically for day care and having accommodations for 100 or more children.

Franchised centers are a somewhat newer entry in the day care field. Here facility design and operational programs are provided for the individual investor, though financial arrangements vary with each franchise. One common difficulty with a franchise package is that the included pre-designed building does not meet local codes and ordinances. Nor does the operational program and budgetary base always fit every state since requirements affecting staff ratio per number of children vary with licensing agencies.

Chain-operated day care centers are also beginning to emerge. In this case the parent owner or corporation owns the centers, develops and centralizes management and operational policy, and hires directors to manage the individual centers. The chain,

like the franchise, develops one design package which thereafter becomes identifiable with its name. The management of the chain day care center usually evaluates the physical plant in relation to its ability to meet operational requirements, while keeping construction, operational, and maintenance costs down, and so produces an anticipated profit return on each unit.

Site Selection

The site selected for a day care center should preferably be in an area where the population will support the facility. Residential areas heavily populated with young families, or near an industrial area which employs large numbers of young women, are typical examples. The location should be easily reached by main thoroughfares, with ample parking for parents bringing or picking up their children. The site must have sufficient ground for a fenced outdoor play area.

Labor

With the cost of labor and fringe benefit packages ever increasing, it is vital for the operational success of a day care center to receive maximum return on investment in kitchen personnel. Kitchen design and selection of equipment must promote simplicity of operation and ease of thorough cleaning.

Productivity

For a day care center to be productive, its design must insure efficient food preparation and service. The margin of profit is inherently minimal, since child care is a service that requires both a high staff ratio for a limited number of children, and foodservice that meets stringent guidelines for quality and quantity; yet the charge for day care has to remain in a range that is affordable for the working parent.

So that the cook's time is used wisely, she must be provided with the tools to carry out her duties. The responsibility for preparing breakfast, lunch, and two snacks does not allow for a poorly planned or unplanned foodservice. It is most likely the cook will be untrained in commercial food preparation, and will have developed her cooking skills in a domestic kitchen. Management should, therefore, provide the cook and foodservice workers with a complete operational program to obtain the optimum return for its invested labor dollar.

It is further recommended that the services of a consulting dietitian be employed by the center to provide expertise in developing an individualized foodservice operational program. If the dietitian can be employed at the beginning of the planning stage for the kitchen at the same time as the food facility layout consultant starts his work, so much the better. Then joint thought can be given to the myriad of decisions that include type of service (such as pre-plated or modified family style); use of permanent ware or single service dishes; menu format; and the equipment required for food preparation, to name a few.

A dietitian can be retained at an hourly fee to develop the foodservice budget, policies and procedures, staffing patterns, job descriptions, menus, recipe sources, purchasing guides and specifications, serving schedules, and cleaning procedures and schedules. Kitchen personnel can be trained by the dietitian. This will free the day care director and teachers to provide an integrated nutrition education program for the children, and even for the parents where appropriate.

Day Care foodservice must provide more than just calories for hungry children. The lunch meal and two snacks should be planned to meet two-thirds of the Recommended Dietary Allowances for the appropriate age of the child. The food should be simply prepared in a manner acceptable to young children, with consideration given to color, shape, and texture. The young child likes "finger foods" and usually does not care for casseroles or mixed dishes.

The foodservices of a day care center can play an important part in the child's nutrition education, and should accept the challenge of helping develop good attitudes toward food. Regular meal hours, together with an adventurous spirit, the willingness to try new foods, and learning to eat a variety of foods will contribute to the child's well-being, now and for the rest of his/her life.

Convenience Foods

Convenience foods, by which I mean totally prepared, ready to heat and serve, are not generally engineered to meet the needs of the day care center. An individual, pre-packaged hot meal, providing child-sized portions—from two to four tablespoons per serving—would not have enough mass to allow for a quality product after heating for service. The cost of packaging such individual meals would raise the food cost above the budget for most centers.

Also, the variety of convenience foods, especially fruits and vegetables, is limited. Yet, the introduction of a wide selection of foods in the day care center is essential to the opportunity for nutrition education of the child. Nor do mixed entree dishes provide enough quality protein for the young child's needs in a two- to four-ounce serving. Convenience foods are designed for the nutritional needs and taste of adults. Desserts and baked items may well be the most appropriate convenience food selections for use in a day care center.

A partial use of convenience food items can, to be sure, enhance the menu, save labor, and provide a back-up for emergency situations. But each such convenience item must be evaluated on its own merit, to determine if it meets the nutritional requirements of the children served, and the food cost budget of the individual center.

Equipment Decisions and Relationships

Because as a rule the cook in a day care center has not been trained for commercial food preparation, she should be provided with a kitchen in which an untrained person can function with maximum efficiency. This calls for well-designed traffic patterns, commercial equipment which is easy to operate and maintain, and adequate dry and refrigerated storage space.

Moreover, storage areas should be properly ventilated to insure optimum temperature control. This will prevent loss of expensive food items, whether through development of weevils and bugs in flours and cereals, or the canned goods bulging and becoming "flippers." Unencumbered work surfaces, a well planned menu, and complete

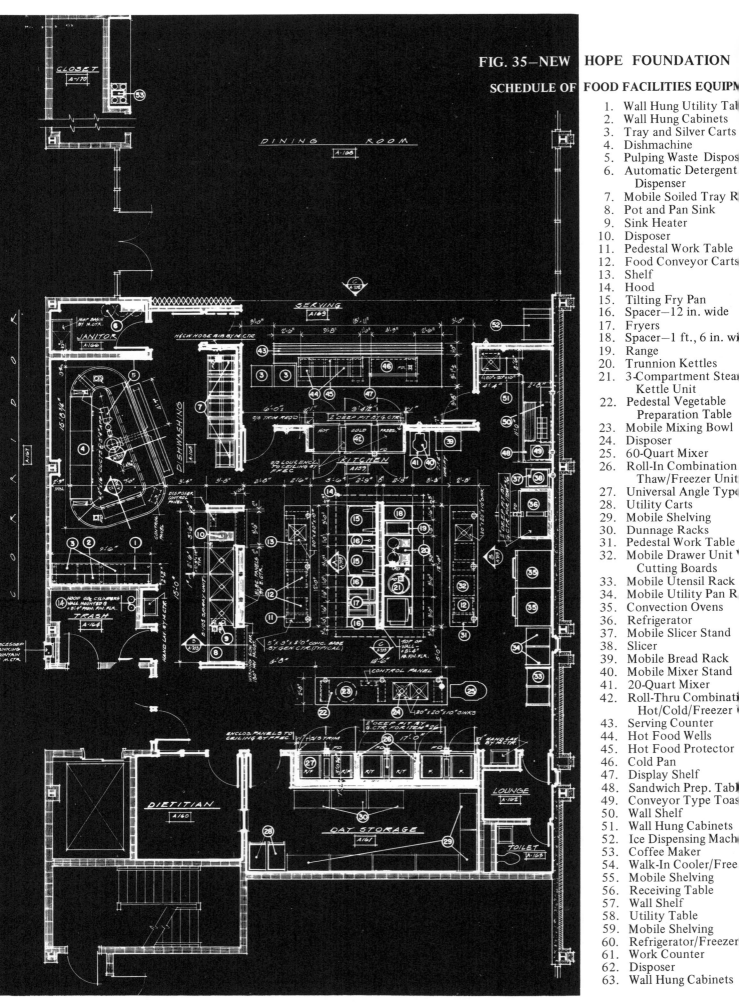

FIG. 35—NEW HOPE FOUNDATION

SCHEDULE OF FOOD FACILITIES EQUIPM

1. Wall Hung Utility Tab
2. Wall Hung Cabinets
3. Tray and Silver Carts
4. Dishmachine
5. Pulping Waste Dispos
6. Automatic Detergent
   Dispenser
7. Mobile Soiled Tray R
8. Pot and Pan Sink
9. Sink Heater
10. Disposer
11. Pedestal Work Table
12. Food Conveyor Carts
13. Shelf
14. Hood
15. Tilting Fry Pan
16. Spacer—12 in. wide
17. Fryers
18. Spacer—1 ft., 6 in. wi
19. Range
20. Trunnion Kettles
21. 3-Compartment Stea
    Kettle Unit
22. Pedestal Vegetable
    Preparation Table
23. Mobile Mixing Bowl
24. Disposer
25. 60-Quart Mixer
26. Roll-In Combination
    Thaw/Freezer Unit
27. Universal Angle Type
28. Utility Carts
29. Mobile Shelving
30. Dunnage Racks
31. Pedestal Work Table
32. Mobile Drawer Unit
    Cutting Boards
33. Mobile Utensil Rack
34. Mobile Utility Pan R
35. Convection Ovens
36. Refrigerator
37. Mobile Slicer Stand
38. Slicer
39. Mobile Bread Rack
40. Mobile Mixer Stand
41. 20-Quart Mixer
42. Roll-Thru Combinati
    Hot/Cold/Freezer
43. Serving Counter
44. Hot Food Wells
45. Hot Food Protector
46. Cold Pan
47. Display Shelf
48. Sandwich Prep. Tab
49. Conveyor Type Toas
50. Wall Shelf
51. Wall Hung Cabinets
52. Ice Dispensing Mach
53. Coffee Maker
54. Walk-In Cooler/Free
55. Mobile Shelving
56. Receiving Table
57. Wall Shelf
58. Utility Table
59. Mobile Shelving
60. Refrigerator/Freezer
61. Work Counter
62. Disposer
63. Wall Hung Cabinets

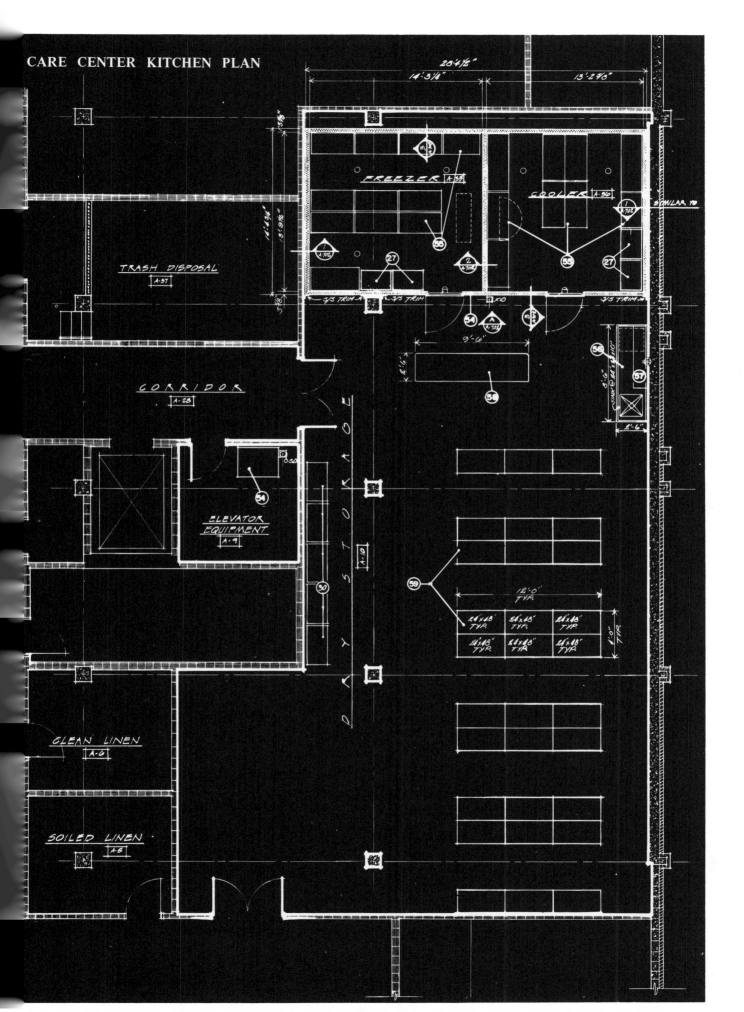

CARE CENTER KITCHEN PLAN

and simple-to-follow recipes are further necessary tools for providing an economical and exemplary foodservice program.

Remember, too, there is little or no down-time, since breakfast is served to early-arriving children, followed by a mid-morning snack, a hot lunch, and a mid-afternoon snack to all the children. Centers operating in the evening must also provide a hot supper meal and a bedtime snack. It takes organization to prepare, serve, and clean up after as many as six meals.

Equipment such as kettles, trunnion kettles, convection ovens, and tilting fry pans should be considered because of their high production capacity, ease of operation, and cleanability, as well as being fairly simple to operate. Work areas should be laid out to eliminate extra steps and wasted motion.

Serving areas should be designed to accommodate serving stations. These stations should include refrigeration for holding such items as milk and cold desserts, and have at least one electrically-heated hot food well. An ideal serving station would also have a storage space for small utensils and a small sink for clean-up.

As part of planning, the non-profit day care center should investigate its eligibility for the Child Care Food Program, administered through the School Lunch Division, U.S. Dept. of Agriculture. This program can provide monies for meals as well as available commodity food items or cash in lieu of these, depending on state options. A Non-Food Assistance Program, operated by the same agency, can also be a source of supplemental funds if the center qualifies. Qualification can affect the menu, type of food preparation, equipment, and amount of refrigerated and dry storage.

Since the basic menu format seldom changes in most day care operations, only small items such as mixers, slicers, utility carts, and the like should be considered for mobility. In most cases, the physical limitations of the building will dictate the amount and feasibility of mobile equipment.

Equipment maintenance should be performed at regular intervals to insure maximum performance and long life. It is also highly desirable to purchase the extended warranties, over and above the standard warranties, offered by most equipment manufacturers. This will insure against unexpected high costs during the first year of operation when cash flow problems are likely to be encountered.

Planning for Change and Growth

The planning process should include consideration of possible growth in the day care center, so that at any future date the physical plant can be expanded to accommodate an additional enrollment. The kitchen should be so designed that it could at any time produce the anticipated additional meals, or have the space and flexibility to accommodate necessary supplemental equipment. If the present structure prohibits this extra space, the allotted kitchen area should be located so that its outside walls can be expanded. As in any foodservice facility it is most difficult to continue food preparation while a remodeling program is under way.

Day care has the potential for rapid growth as a service industry. By insuring good planning, facilities, and programs, we will contribute to our tomorrow by providing quality care for today's children.

Day care center cooks seldom have had experience in commercial food preparation. For them to achieve maximum efficiency kitchen equipment must be selected that is easy to use and easy to clean as shown at left. Camera angle distorts aisle width which is actually adequate for easy use by more than one worker. Filler for steam kettle is another item selected to ease operation.

Height of ovens is designed to make pan placement easy for women workers. Ample aisle and brace that holds open oven door make work easy for inexperienced/busy cooks.

Above left, three-tank dishwashing set-up has booster heater, plus sign above faucets warning of water's heat and urging extreme care. Across the aisle from the dishwashing set-up is accessible hand washing unit pictured at right above.

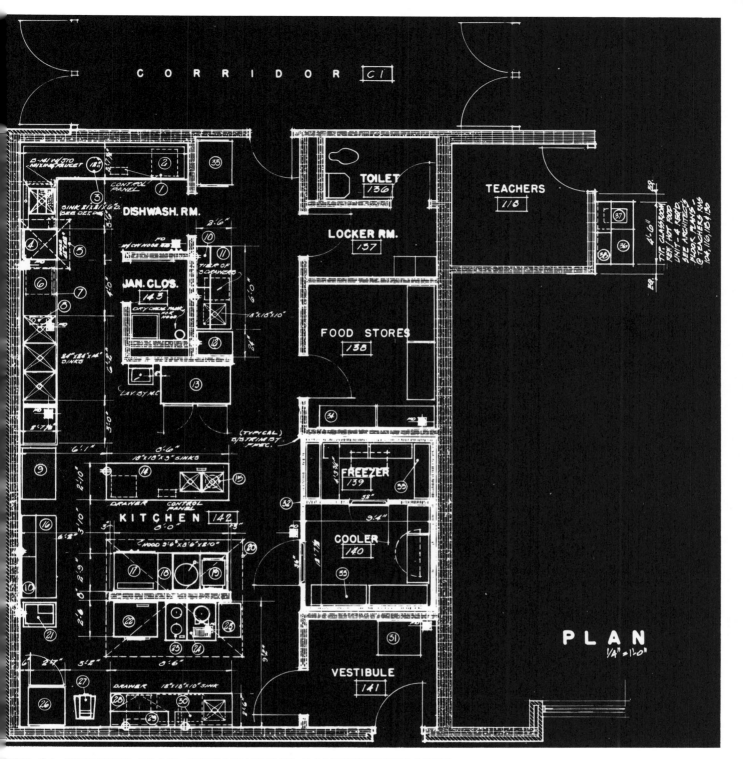

FIG. 36—KITCHEN PLAN, INDIANAPOLIS DAY NURSERY ASSN.

SCHEDULE OF FOOD FACILITIES EQUIPMENT

1. Soiled Dish Table	13. Refrigerator	26. Freezer
2. Trash Container	14. Cook's Table	27. Mixer
3. Disposer	15. Disposer	28. Baker's Table
4. Dish Machine	16. Work Table	29. Wall Cabinet
5. Hood	17. Convection Oven	30. Shelf
6. Booster Heater	18. Spacer	31. Compressors and Rack
7. Clean Dish Table/Pot and	19. Steamer/Kettle Unit	32. Walk-In Cooler/Freezer
Pan Sink	20. Hood	33. Shelving
8. Sink Heater	21. Mobile Slicer and Stand	34. Shelving
9. Mobile Pot and Pan Rack Cart	22. Oven	35. Mobile Dish Carts
10. Wall Cabinets	23. Baker's Range	36. Refrigerated Cabinet
11. Work Station	24. Trunnion Kettle	37. Hot Food Cabinet
12. Utility Cart	25. Pan Rack	38. Wall Cabinets

Foodservice for the Elderly

Philip Golden

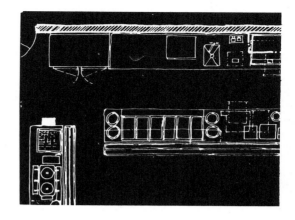

BASICALLY, THERE are two types of institutions to house the elderly. The first is for the older person who is in good health; such a facility is, essentially, a hotel.

The second type of facility is for the elderly person who is not in the best of health and needs dietary attention similar to that in a hospital where the special, or therapeutic, diet becomes an important part of dietary requirement in the kitchen.

Unfortunately some institutions housing the elderly poor and ill give inadequate thought to the complexities of the required diets. There is no mystery in doing this; it simply requires observation and a knowledge of the operating requirements. For instance, occasionally in feeding the elderly, religious preferences must be considered. A case in point is orthodox Kosher foodservice which requires two separate preparation and cooking facilities—one set for dairy foods (milk and milk products), and a separate set for meat and meat products. And, should pre-Koshered meats not be easily available, consideration must be given to provision of on-premise Koshering facilities.

All foodservice facility planning should commence with professional fundamentals. We shall begin there, too. Later on, we will discuss those refinements that distinguish planning for the elderly.

In designing a workable facility plan, regardless of the clientele, the most important guide is the proposed menu. Knowing what foods are to be prepared and served gives us a "leg up" on the planning.

We must next determine the institution's proximity to markets so that supplies, both perishable and non-perishable, may be stored in sufficient quantities for the required meals within acknowledged time frames. Failure to do this can result in a crowded storeroom where, because of improper planning, the first-in becomes the last out.

Sanitation Initial Step in Plan

It is mandatory that sanitation be *planned* into a facility at the outset. When a kitchen is planned clean, we can easily program personnel to keep it clean. If it is planned "dirty" it never will be clean. Environmental sanitation must be planned; it doesn't just happen.

Another element of good planning is mobility of equipment. If a piece of equipment does not have a mechanical connection (pipes, wires, ducts, etc.) it should be on wheels. Smaller items, e.g. small mixers and food slicers, should be mounted on mobile tables. Bringing the machine to the food not only saves preparation time and labor, it gives greater cost effectiveness to these pieces of equipment.

In areas of high probability of spillage, such as steam kettles, steamers, tilting braising pans and vertical cutter mixers, there is a constant attack by the food product overflow on the tile floor. This has a tendency to erode the cement grout that holds down the tile. Thus, it is highly recommended that stainless steel drainer pans be made an integral part of the floor and, in addition, the remainder of the floor (where quarry tile is used) be set with an epoxy grout between the tiles to prevent them from lifting. Alternatively, monolithic vinyl floors have proven feasible in some instances.

Walk-in refrigerators and freezers should have floors integral with the outside kitchen floor so that loaded wheeled carts may be pushed directly into the boxes. By allowing the largest manageable loads, we reduce to a minimum the number of trips into these refrigerators. When refrigerator shelving is used it should be totally mobile. This not only insures cleanability of the refrigerators, but permits effortless rotation of food stocks. Refrigerator doors should have large glass vision panels to allow personnel to monitor the interior and contents.

Normally, in this type of institution, steam is regularly available and so becomes a good source of cooking energy to replace gas and electricity. We have found great acceptance of the tilting table top steam kettle in the 20 and 40 quart sizes. This cooking tool can all but eliminate the use of hot top ranges. The ability to cook without the concern of having the food burn, is as attractive as the reduction in the need to move, remove, store, clean and restore the heavy pots usually used with hot top ranges. These small steam kettles are filled with food product, the food cooked, the finished product removed, the kettle quickly cleaned in place, and then it is ready for the next batch of food.

Remember, too, that we are often dealing here with large quantity cooking, with numbers ranging from 500 to 5,000 meals daily, so we must think in terms of equipment that is capable of handling such quantities. A little pan or pot is not the answer. Here we must think in terms of a food production factory and include large quantity processing equipment.

Consider, for example, a machine that makes 200 portions of tossed salad or 25 lb. of cabbage slaw in less than a minute. Or, a pair of roll-in convection ovens that can roast 16 to 18, 28-lb. turkeys in less than 3-½ hours, and are self-cleaning to boot. Or, a tilting braising pan that can produce 50 potato pancakes in less than four minutes. This type of equipment makes a facility

operate economically and reduces the number of staff required to operate the kitchen.

For example, in one institution that serves more than 3,000 meals daily, the kitchen staff was reduced by 11 in less than two years. Because the union base pay plus fringe benefits were averaging $12,000 yearly per employee, we realized savings in excess of $132,000. In less than three years, this kitchen will pay for itself.

BASIC PLANNING

Product flow is the heart of all foodservice facility planning. Everything else is supplemental and should be complementary. Thus, the sequence of procedures must flow in a logical, orderly manner to allow the facility to function well. There is no magic or luck involved in a good working kitchen. It is the result of a plan that has been thought out, anticipating the needs of the recipients.

There are seven basic steps that comprise any foodservice operation. They are:

1. Receiving   5. Processing
2. Checking   6. Distribution
3. Storing   7. Cleanup.
4. Preparation

This is precisely the sequence that must be followed to make any foodservice facility work. Careful planning for each of these functions will allow the operation to perform easily, well, and economically; improper planning will increase payroll dangerously.

A basic correlation to this is a well-lighted facility. Storerooms and walk-in refrigerators that require a flashlight to find what you are looking for present a hazard. Loading platforms that are nothing more than cubicles are disasters looking for a place to happen.

Receiving

The first function, receiving, too often suffers from insufficient planning. Here are several things that deserve consideration.

- A loading platform, preferably 44 inches above the road with a load leveller elevator to accommodate uneven truck floor heights in case the truck does not have a mechanical lift gate.
- A roll-on platform scale, preferably with a printing device, to provide a true

record of the merchandise received. This unit will soon pay for itself. These are available with pound and kilo printouts.

• A table, preferably on wheels, to allow incoming merchandise packages to be opened for inspection.

• A single compartment sink to wash the remnants of broken bottles and jars as well as the soiled hands of the receiving clerk.

• Strategically-placed floor drains, and an environmental sanitation station consisting of a hot and cold water, or steam and cold water mixing device with a detergent-injector attachment. Include not less than 50 ft. of hose and an assortment of nozzles. (This type of washdown station should be repeated in such a pattern that the entire facility is covered. This is especially important in the cooking area where a soiled environment is constantly being created.)

• A receiving office located for direct visual control of the loading dock as well as the checking area. If the shape of the available space does not allow this, then closed circuit television should be considered as a means of monitoring.

• A space for storage of returning "empties," such as plastic cases and containers, milk cans, etc.

Storage

From the receiving area, we must move products to a place of storage. Storage facilities fall into one of two categories; those for perishables and those for nonperishables.

Perishables require two distinct types of holding, termed high temperature and low temperature storage. High temperature in this parlance is storage above freezing, preferably 32° to 40°F., while low temperature usually refers to below 0°F., commonly used to store frozen foods (not freeze these foods, mind you; that should be done at or below minus 40°F.).

Prefabricated walk-in refrigerators are preferred, essentially because of the ease of erection and installation, and the fact that these are considerably more economical over the long run than the traditional "cork and cement" type. The latter have plaster interior walls and mastic ceiling; the plaster being

hygroscopic absorbs moisture, smells, and flavors and, in time, starts to crumble.

The interior surfaces of prefabricated refrigerators are made of metal, either aluminum or stainless steel, and so are impervious to moisture or odors. In addition, should it one day become desirable to change a high temp refrigerator into a low temp, all that's required is to change the size and type of interior blower coil and the refrigeration condenser.

It is sometimes advisable in large walk-ins to use skids or pallets in lieu of the traditional refrigerator shelves. These allow handling large quantities with economy of labor. Floor drains to catch drainage from the blower coil condensation should be located so that employees do not trip over exposed drain pipes. Be sure the drain lines from the freezer blower coils are wrapped in heater strips or you might create the longest popsicle in the world.

The other end of the basic type of storage is for non-perishables—supplies and dry groceries, as well as cleaning chemicals.

Any storeroom should, of course, be well ventilated. Where there is broken lot shelving, the lowest shelf should be high enough off the floor to allow a mop to clear, or for the floor to be hosed down without water splashing on cartons. For large operations where products come in by the pallet load, live skids or pallets are advisable. In extremely large institutions, a small fork-lift truck is of great help in moving pallets.

It is recommended that a series of floor drains and at least a hose cock, if not a washdown station, be provided in storerooms to insure environmental sanitation. Chemicals should be stored separately.

Preparation

Fundamentally, preparation areas require work tables and sinks, as well as waste removal facilities. Economic cost effectiveness is created by the addition of labor-saving preparation equipment.

This would include such machines as a vertical cutter mixer that can cut salad for a 200-bed hospital in less than five minutes or chop 25 lb. of cabbage slaw in a similar time. The same machine can whip potatoes, chop frozen meat, make bread crumbs from fresh bread and even make mayonnaise.

A professional preparation area should also have a food cutting machine that can shred and angle cut, as well as julienne and cube vegetables. For good work efficiency, the area could also include an automatic food slicer with an inclined chute, and a small food mixer to prepare small quantities of food or dressings without wasteful running around the kitchen.

Because the floor under a vertical cutter mixer is subject to much moisture, both as a result of work and when the machine is tilted during the cleanup operation, I recommend including a flush-mounted, stainless steel drainer pan. The drainer trough is surmounted with a subway grate that allows the drain water to wash down into the waste pipe outlet while the operator is standing on the grate. The use of the subway grate also allows the machine to be unloaded using a wheeled cart which can be rolled right up to the machine. (See Figure 37.)

Mounted above the work tables should be rotating utensil racks that move with the tables. This insures handy access to the tools being used. Stainless steel tables are great, but we need surfaces to cut on and these should be synthetic or plastic cutting boards that can be washed in a sink or dishmachine.

As part of the preparation operation, the kitchen should be supplied with mobile carts, either the three-level or the multi-deck type. A reach-in refrigerator should be part of the vegetable and salad preparation area, for

FIG. 37—DRAINER PLAN FOR VERTICAL CUTTER/MIXER

To preserve the floor below from moisture that collects as a result of operation of the vertical cutter/mixer, the installation of a flush-mounted, stainless steel drainer pan with a subway grate above it permits water to wash down into the waste pipe outlet while worker using cutter/mixer stands alongside. A cart can also be wheeled right to the machine for unloading over the grate.

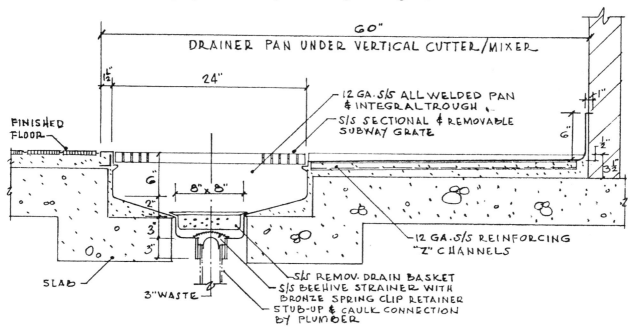

SECTION AT DRAINER PAN

ingredients like mayonnaise, garnitures, open cans of food, and foods in progress, such as cottage cheese, and so on.

As a complement to the ingredient refrigerator, there should be roll-in refrigerators of sufficient capacity to hold finished racks of portioned salads, desserts, and the like. These units should have floors flush with the kitchen floor so that filled carts can be moved in and out without jarring or upsetting the finished plates.

In the meat preparation area we have found a meat saw to be useful. When severing a quantity of poultry parts and the like, this machine eliminates the need for much hand work. And, depending on whether meat is bought ground or not, a meat grinder or a grinder attachment on a mixing machine can be a useful device.

Processing Hot Food Cooking

In planning and specifying cooking and baking equipment we must again consider the large quantities of food being processed. The "Look and Cook" school can no longer be the method. Cooking must be the "Time and Temperature" kind, with absolute control for consistency of product.

Our experience shows that top-of-the-range cooking is no longer viable, nor is the oven under the range top. We no longer have the luxury of time that allowed the chef to load one range oven at a time and come back and bend down every time he needed to inspect the stage of doneness of the product.

Nor can we any longer afford the time for pot and pan washing by hand. The use of tabletop tilting kettles and braising pans allows for greater productivity where food is cooked in a utensil. Whether roasted, cooked or pan fried, the finished product can be emptied into a serving pan and the cooking vessel cleaned on the spot without removing and replacing it with another. Large tilting kettles, that allow cleaning from the front instead of the top, reduce the cleaning time required. The same is true for large tilting braising pans with their own water supply. As previously indicated, each piece of equipment that produces moisture or food debris should rest on stainless steel drainer pans. (See Figure 38, p. 123.)

Either high or low pressure steamers are effective, efficient, and recommended for the hot food prep area. For one thing, cooking is done in the pan the food is to be served in. For another, either is a valuable tool for rewarming already cooked and panned food, a backup for weekends or holidays, strikes, convenience entrees, etc.

High velocity, unitized ventilation units are normally best for this kind of foodservice facility. A water wash unit as part of the ventilator system reduces grease accumulation in the hood and duct. Interestingly, when much of the cooking is done either in steam kettles or convection ovens, the necessity for fire extinguishing systems is greatly reduced.

Fire Protection

For highly effective as well as economical fire extinguishing equipment we recommend the "dry chemical" type. This floods the endangered area automatically and saponifies the grease, forming a kind of soap that may be washed down. Thus this unit stops the fire and cleans the equipment at one and the same time.

To insure sanitation, it is our practice where we have an "island" type of cooking line to maintain a space of at least three feet between the backs of the equipment. Where equipment parallels a wall, there should be at least 2 feet between the back of the cooking equipment and the wall. This design allows the operator to clean 360 degrees around the equipment.

Should ranges be necessary, it is preferable to specify range tops only. In general, "modular" equipment, including broilers, fryers, and the like, should be used since the entire bank of cooking equipment can be mounted on either an elevated stainless steel pedestal base or legs to insure better cleanup.

Ranges are not mandatory. In one institution, serving more than 3,000 meals daily, the kitchen has only two range tops; in nearly two years of operation, these range tops have been used no more than ten times. Another bonus in this reduction of pot and pan use was that the pot washing room could be drastically reduced in size.

Make sure in your planning that the cooks have an abundance of tables to work on, that there are sinks specially located for their convenience (efficiency) and that the work tables have revolving utensil racks.

We find that a bain marie is a handy hot food holding device (for smaller quantities) and should be part of the facility. In addition, portable food warmers should work in conjunction with the cooking equipment to hold the prepared hot food in a hot and moist condition until moved for service.

Again, because the cooking area will inevitably become wet and dirty, it is advisable to have strategically-placed floor drains as well as washdown stations.

We have, thus far, talked about the processing of hot food. Cold food processing, comprising mainly salads, desserts, and cold plate entrees, basically requires considerable flat space for plate layout. This takes the form of many table tops, plus portable carts to hold cold ingredients for plate assembly. To expedite this assembly, there should be a complement of multi-tiered racks that can take the completed, wrapped plates on trays to storage in roll-in refrigerators.

Distribution

In considering distribution we must recall that there are two types of foodservice for the elderly: Foodservice for the resident who is healthy and leading a normal ambulatory life, and also for the elderly person not in the best of health.

FIG. 38—DRAINER PANS UNDER TILTING BRAISING PANS, KETTLES

Tabletop tilting kettles and tilting braising pans with their own water supply (at far right) offer reduction in cleaning time plus comfortable working conditions for personnel using them if installed on stainless steel drainer pans. (Picture shows equipment in reverse position to plan below which details recommended drainer pan.)

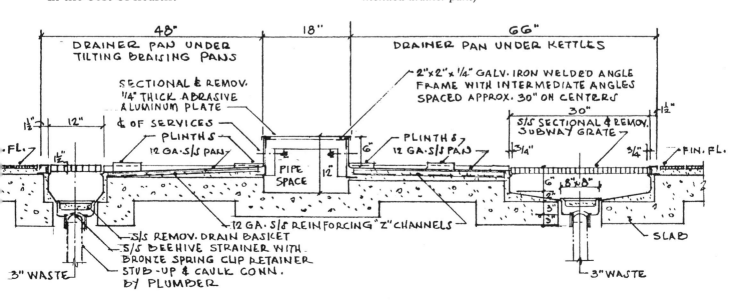

SECTION AT DRAINED PAN

Foodservice for the former is usually served in a communal dining room. In those residences that are concerned with both mental and physical well-being, foodservice takes on the atmosphere of a resort hotel. (The menus shown (pp. 126–135) indicate the lengths to which management goes to make their charges, if not happy, at least content.) The healthy resident is served from either the main or a satellite kitchen to assure the food served is attractive, palatable, and at proper temperature.

For the non-ambulatory resident or patient, or those who are partially mobile, we have found that serving the complete meal on a tray is the most convenient method of food delivery. A typical meal consists of a juice, soup, entree or salad, dessert and beverage (hot or cold), together with bread, spread, salt, pepper, etc. When the patient receives the tray the entire meal is presented.

We are now faced with two further decisions: 1) The method of insuring proper temperature of served foods; and 2) the type of tableware to be used.

Food Delivery

Delivery of a food tray to an elderly remote resident or patient presents a problem similar to that in a large hospital; how does the recipient get a hot—not lukewarm—meal?

Our method, which has enjoyed considerable success measured by patient acceptance, is a hybrid. We use a Dinex cup (two nested plastic cups with styrofoam between) for hot beverages and a similarly constructed bowl for hot soup; both have disposable covers. Onsite testing has yielded hot products as long as 45 minutes after leaving the kitchen. We also use a styrofoam egg caddy that keeps a soft boiled egg in a palatable state for as long as 25 minutes after leaving the kitchen.

For the entree, we have successfully used the Finessa system. This is a base liner with a totally enclosed alloy pellet, a heated dinner plate with hot food, and a heated plate cover. Except for senile patients, there have been no complaints about cold food. On the contrary, there have been many compliments, and this from the oldsters is praise indeed!

If one is to be truly considerate of the older person and wishes to emulate a homelike atmosphere, no tableware but china or permanent plastic will do. On the other hand economics often dictate that single service or disposable ware be considered.

The personnel and amount of space and equipment required to use china, glass, and metal cutlery can be significant. We must store the ware prior to use, then move and dispense it with carts and self-levelling dispensers. When soiled we must collect it in tote boxes and soiled ware carts and provide sets of dishtables, a dishmachine as well as detergents and wetting agents, and ventilation systems for the dishwashing room, and the equipment to provide at least elemental environmental sanitation. In addition we need the personnel to run the warewashing operation, 365 days a year, three meals each day.

Dishes for the Day's Most Exciting Event

Remember, though, there are disposables and there are disposables. You can pay four cents for a nine-inch dinner plate or buy one for one-third of that. And, unfortunately, when a purchasing agent or facilities manager or the supplier is pushed to the wall for economies a too-light weight of plate is substituted; then the patient or resident suffers, while the effort and care that went into the whole meal is diminished. And the meal is one of the few events the elderly look forward to, to break up the continuum of monotony they must live with.

But the picture is not one-sided. The use of single service tableware presents its own set of problems. First we must collect the spent tableware, and remove it to a remote collection point, which requires either manpower or equipment. Then we face the major problem of disposal. There are several possibilities, but all are costly.

The simplest is just to throw it away but the resulting bulk plays havoc with trash removal costs or we can employ a vacuum waste handling system or compact it to reduce the bulk. Or we can shred it and emulsify the waste. This must be either flushed down the drain (now more and more frowned upon by communities since it puts an unanticipated burden on already overloaded sewer systems), or use a closed system that transports the emulsified waste to a remote spot where much of the water is extracted and recirculated back into the system.

Even this system has its drawbacks. The end product now has approximately 70 percent water content, so a cubic yard of the waste pulp weighs approximately 1,100 to 1,300 lb. against 250 to 450 lb. per cubic yard of usual institutional waste.

It should also be remembered that if waste is collected in the raw, that is un-compacted or unpulped in plastic bags, then it is advisable to have a refrigerated garbage room to reduce the possibility of the waste material putrefying.

Cleanup

There are three segments that comprise the cleanup operation. The first is the soiled tableware used by the patient/resident. The second is cleaning the preparation and cook-ing utensils and equipment, including carts. The last is environmental sanitation; cleaning the floors and walls after everything else has been cleaned.

Soiled tableware is collected either in the dining room and returned to the dishwashing room, or patient trays are collected on the floors and loaded in the delivery carts to be returned to the warewashing area where both the ware and carts are washed.

Dishwashing Equipment Design

Depending on the resident or patient count, a properly sized dishmachine should be designed into a properly laid out set of dishtables. This requires analyzing the work flow—scrapping tableware, handling the soiled ware, disposing of meal scraps from the dishes, and handling the clean ware.

We recommend mobile undercounter soak sinks that will not clutter the top of the soiled dishtable but allow the operator to move a rack of soaked tableware directly into the dishmachine.

Some method of discarding the ac-cumulated post-meal waste should be in-cluded in the warewashing plan. This might be an integral waste collector and/or pul-verizer in the soiled dishtable, or a mobile, plastic bag-lined garbage can.

When using disposables for elderly patients we have found that dumping the contents of the tray (in many instances the tray is recycled) into a plastic bag on the patient floor eliminates returning it to the kitchen and reduces cleanup time.

The location of unsightly waste recep-tacles, commonly called dumpster containers, should be far from the loading platform. To aid in the movement of the waste, which can be categorized as organic and inorganic types, there are a number of methods available.

Bulk waste may be handled in a vacuum tube that transports the waste to a remote terminus at a speed approaching 60 miles per hour. If this equipment is part of the entire institution's waste handling system, foodservice waste can be programmed to an indicated terminus for collection, compac-tion, destruction, and/or energy conversion. (This latter might contribute to an increased economic viability of the foodservice facility.)

In situations where there are no mechan-ical alternatives provisions should be made for low-temperature storage of organic waste in a washable walk-in refrigerator. In this instance, facilities should be provided for washing and sanitizing the refuse cans.

The use of small tabletop tilting kettles, braising pans, and steamers markedly reduces the necessity for large potwashing facilities and the personnel to operate them. However, if there are a large number of pots and pans as well as mobile carts, it is advisable to include a roll-in mechanical pot and cart washer which does an exceptional job in cleaning and sanitizing. Both the dishmachine and the cart and pot washer should have detergent injectors as well as an abundant supply of 180° F. hot water for final sanitizing.

Environmental sanitation is of critical importance. If facilities are not provided for ease and accessibility of "washdown" sta-tions, it will cost excessive time, money, and personnel to accomplish the required degree of cleanliness. A recommended washdown station has a mixing valve accepting both cold water and steam, and also giving hot water, cold water, or steam as desired. It comes with deter-gent and chemical injector accessories and hoses. Fifty feet of hose has been found to be the best length. The unit has its own storage.

We cannot too strongly urge designers and planners to have guts. Do not be satisfied with the traditional "design out of the cata-log" concepts. There are better solutions. We have had exceptionally pleasant receptions from product manufacturers after showing them where they could improve their product (and also their profit).

5-WEEK CYCLE MENU
FIRST WEEK CYCLE
Daughters of Jacob Nursing Home Co., Inc.

This Week's Menu: Monday June 9 Thru Sunday June 15

RESIDENTS BREAKFAST	RESIDENTS LUNCH	RESIDENTS SUPPER
MONDAY	Cream of Celery Soup	Vegetable Farina Soup
Orange Juice	Cottage Cheese	Fish Sticks
Farina	Noodle Pudding	Spaghetti in Tomato Sauce
One Medium Cooked Egg	Sliced Carrots	Green Beans
Roll-SF Bread-SF Margarine	Puree Carrots	Puree Green Beans
Jam-Diabetic Jam	Vanilla Pudding	Bread-SF Bread-SF Margarine
Coffee-Milk	Diab. Chocolate Pudding	Jello
Bland-Sanka	Bread-SF Bread-SF Margarine	Diabetic Jello
	Coffee-Milk	Coffee W/Non Dairy Creamer
	Bland-Sanka	Bland-Sanka
TUESDAY	Egg Drop Soup	Potato Soup
Blended Juice	Roast Shoulder of Veal	Medium Cooked Egg
Oatmeal	Puree Ground Veal	Kasha Varnishka
Roll-SF Bread-SF Margarine	Paprika Rice W/Mushrooms	Carrots & Peas
Jam-Diabetic Jam	Sliced Beets	Puree Peas
Coffee-Milk	Puree Beets	Bread-SF Bread-SF Margarine
Bland-Sanka	Bread-SF Bread	Pears
	Plums	Diabetic Pears
	Diabetic Plums	Puree Pears
	Puree Peaches	Coffee W/Non Dairy Creamer
	Tea-Lemon	Bland-Sanka
WEDNESDAY	Milk Flake Soup	Mushroom Barley Soup
Pineapple Juice	Farmer Cheese	Baked Fish
Wheatena	White-N-Gold Potato Latkes	Parslied Mashed Potatoes
Roll-SF Bread-SF Margarine	Sliced Tomato	Spinach A La Arnold
Jam-Diabetic Jam	Applesauce	Fresh Fruit
Coffee-Milk	Diabetic Applesauce	Puree Fruit
Bland-Sanka	Bread-SF Bread-SF Margarine	Bread-SF Bread-SF Margarine
	Coffee-Milk	Coffee W/Non Dairy Creamer
	Bland-Sanka	Bland-Sanka
THURSDAY	Vegetable Soup	Puree Mongole Soup
Stewed Prunes	Stuffed Cabbage	Salami Omelette
Puree-Prune Juice	Bland-Hamburger	Baked Potato
Oatmeal	Puree Ground Beef	Mixed Vegetables
Roll-SF Bread-SF Margarine	Potato Patty	Puree Vegetables
Jam-Diabetic Jam	Mixed Beans	Bread-SF Bread
Coffee-Milk	Puree Wax Beans	Fruit Cocktail
Bland-Sanka	Bread-SF Bread	Diabetic Fruit Cocktail
	Apricots	Puree Fruit
	Diabetic Apricots	Tea-Lemon
	Puree Apricots	
	Tea-Lemon	

This Week's Menu: Monday June 9 Thru Sunday June 15 (Cont.)

RESIDENTS BREAKFAST	RESIDENTS LUNCH	RESIDENTS SUPPER
FRIDAY		
Apple Juice	Mamaliga	Matzo Ball Soup
Wheatena	Cottage Cheese	Stewed Chicken
Roll-SF Bread-SF Margarine	Sour Cream	Puree Chicken
Jam-Diabetic Jam	Ripe Banana	Farfel
Coffee-Milk	Bread-SF Bread-SF Margarine	Chopped Broccoli
Bland-Sanka	Cookies	Puree Green Vegetable
	Diabetic Cookies	Individual Chaleh
	Coffee-Milk	Sponge Cake
	Bland-Sanka	Tea-Lemon
SATURDAY		
Orange Juice	Consomme W/Rice	Tomato Rice Soup
Rice Krispies	Stewed Steak	Gefilte Fish on Lettuce
2 Slices Chaleh	Puree Ground Beef	Hard Cooked Egg
SF Margarine-Jam	Potato Pudding	Sliced Tomato
Diabetic Jam	Yellow Squash	Melba Toast
Coffee-Milk	Puree Yellow Vegetable	Bread-SF Bread-SF Margarine
Bland-Sanka	Individual Chaleh	Stewed Rhubarb
	Sliced Pineapple	Diabetic Rhubarb
	Diabetic Pineapple	Coffee W/Non Dairy Creamer
	Puree Fruit	Bland-Sanka
	Tea-Lemon	
SUNDAY		
Blended Juice	Schav W/½ Matzo	Egg Drop Soup
Oatmeal	Herring in Cream Sauce	Chicken Paprika
One Soft Cooked Egg	Puree Chopped Herring	Puree Chicken
Roll-SF Bread-SF Margarine	Muenster Cheese	Steamed Rice
Jam-Diabetic Jam	Sliced Tomato	Cauliflower W/Bread Crumbs
Coffee-Milk	Soft Bagel-SF Margarine	Bread-SF Bread
Bland-Sanka	Tapioca Pudding	Jello
	Diabetic Pudding	Diabetic Jello
	Coffee-Milk	Tea-Lemon
	Bland-Sanka	

Between Meal Nourishments of Orange & Prune Juice, Tea, Sanka, Melba Toast, Cookies & Diabetic Cookies are available for patients.

PLEASE REMEMBER THAT OUR MENUS ARE VARIED TO PLEASE DIFFERENT TASTES
DAILY MENUS ARE MODIFIED FOR SPECIAL DIETS

5-WEEK MENU CYCLE (Cont.)
SECOND WEEK CYCLE
Daughters of Jacob Nursing Home Co., Inc.
This Week's Menu: Monday June 16 Thru Sunday June 22

RESIDENTS BREAKFAST	RESIDENTS LUNCH	RESIDENTS SUPPER
MONDAY		
Orange Juice	Borsht W/½ Matzo	Pea Soup
Wheatena	Cottage Cheese	Medium Cooked Egg
Roll-SF Margarine-Jam	Buttered Noodles	Baked Potato
Diabetic Jam	Green Beans	Spinach A La Arnold
Coffee-Milk	Pureed Green Beans	Bread-SF Bread-SF Margarine
Bland-Sanka	Bread-SF Bread-SF Margarine	Fresh Fruit
	Butterscotch Pudding	Puree Fruit
	Diabetic Pudding	Coffee W/Non Dairy Creamer
	Coffee-Milk	Bland-Sanka
	Bland-Sanka	
TUESDAY		
Stewed Prunes	Scotch Broth	Tomato Rice Soup
Puree-Prune Juice	Fricasse Gizzard & Meatballs	Fried Fish
Farina	Puree Chicken	Puree-Baked Fish
Roll-SF Margarine-Jam	Paprika Rice	Mashed Squash
Diabetic Jam	Sliced Beets	Green Peas
Coffee-Milk	Puree Beets	Puree Peas
Bland-Sanka	Bread-SF Bread	Bread-SF Bread-SF Margarine
	Stewed Rhubarb	Whipped Jello
	Diabetic Rhubarb	Diabetic Jello
	Tea-Lemon	Coffee W/Non Dairy Creamer
	Bland-Sanka	Bland-Sanka
WEDNESDAY		
Orange Juice	Minestrone Soup	Vegetable Soup
Mamaliga	2 Griddle Cakes W/Syrup	Baked Fish Filet
Roll-SF Margarine-Jam	Farmer Cheese	Mashed Potato
Diabetic Jam	Sliced Tomato on Lettuce	Mixed Vegetables
Coffee-Milk	Puree-Pureed Carrots	Puree Vegetables
Bland-Sanka	Bread-SF Bread-SF Margarine	Bread-SF Bread-SF Margarine
	Custard	Stewed Dried Fruit
	Diabetic Custard	Puree Fruit
	Coffee-Milk	Coffee W/Non Dairy Creamer
	Bland-Sanka	Bland-Sanka
THURSDAY		
Blended Juice	Mushroom Barley Soup	Spinach Soup
Oatmeal	Roast Lamb	Vegetable Chow Mein
Roll-SF Margarine-Jam	Puree-Ground Lamb	Rice
Diabetic Jam	Parslied Potatoes	Chinese Noodles
Coffee-Milk	Oriental Vegetables	Medium Cooked Egg
Bland-Sanka	Puree-Pureed Vegetables	Bread-SF Bread-SF Margarine
	Bread-SF Bread	Fresh Fruit
	Apricots	Pureed Fruit
	Diabetic Apricots	Coffee W/Non Dairy Creamer
	Puree Apricots	Bland-Sanka
	Tea-Lemon	
	Bland-Sanka	

This Week's Menu: Monday June 16 Thru Sunday June 22 (Cont.)

RESIDENTS BREAKFAST	RESIDENTS LUNCH	RESIDENTS SUPPER
FRIDAY		
Pineapple Juice	Potato Soup	Noodle Soup W/Kreplach
Farina	American & Muenster Cheese	Gan Eden Chicken
Roll-SF Margarine-Jam	Lettuce & Tomato	Puree Chicken
Diabetic Jam	Puree-No Lettuce	Potato Pudding
Coffee-Milk	Soft Bagel	Chopped Broccoli
Bland-Sanka	Cream Cheese	Puree Vegetables
	Palatschinken	Indiv. Chaleh
	Diabetic Palatschinken	Jello
	Coffee-Milk	Diabetic Jello
	Bland-Sanka	Tea-Lemon
		Bland-Sanka
SATURDAY		
Blended Juice	Consomme W/Rice	Tomato Rice Soup
Corn Flakes	Pot Roast	Tuna Salad
2 Slices Chaleh	Puree-Ground Beef	Macaroni Salad
SF Margarine-Jam	Matzo Pudding	Tossed Salad
Dietetic Jelly	Green Beans	Puree Vegetable
Coffee-Milk	Puree Green Beans	Bread-SF Bread-SF Margarine
Bland-Sanka	Indiv. Chaleh	Sliced Pineapple
	Fruit Cocktail	Diabetic Pineapple
	Diabetic Fruit Cocktail	Puree Fruit
	Puree Fruit	Coffee W/Non Dairy Creamer
	Tea-Lemon	Bland-Sanka
	Bland-Sanka	
SUNDAY		
Orange Juice	Cream of Celery Soup	Asparagus Soup
Oatmeal	Cottage Cheese	Roast Chicken W/Cranberry Sauce
Roll-SF Margarine	Sour Cream	Puree Chicken
Jam-Diabetic Jam	Peach & Pear Halves	Mashed Potato
Coffee-Milk	Diabetic Peach & Pear Halves	Cauliflower W/Bread Crumbs
Bland-Sanka	Mech. Soft Puree Peach	Puree Vegetable
	Bread-SF Bread-SF Margarine	Bread-SF Bread
	Ice Cream	Applesauce
	Diabetic Ice Cream	Diabetic Applesauce
	Coffee-Milk	Tea-Lemon
	Bland-Sanka	Bland-Sanka

Between Meal Nourishments of Orange & Prune Juice, Tea, Sanka, Melba Toast, Cookies & Diabetic Cookies are available for patients.

PLEASE REMEMBER THAT OUR MENUS ARE VARIED TO PLEASE DIFFERENT TASTES
DAILY MENUS ARE MODIFIED FOR SPECIAL DIETS

5-WEEK MENU CYCLE (Cont.)
THIRD WEEK CYCLE
Daughters of Jacob Nursing Home Co., Inc.
This Week's Menu: Monday June 23 Thru Sunday June 29

RESIDENTS BREAKFAST	RESIDENTS LUNCH	RESIDENTS SUPPER
MONDAY		
Pineapple Juice	Milk Rice Soup	Pea Soup
Mamaliga	Cottage Cheese Souffle	Tomato Herring
Roll-SF Margarine-Jam	Baked Potato	Potato Salad
Diabetic Jam	Creamed Spinach	Lettuce & Tomato
Coffee-Milk	Bread-SF Bread-SF Margarine	Puree-No Lettuce
Bland-Sanka	Tapioca Pudding	Reg. & Diab.-Sliced Pickle
	Diabetic Chocolate Pudding	Sliced Bagel & SF Margarine
	Coffee-Milk	Peaches
	Bland-Sanka	Diabetic Peaches
		Puree Peaches
		Coffee W/Non Dairy Creamer
		Bland-Sanka
TUESDAY		
Stewed Prunes	Consomme Julienne	Noodle Soup
Farina	Beef Pot Pie	Fried Vegetable Cutlet W/Tomato
Roll-SF Margarine-Jam	Puree-Ground Beef	Mushroom Sauce
Diabetic Jam	Pureed Vegetable	Hard Cooked Egg
Coffee-Milk	Puree-Mashed Potato	Baked Potato
Bland-Sanka	Cole Slaw	Bread-SF Bread-SF Margarine
	Jello	Fresh Fruit
	Diabetic Jello	Coffee W/Non Dairy Creamer
	Bread-SF Bread	Bland-Sanka
	Tea-Lemon	
WEDNESDAY		
Blended Juice	Minestrone Soup	Mushroom Barley Soup
Wheatena	Plain Tuna on Lettuce W/Lemon	Baked Fish
Soft Cooked Egg	Wedge	Mashed Potatoes
Roll-SF Margarine-Jam	Swiss Gruyere Cheese Wedge	Green Beans Almandine
Diabetic Jam	Sliced Tomato	Puree Green Beans
Coffee-Milk	Baked Custard	Stewed Dried Fruit
Bland-Sanka	Diabetic Custard	Pureed Fruit
	Bread-SF Bread-SF Margarine	Bread-SF Bread-SF Margarine
	Coffee-Milk	Coffee W/Non Dairy Creamer
	Bland-Sanka	Bland-Sanka
THURSDAY		
Orange Juice	Broth W/Noodles	Vegetable Soup
Oatmeal	Meatloaf	Soft Cooked Egg
Roll-SF Margarine-Jam	Puree-Ground Beef	Kasha Varnishka
Diabetic Jam	French Fried Potatoes	Carrot Tzimmes
Coffee-Milk	Puree-Mashed Potatoes	Diabetic Carrots
Bland-Sanka	Yellow Squash	Puree Carrots
	Puree Vegetables	Fruit Cocktail
	Fresh Fruit	Diabetic Fruit Cocktail
	Puree Fruit	Puree Fruit
	Bread-SF Bread	Bread-SF Bread-SF Margarine
	Tea-Lemon	Coffee W/Non Dairy Creamer
		Bland-Sanka

This Week's Menu: Monday June 23 Thru Sunday June 29 (Cont.)

RESIDENTS BREAKFAST	RESIDENTS LUNCH	RESIDENTS SUPPER
FRIDAY		
Apple Juice	Potato Soup	Egg Drop Soup
Farina	Blintzes W/Sour Cream	Chicken Cacciatore
Roll-SF Margarine-Jam	Cucumbers W/Dill Dressing	Puree Chicken
Diabetic Jam	Puree Vegetables	Rice Pilaf
Coffee-Milk	Applesauce	Chopped Broccoli
Bland-Sanka	Diabetic Applesauce	Puree Peas
	Bread-SF Bread-SF Margarine	Individual Chaleh
	Coffee-Milk	Whipped Jello
	Bland-Sanka	Diabetic Jello
		Tea-Lemon
SATURDAY		
Blended Juice	Chopped Chicken Liver	Tomato Rice Soup
Special "K"	Fresh Tongue in Gravy	2 Gefilte Fish W/Horseradish
2 Slices Chaleh	Puree Tongue	Tossed Salad
SF Margarine-Jam	Mashed Potatoes	Melba Toast
Diabetic Jam	Wax Beans	Brownie
Coffee-Milk	Puree Wax Beans	Diabetic Marble Cake
Bland-Sanka	Individual Chaleh	Bread-SF Bread-SF Margarine
	Pears	Coffee W/Non Dairy Creamer
	Diabetic Pears	Bland-Sanka
	Puree Pears	
	Tea-Lemon	
SUNDAY		
Pineapple Juice	Vegetable Soup	Egg Drop Soup
Oatmeal	Cottage Cheese & Sour Cream	Stewed Chicken
Roll-SF Margarine-Jam	Tossed Salad	Puree Chicken
Diabetic Jam	Radishes & Scallions	Farfel W/Mushrooms
Coffee-Milk	Puree Green Vegetable	Zucchini W/Tomatoes
Bland-Sanka	Fruit Ice	Puree Vegetable
	Diabetic Ice Cream	Bread-SF Bread
	Bread-SF Bread-SF Margarine	Apricot Halves
	Coffee-Milk	Diabetic Apricots
	Bland-Sanka	Pureed Apricots
		Tea-Lemon

Between Meal Nourishments of Orange & Prune Juice, Tea, Sanka, Melba Toast, Cookies & Diabetic Cookies are available for patients.

PLEASE REMEMBER THAT OUR MENUS ARE VARIED TO PLEASE DIFFERENT TASTES
DAILY MENUS ARE MODIFIED FOR SPECIAL DIETS

5-WEEK MENU CYCLE (Cont.)
FOURTH WEEK CYCLE
Daughters of Jacob Nursing Home Co., Inc.
This Week's Menu: Monday June 30 Thru Sunday July 6

RESIDENTS BREAKFAST	RESIDENTS LUNCH	RESIDENTS SUPPER
MONDAY		
Blended Juice	Milk Flake Soup	Green Pea Soup
Wheatena	Herring in Cream Sauce	Vegetable Chopped Liver on Lettuce
Roll-SF Margarine-Jelly	Puree-Chopped Herring	Hard Cooked Egg
Diabetic Jelly	Sliced Cheese	Potato Salad
Coffee-Milk	Tossed Salad	Puree-Mashed Potato
Bland-Sanka	Puree-Pureed Vegetables	Roll-SF Margarine
	Soft Bagel & Cream Cheese	Citrus Sections
	Rice Pudding	Diabetic Citrus Sections
	Coffee-Milk	Coffee W/Non Dairy Creamer
	Bland-Sanka	Bland-Sanka
TUESDAY		
Stewed Dried Fruits	Veal Bone Soup	Mushroom Barley Soup
Puree-Prune Juice	Stewed Meatballs	Fish Cakes
Farina	Puree-Ground Beef	Spaghetti W/Tomato Sauce
Bread-SF Bread-SF Margarine	Rice	Green Beans
Jam-Diabetic Jam	Chopped Broccoli	Puree Green Beans
Coffee-Milk	Puree Vegetables	Bread-SF Bread-SF Margarine
Bland-Sanka	Bread-SF Bread	Fresh Fruit
	Jello	Puree Fruit
	Diabetic Jello	Coffee W/Non Dairy Creamer
	Tea-Lemon	Bland-Sanka
WEDNESDAY		
Orange Juice	Borsht W/½ Matzo	Vegetable Soup
Oatmeal	Cottage Cheese & Sour Cream	Medium Cooked Egg
Roll-SF Margarine-Jam	Peach & Pear Halves	Vegetable Chow Mein
Diabetic Jam	Diabetic Peach & Pear Halves	Rice
Coffee-Milk	Bread-SF Bread-SF Margarine	Chinese Noodles
Bland-Sanka	Baked Custard	Bread-SF Bread-SF Margarine
	Diabetic Custard	Pineapple Ring
	Coffee-Milk	Coffee W/Non Dairy Creamer
	Bland-Sanka	Bland-Sanka
THURSDAY		
Apple Juice	Cabbage Soup	Asparagus Soup
Mamaliga	Puree & Bland-Consomme	Baked Fish Filet
Roll-SF Margarine-Jam	Corned Beef W/Mustard	Mashed Potato
Diabetic Jam	SF-Stewed Steak	Cole Slaw
Coffee-Milk	Puree-Ground Beef	Puree Vegetables
Bland-Sanka	Boiled Potato	Bread-SF Bread-SF Margarine
	Green Peas	Stewed Rhubarb
	Puree Peas	Puree Fruit
	Bread-SF Bread	Coffee W/Non Dairy Creamer
	Plums	Bland-Sanka
	Diabetic Plums	
	Puree Fruit	
	Tea-Lemon	

This Week's Menu: Monday June 30 Thru July 6 (Cont.)

RESIDENTS
BREAKFAST

RESIDENTS
LUNCH

RESIDENTS
SUPPER

FRIDAY

Blended Juice
Cream of Rice
One Medium Cooked Egg
Roll-SF Margarine-Jam
Diabetic Jam
Coffee-Milk
Bland-Sanka

Cream of Celery Soup
Tuna Salad
Macaroni Salad on Lettuce W/-
   Sliced Tomato
Bread-SF Bread-SF Margarine
Ice Cream
Diabetic Ice Cream
Coffee-Milk
Bland-Sanka

Matzo Ball Soup
Braised Chicken Legs
Puree Chicken
Sweet Potato & Prune Tzimmes
Mixed Vegetables
Puree Green Vegetable
Individual Chaleh
Honey Cake
Diabetic Marble Cake
Tea-Lemon

SATURDAY

Orange Juice
Rice Krispies
2 Slices Chaleh
SF Margarine-Jam
Diabetic Jam
Coffee-Milk
Bland-Sanka

Egg Drop Soup
Boiled Brisket of Beef W/-
   Sliced Pickle
Puree-Ground Beef
Noodle Pudding
Stewed Zucchini Squash
Puree Vegetable
Individual Chaleh
Jello
Diabetic Jello
Tea-Lemon

Tomato Rice Soup
Hot Carp W/Horseradish
Hosp. Hot Filet
Mashed Potatoes
Pickled Beets
Puree Beets
Bread-SF Bread-SF Margarine
Plums
Diabetic Plums
Puree Fruit
Coffee W/Non Dairy Creamer
Bland-Sanka

SUNDAY

Blended Juice
Oatmeal
One Medium Cooked Egg
Roll-SF Margarine-Jam
Diabetic Jam
Coffee-Milk
Bland-Sanka

Cream of Spinach Soup
Farmer Cheese
Breaded Baked Eggplant Steak
Sliced Tomato on Lettuce
Puree-No Lettuce
Bread-SF Bread-SF Margarine
Fruit Cocktail
Diabetic Fruit Cocktail
Puree Fruit
Coffee-Milk
Bland-Sanka

Consomme W/Farfel
Chicken Paprikash
Puree Chicken
Steamed Rice
Parslied Sliced Carrots
Puree Carrots
Bread-SF Bread
Fresh Fruit
Puree Fruit
Tea-Lemon

Between Meal Nourishments of Orange & Prune Juice, Tea, Sanka, Melba Toast, Cookies & Diabetic Cookies
are available for patients.

PLEASE REMEMBER THAT OUR MENUS ARE VARIED TO PLEASE DIFFERENT TASTES
DAILY MENUS ARE MODIFIED FOR SPECIAL DIETS

5-WEEK MENU CYCLE (Cont.)
FIFTH WEEK CYCLE
Daughters of Jacob Nursing Home Co., Inc.
This Week's Menu: Monday July 7 Thru Sunday July 13

RESIDENTS BREAKFAST	RESIDENTS LUNCH	RESIDENTS SUPPER
MONDAY		
Orange Juice	Milk Farfel Soup	Potato Soup
Wheatena	Cottage Cheese	Tuna Loaf W/Tomato Mushroom-
One Medium Cooked Egg	Sour Cream	Sauce
Roll-SF Margarine-Jam	Potato Latkes	Succotash
Dietetic Jam	Tossed Salad	Puree-Mashed Potatoes
Coffee-Milk	Puree-Sliced Tomato	Pickled Beets
Bland-Sanka	Bread-SF Bread-SF Margarine	Puree Green Vegetable
	Applesauce	Bread-SF Bread-SF Margarine
	Diabetic Applesauce	Jello
	Coffee-Milk	Diabetic Jello
	Bland-Sanka	Coffee W/Non Dairy Creamer
		Bland-Sanka
TUESDAY		
Blended Juice	Egg Drop Soup	Vegetable Soup
Oatmeal	Veal Paprikash	2 Gefilte Fish
Roll-SF Margarine-Jam	Puree Veal	Horseradish
Dietetic Jam	Broad Noodles W/Sauteed Onions	Sliced Tomato on Lettuce
Coffee-Milk	Green Beans Almandine	Puree-No Lettuce
Bland-Sanka	Puree Green Beans	Bread-SF Bread-SF Margarine
	Bread-SF Bread	Fresh Fruit
	Plums	Pureed Fruit
	Dietetic Plums	Coffee W/Non Dairy Creamer
	Tea-Lemon	Bland-Sanka
WEDNESDAY		
Orange Juice	Schav W/Matzo	Spinach Soup
Farina	Sliced American & Muenster	Baked Fish
Roll-SF Margarine-Jam	Cheese W/Lettuce & Tomato	Mashed Potato
Dietetic Jam	Puree-No Lettuce	Mixed Vegetables
Coffee-Milk	Soft Bagel W/Cream Cheese	Puree Green Vegetables
Bland-Sanka	Baked Custard	Bread-SF Bread-SF Margarine
	Diabetic Custard	Whipped Jello
	Coffee-Milk	Diabetic Jello
	Bland-Sanka	Coffee W/Non Dairy Creamer
		Bland-Sanka
THURSDAY		
Apple Juice	Potato Soup	Mushroom Barley Soup
Oatmeal	2 Blintzes W/Sour Cream	Soft Cooked Egg
Roll-SF Margarine-Jam	Cucumber Salad	Potato Knish
Dietetic Jam	Applesauce	Peas & Carrots
Coffee-Milk	Bread-SF Bread-SF Margarine	Puree Peas
Bland-Sanka	Coffee-Milk	Bread-SF Bread-SF Margarine
	Bland-Sanka	Apricots
		Diabetic Apricots
		Coffee W/Non Dairy Creamer
		Bland-Sanka

This Week's Menu: Monday July 7 Thru Sunday July 13 (Cont.)

RESIDENTS BREAKFAST	RESIDENTS LUNCH	RESIDENTS SUPPER
FRIDAY		
Stewed Prunes	Cream of Mushroom Soup	Noodle Soup
Puree-Prune Juice	French Toast W/Syrup	Steamed Chicken
Mamaliga	Diabetic Syrup	Puree Chicken
Roll-SF Margarine-Jam	Farmer Cheese	Chaleh
Dietetic Jam	Tossed Salad	Potato Kugel
Coffee-Milk	Puree Vegetable	Chopped Broccoli
Bland-Sanka	Fresh Fruit	Sponge Cake
	Puree Fruit	Diabetic Cake
	Coffee-Milk	Tea-Lemon
	Bland-Sanka	
SATURDAY		
Blended Juice	Chopped Liver on Lettuce	Tomato Soup
Cornflakes	Puree-No Lettuce	Chopped Herring
Sliced Chaleh	Braised Flanken	Hard Cooked Egg
SF Margarine-Jam	Puree-Beef	Sliced Tomato
Diabetic Jam	Mashed Potato	Bread-SF Bread-SF Margarine
Coffee-Milk	Sliced Carrots	Apple Cake
Bland-Sanka	Puree Carrots	Diabetic Apple Cake
	Indiv. Chaleh	Coffee W/Non Dairy Creamer
	Strawberry W/Pineapple Bits	Bland-Sanka
	Diabetic Strawberries W/Pineapple	
	Puree Fruit	
	Tea-Lemon	
SUNDAY		
Pineapple Juice	Milk Flake Soup	Broth W/Rice & Parsley
Oatmeal	Muenster Cheese Souffle	Baked White Fish
Roll-SF Margarine-Jam	Baked Potato	Hospital: Filet
Diabetic Jam	Yellow Squash	Sweet Potato Prune Tzimmes
Coffee-Milk	Puree Vegetable	Mixed Beans
Bland-Sanka	Bread-SF Bread-SF Margarine	Puree Green Vegetable
	Ice Cream	Fruit Cocktail
	Diabetic Ice Cream	Diabetic Fruit Cocktail
	Coffee-Milk	Puree Fruit
	Bland-Sanka	Coffee W/Non Dairy Creamer
		Bland-Sanka
		Bread-SF Bread-SF Margarine

Between Meal Nourishments of Orange & Prune Juice, Tea, Sanka, Melba Toast, Cookies & Diabetic Cookies are available for patients.

PLEASE REMEMBER THAT OUR MENUS ARE VARIED TO PLEASE DIFFERENT TASTES
DAILY MENUS ARE MODIFIED FOR SPECIAL DIETS

Montefiore-Beth Abraham

Kitchen in plan at right serves 800 residents at Montefiore-Beth Abraham in the Bronx, N.Y. The foodservice requires only 65 employees in the tightly-planned production area for this total extended care facility.

Designed by: Philip Golden, Consultants Collaborative, Inc.

EQUIPMENT LIST
1. Sink
2. Store Room Shelving
3. Fire Extinguishing System
4. Work Table
5. Overshelf
6. Food Cutter w/table
7. Disposal to Pulper
8. Sinks w/Drainboard
9. Slicer
10. Drainer Pan
11. Faucet
12. Vertical Cutter Mixer
13. Mixing Valve
14. Hand Sinks
15. Pot Rack
16. Pot Sink
17. Booster Heater
18. Pot Washer
19. Cooks Table
20. Mixer
21. Kettles
22. Equipment Stand
23. Steamer
24. Ovens
25. Ventilator
26. Broiler
27. Tilting Fryer
28. Kettle Stand
29. Ranges
30. Table w/Overshelf
31. Meat Saw
32. Cart Washer
33. Refrigerator
34. Counter
35. Hot Plate
36. Food Warmer
37. Cold Counters
38. Hot Counters
39. Conveyors
40. Food Carts

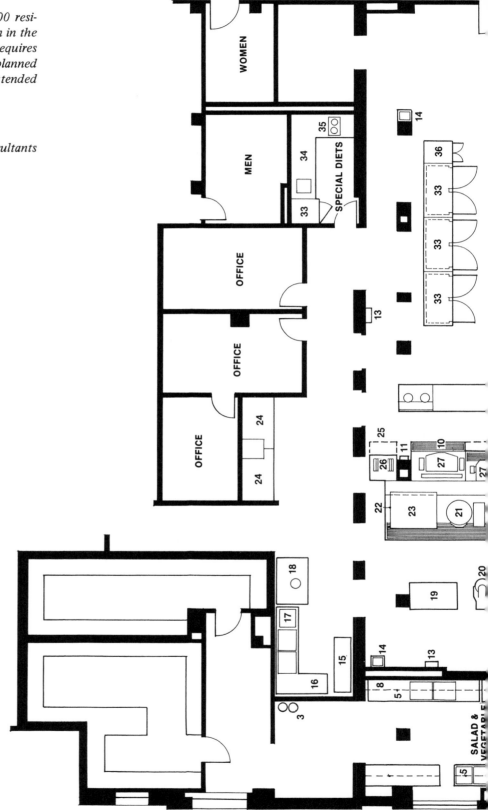

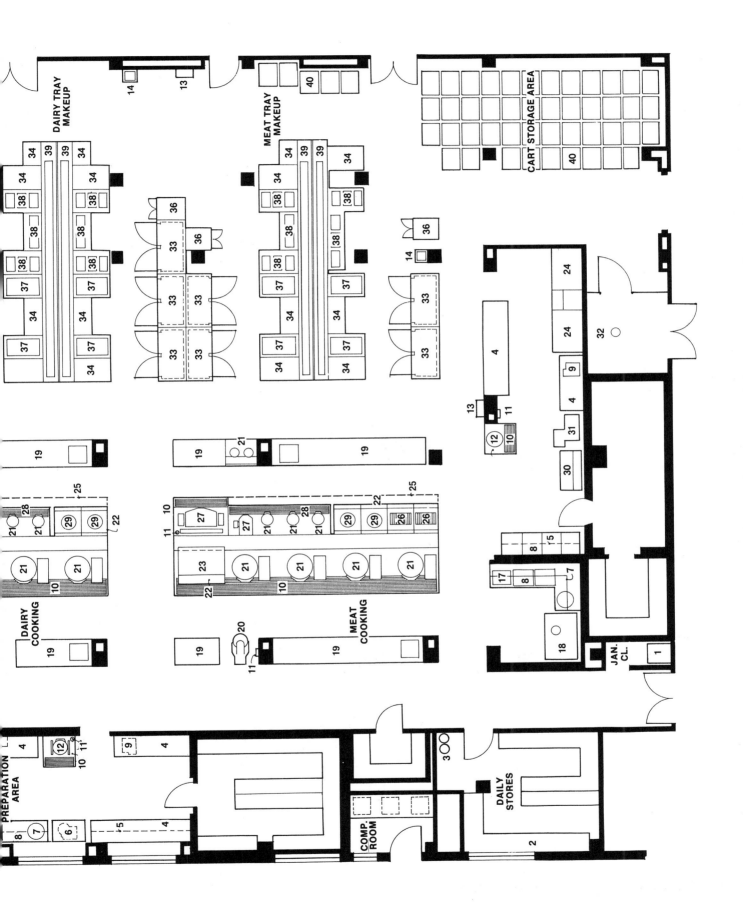

Salzman Pavilion for the Jewish Home for Aged

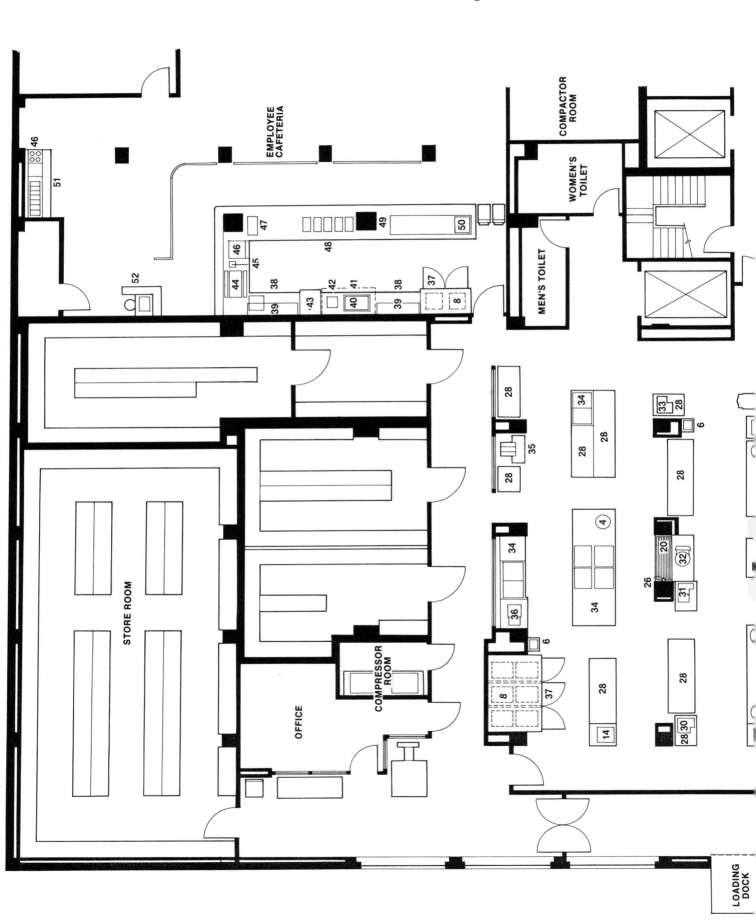

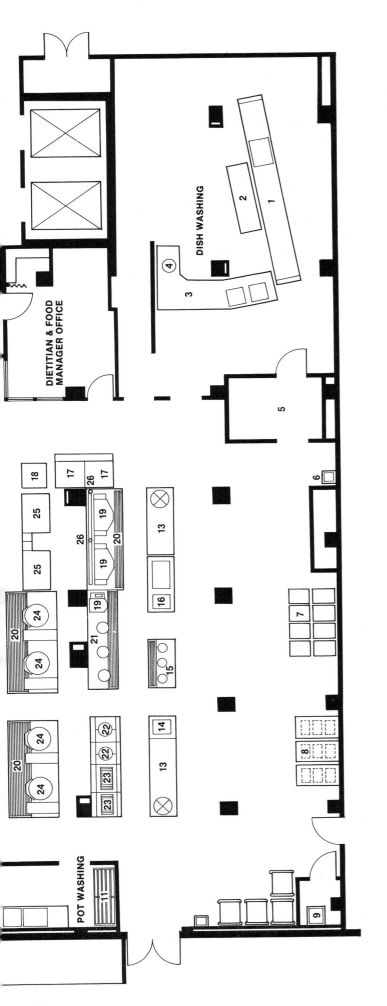

Salzman Pavillion for the Jewish Home for Aged, Bronx, N.Y. cares for 890 residents, 120 of whom have health-related problems. Of the 98 workers in the dietary department, 27 are assigned to the kitchen. The operation has been opened only a little less than 2 years in which time the number of dietary personnel has been reduced by 24, most of them kitchen workers.

Designed by: Philip Golden, Consultants Collaborative, Inc.

EQUIPMENT LIST
1. Dishwasher
2. Portable Table
3. Dish Table w/Soak Sinks
4. Waste Disposal
5. Cart Wash w/Drainer Pan
6. Hand Sink
7. Tray Carts
8. Cold Food Carts
9. Mop Rack w/Detergent Shelf
10. Mobile Food Warmers
11. Portable Pot Rack
12. Pot Sinks & Drainboards w/Overshelf
13. Cooks Table
14. Sink
15. Steam Kettles w/Stand
16. Table w/Bain Marie & Sink
17. Steamers w/Stand
18. Convection Oven
19. Tilting Braising Pans
20. Drainer Pan
21. Tilting Kettles w/Stand
22. Ranges w/Stand
23. Broilers w/Stand
24. Kettles-Tilting
25. Roll-In Convection Ovens
26. Faucet
27. Mixer
28. Table
29. Mixer
30. Slicer
31. Vegetable Cutter
32. Vertical Cutter/Mixer
33. Slicer
34. Sink & Drainboard
35. Meat Saw
36. Potato Peeler
37. Roll-In Refrigerator
38. Counter
39. Overshelves
40. Griddle
41. Ventilation/Fire Extinguishing System
42. Toaster
43. Food Warmer
44. Coffee Urn
45. Creamer
46. Portable Cup Dispenser
47. Ice Cream Cabinet w/Compressor
48. Hot Food Counter
49. Cafeteria Counter
50. Cold Pan w/Compressor
51. Condiment Stand
52. Cashier Stand

Public Cafeteria

*John C. Cini
and
William V. Eaton*

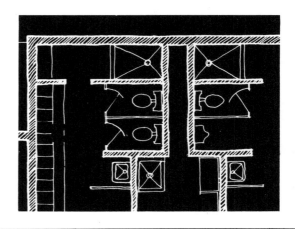

THE CONCEPT of the public cafeteria seems to have originated in San Francisco shortly after the turn of the century, though the origin of the concept is difficult to establish. In any event, public cafeterias of note did not begin to appear until 1920, when J.A. Morrison, Sr. opened his first such operation in Mobile, Alabama. Unlike the present image of a public cafeteria, Mr. Morrison's operation had more the flavor of an exclusive restaurant. The check average was high, service was extensive, table cloths and napkins were used and, in general, the concept was more that of an exclusive buffet than what we now think of as a cafeteria.

The economic pressures of the 1930s caused a redefinition of public cafeterias. There was a pressing need for public food-service, yet disposable income was almost nonexistent, necessitating a less expensive way to eat. By adopting the Morrison concept—ample quantity for a low price with the highest quality raw product available— a complete cafeteria meal during the Depression years could be had for 21¢! There were even such promotional gestures as free dessert night and family night. From these beginnings emerged the public cafeterias of today.

The first public cafeterias were of the "straight line" type, offering a selection of salads, desserts, hot foods, and a more limited selection of beverages. The basic cafeteria concept today has not changed with the exception of the menu, which has been expanded considerably to parallel the more educated palate of the American consumer.

Any discussion of public cafeterias should begin with site and market analysis.

SITE SELECTION AND MARKET ANALYSIS

Choosing a site for a public cafeteria that has viability depends on a number of interrelated factors. As with any public food-service, the site should be either within a heavily trafficked area or easily accessible to potential clientele. One of the most popular sites for public cafeterias is a suburban shopping mall. These usually offer the combined advantages of heavy shopper traffic, parking for patrons who are coming to dine without shopping, and the opportunity for the "impulse" sale in capturing the patron who happens to pass the cafeteria and is drawn in. Other sites also can prove viable, including downtown office buildings and freestanding units associated with shopping areas, and each will be discussed individually.

A shopping mall, assuming it is successful, assures a constant stream of traffic passing the cafeteria entrance; simply the availability of a convenient foodservice facility will result in substantial business. Because shopping trips involving a mall often have a tendency to extend near or into a meal period, it is logical for women shopping together, young families, or elderly couples to patronize it simply for convenience which is not paired with extravagant expense. Moreover, it's a logical spot to relax and the hectic pace of today's life often prohibits sitting and relaxing without accomplishing some other function, such as eating.

Other criteria used in the site selection for public cafeterias are similar to those for public restaurants. The assurance of a market is of first importance.

The second major factor is parking. While this is critical to mall and freestanding facilities, it is of substantially less importance when the location is a downtown office building. In that circumstance it is assumed that the majority of patrons will have arrived within the area for work that morning and have no need for parking adjacent to the cafeteria.

A number of other site-related points should be considered. Foot traffic is important since the more exposure a facility has, the more it will be patronized. A prominent location in the shopping mall is also important. It should be visible from as many stores as possible, particularly from the major stores in the center, and hopefully from the competition.

Still another factor must be kept in mind. If the entrance to the cafeteria is within the mall, is the central space in the mall to be open evenings and weekends, particularly on Sunday? If that space is closed, it becomes necessary to plan an easily identified exterior entrance, so the patronage you develop in the surrounding area has access to your facility when the mall is closed.

MENU STRUCTURE

The menu for any public cafeteria must be structured to meet the requirements of its proposed clientele. The major clientele, most of whom frequent the area, must be assessed, and the menu molded around their particular wants and needs. This is unlike the public restaurant, where the type of menu is determined first, followed by an assessment of that menu's marketability in a given area.

The public restaurant can select from many menu categories such as steak house, seafood, family restaurant, Italian cuisine, luxury dining, among others. The public cafeteria does not have this flexibility. If in a shopping center, then the menu requirements and cost considerations common to shoppers at the center must be met. For the same reasons a freestanding cafeteria must match the market in its immediate surroundings, while a cafeteria in a downtown office building must primarily serve the noontime office worker. To a great extent then, both the site and menu—and even the menu cost structure—follow from this same market analysis.

Again, with a public restaurant, you may peg your check average at five, ten, or whatever dollars, tailor the menu to meet the price range and, with adequate advertising and the assumption that a market exists, you have the opportunity to be successful. In a public cafeteria where the market is already determined and the likelihood of people traveling great distances to dine at the cafeteria is unlikely, the menu pricing and consequently the menu selections become a factor in selection of the site.

Care must be taken to develop a menu of sufficient length and with a price range to meet the varied tastes and preferences of the market. This is necessary because you are not attempting to select a small segment of the market, but to appeal to the market as a whole and obtain a substantial share of that market.

Once your site has been selected and your menu and price structure established, you are in a position to begin the process of design.

DESIGN PARAMETERS

No matter how simple the cafeteria appears at the outset, there are many complex decisions that must be made during the early stages of design to mold the finished product that will best serve the market. The first such is that of the design. Basically, there are three design styles for cafeterias today: straight line, hollow square, and random or free flow.

Straight Line

The straight line is the simplest, and earliest form of cafeteria design. It is, as the term implies, a straight line where the menu items are displayed one after another, between the trays at one end and the cashier at the other. We will discuss, later in the text, the arrangement and orientation of the variety of menu items.

The straight line is most effective when the number of patrons to be served during any hour does not exceed 400. And that is the primary limiting factor in the efficient use of a straight line cafeteria: the speed with which patrons can be processed by the cashier. Cashier capacities range from four per minute to eight or nine per minute, with the speed reflecting the efficiency of the cashier, the sophistication of the register, the orientation of the cafeteria line and, to some extent, the breadth of the menu.

The industry average for a straight line is between five-and-a-half and six patrons per minute. This speed is most acceptable and has, in fact, been brought about only recently with the introduction of sophisticated cash registers. This new generation of cash register offers item keys in lieu of money keys. The menu item is listed by name on the register key and the price of the item is programmed into the machine. The prices are easily reset, and the registers are available with up to 120 keys, allowing the entire breadth of any reasonable cafeteria menu to be included.

The obvious advantages with this system are speed, accuracy, and inventory control. A cashier who is not required to remember prices or do mental arithmetic is obviously more accurate and substantially quicker. The added feature of inventory control has enormous advantages for the foodservice manager in reviewing specific sales records or, for that matter, monitoring the minute-by-minute sales profile.

A second, and equally limiting bottleneck, is the speed with which beverages can be dispensed. Beverages are much like cashiering in that essentially all patrons stop for a beverage; whereas only 70 to 75 percent will select an entree. Thus, industry averages show a served beverage speed of only six and eight patrons per minute, and even this speed takes into account the prepouring or predrawing of beverages to a small par just prior to service.

A third, and less limiting factor, is the speed with which entrees can be served, because only about three-quarters of the patrons select a hot entree. The remainder select salad plates, pre-wrapped sandwiches, or partial meals, and therefore do not place a burden on the entree service station. Each entree server can accommodate approximately three patrons per minute if the food items are ready for service, i.e., not carved to order. Normally, this station is divided between two or three persons handling entrees and potato/vegetable side orders separately.

How, then, to overcome the capacity limitations of the single line cafeteria? By duplicating or separating the limiting functions. If the cashier is the limiting factor, that function can be separated from the cafeteria line and a twin unit placed at a reasonable distance from the end of the line. This, theoretically, doubles the capacity of the line.

In fact, this merely shifts the limiting factor. Then the next slowest function, beverage service, becomes the new limiting factor. Duplication of beverage service is a much more expensive alternative, involving additional capital funds for equipment and space, and operating funds for staffing. This alternative of duplicating the beverage service must be carefully reviewed to insure its economic feasibility.

Modifications to the Single Line Concept

In recent years the conventional single line cafeteria has frequently been modified to provide a broader menu. The most notable addition is to-order foods, whether cold sandwiches or grilled items. Expansion into these areas results in a thin line separating the single line concept from the hollow square or free form concept. An example of a typical straight line cafeteria, serving up to 800 patrons per meal, is shown in Figure 39 on the facing page.

FIG. 39–TYPICAL STRAIGHT LINE SERVING AREA, 800 PATRONS PER MEAL

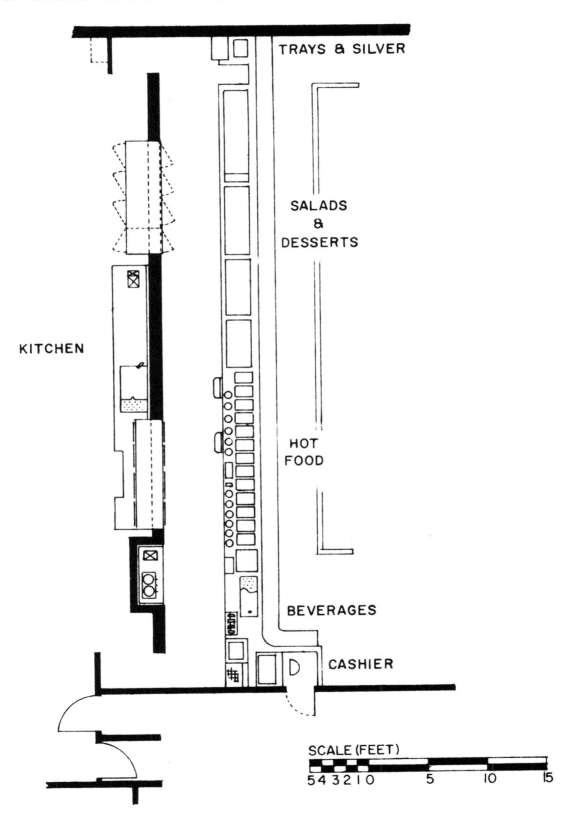

TRAYS & SILVER

SALADS
&
DESSERTS

KITCHEN

HOT
FOOD

BEVERAGES

CASHIER

SCALE (FEET)

5 4 3 2 1 0   5   10   15

Hollow Square

The first major change from the straight line design was to what is commonly called the "Hollow Square." Two major concepts distinguish the hollow square; the first is two separate serving lines feeding together, and the second is separating the beverage facility. Figure 40 (facing page) illustrates a typical hollow square concept.

As shown, the hollow square takes the form of an inverted "U" with the beginning point of the twin serving lines at the end of the two legs. The legs of the "U" serve as the cold food/dessert areas, with the base of the inverted "U" accommodating twin hot food lines joined at the center. The beverage facilities are separated from the twin lines and occupy the center space between the legs. When combined with a maximum of four remote cashiers a hollow square can triple the capacity of a conventional single line cafeteria. Variations on the concept include different menus offered on the two legs, such as the conventional meal with hot entrees on one leg, and salads, sandwiches and grilled foods on the second leg.

Hollow squares do not have the inherent versatility of allowing any extensive to-order items, although variations similar to those in single line arrangements are occassionally included. The basic value of the hollow square is to increase capacity without a parallel increase in labor. The dual hot food stations are fed from the same point in the kitchen and staffed by less than double the number of servers required for single line service. The dual beverage line requires fewer personnel than two single lines and often less equipment; using recently developed, sophisticated, carbonated beverage and coffee makers, single units can serve multiple stations.

Random/Free Form System

The most recent innovation in public cafeteria design has been the development of the "random" or "scatter" system. ("Free form," "scramble" and "shopping center" are other names frequently applied.) This system was first pioneered in the 1940s for industrial foodservice in the belief that regular users would not be confused by the non-linear arrangement of counters.

Foodservice operators more recently have come to realize that the patron is more sophisticated now. Perhaps he has been exposed to the free form/random system in his plant or office building, but even if he has not his basic intelligence, supplemented with graphics, overcomes any confusion. Figure 41 (page 146) depicts an example of this system.

Conceptually, the free form/random system incorporates a separate station for each menu classification such as:

Cold Foods and Salads
Desserts
Hot Entrees
Delicatessen Sandwiches
Hot Carved Meat Sandwiches
Grilled Items
Beverages
Milk and Ice Cream
Condiments and Dressings

as well as separate stations for trays/silver and cashiers.

Depending upon patron menu preferences, the number of stations offering each item—or the possibility of combining two or more menu classifications—can be determined. The chief advantage of the free form/random system is the ability of the patron to move quickly from station to station and pass through the cashiers without waiting behind patrons at stations where he has no intention of making a selection.

The fact that the tray slides do not connect from counter to counter enforces the shopping concept and eliminates the need to slide one's tray along regardless of any intention to make a selection at a particular counter. In theory, the capacity of a free form/random system is limited only by the capacity of the cashiers, and the design is such that additional cashiers can be provided with a minimum of renovation.

An added advantage of this system over the hollow square is that although a preliminary menu decision may have been made by the patron, if he sees the station serving his preference is crowded, he can change without any delay. Another advantage is the ability to serve an extremely wide menu

FIG. 40–TYPICAL HOLLOW SQUARE SERVING AREA, 1,500 PATRONS PER MEAL

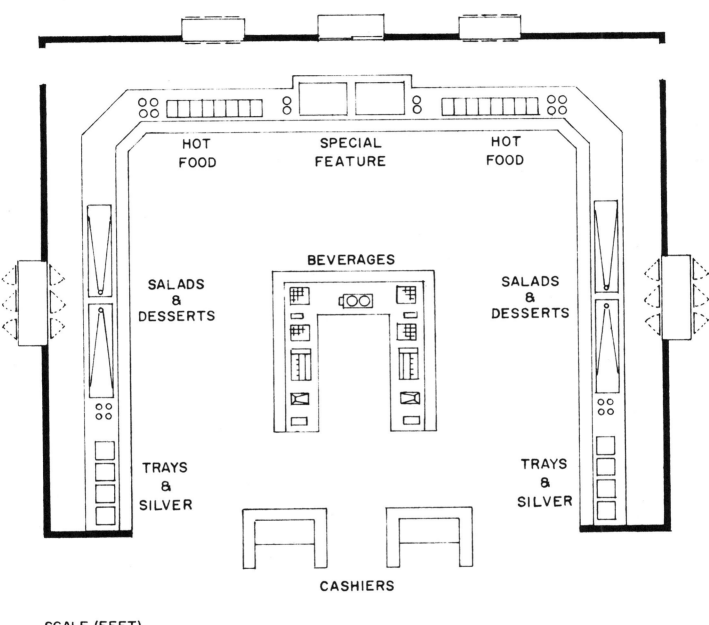

HOT
FOOD

SPECIAL
FEATURE

HOT
FOOD

SALADS
&
DESSERTS

BEVERAGES

SALADS
&
DESSERTS

TRAYS
&
SILVER

TRAYS
&
SILVER

CASHIERS

SCALE (FEET)

5 4 3 2 1 0   5   10   15

FIG. 41–TYPICAL FREE FLOW/SCATTER SERVING AREA, 3,000 PATRONS PER MEAL

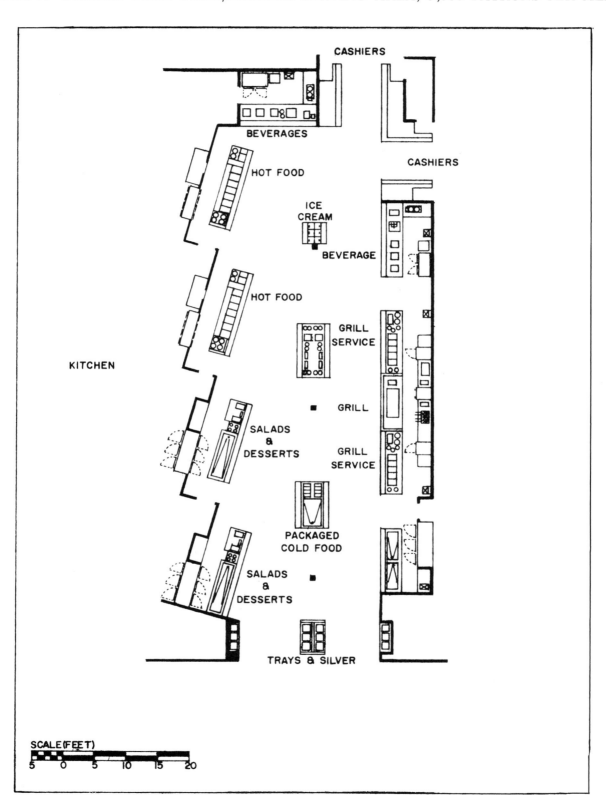

variety, and to develop each station as an individual boutique. Much of the commercialism of the conventional straight line or hollow square cafeteria is masked and the patron is made to feel more comfortable.

Further Design Decisions

To continue our basic decision process toward the design of a public cafeteria, we face two additional major decisions which must be made before allocation of space can commence. They are 1) permanent ware *versus* disposable dishware, and 2) conventional food production *versus* convenience food. To a great extent, the first decision follows from the style of service to be provided. Disposable ware is rarely the equal of permanent ware in aesthetics and ambience. Except in extremely unusual circumstances, where the use of permanent ware is impossible, we would not expect to see a public cafeteria using such material except for carry-out orders.

Aside from the aesthetic problem, the continuing petroleum shortage has made the cost of the "better grade" disposables almost prohibitive.

The second area of decision, convenience *versus* conventional food production, requires a more complex analysis. The term "convenience food" has many different meanings and one must define the term before decisions can be made. Certainly, almost any public cafeteria will use frozen vegetables and certain pre-prepared entrees, purchased (as opposed to on-premise baked) bread, rolls, pies, and cakes, and so on. These are all convenience foods and are quite acceptable from the standpoint of cost and gastronomy.

But the use of convenience foods can be much greater and involve a large proportion of frozen pre-prepared entrees. Should this be the case, substantially less area for the production kitchen may be required. To some extent, this reduced production kitchen would be supplanted by increased storage, though not on a one to one ratio. The final decision here must consider both the economics of convenience foods and the availability of acceptable products.

Determining the Basic Design

We have, so far, discussed the types of cafeterias and some of the decisions that must be made when undertaking the preliminary design. We have not addressed ourselves to the method by which we choose the size and, therefore, style of cafeteria, and we must do so before we embark further into design.

SIZING—The sizing of a public cafeteria depends upon both site selection and market analysis. If the site selected is a freestanding facility, an extensive market analysis should be made to determine the expected patronage. If the site selected is a shopping center or office building, the amount of space available may well determine the style of cafeteria. Even so, a less extensive market study should be undertaken to prove the viability of the location based on the number of seats projected.

If we were to assume an unrestrained space for this initial design exercise, we would then rely on the market analysis to dictate the number of patrons expected during a given meal period, and develop our style and size from this figure. The total patronage at any public cafeteria will depend upon the accessibility of the cafeteria to the dining public, pressure of other competition and, of course, the conduct of the operation itself. We will assume, for design purposes, that the resultant operation will be excellent and that the menu variety and price structure are matched to the market area.

The optimum service levels for a 2½- to 3-hour meal period for the three styles of cafeteria are as follows:

Straight line—500 to 800 persons per meal

Hollow Square—1,000 to 2,200 persons per meal

Free Form/Random—1,500 to 6,000 persons per meal.

The wide range of service capabilities of the hollow square is achieved by opening both legs of the "U" only for the peak meal period. Where a single line will not suffice but two full lines are not warranted, the hollow square fills a wide range of needs.

The capacity of the free form/random system is limited only by the total space available. Simply by adding serving stations and cashiers, the capacity is increased. Access to dining rooms can pose a problem from the standpoint of distance, because as the dining room size increases, the distance the patron must walk from the cashier to his seat increases. This problem also is commonly solved with a series of exits from the serving area to a series of smaller, more intimate dining areas. Still, we would normally not project more than 1,500 seats in any area which, under optimum circumstances, would allow a maximum of 4,000 patrons. Beyond this figure, we would investigate the possibility of providing a series of separate serving areas, possibly offering different styles of cuisine, but all gathered around a central commissary kitchen.

In order to size the serving area of any cafeteria, we must first know the menu. The length of a straight line cafeteria is determined by the variety of menu to be offered. The typical example shown in Figure 39, with a 65 to 70 ft. counter, allows the display of a menu range as follows:

    12 varieties of salad
    10 varieties of dessert
    2 soups
    5 or 6 entrees
    8 to 10 side orders
    2 to 3 breads
    A full complement of beverages, including carbonated and non-carbonated, milk, coffee, and ice water.

A somewhat less ambitious menu would require proportionately less space although we could not project displaying an adequate menu on less than 45 to 50 ft. Obviously, adequate tray slide dimension and patron aisle space is required as well as queuing space for persons waiting to enter the serving line.

Sizing a hollow square is affected by much the same considerations as the straight line. The procedure for arranging displays and the length of display required is not changed, although it would be reasonable to expect only a single, central hand-carved meat station at the intersection of the two hot food tables, should that be a featured portion of the menu.

The length of the beverage counter would be the same as for a straight line with the exception that milk and ice cream could easily be placed along the end of the counter, thereby shortening the overall length. The example shown in Figure 40 would accommodate the full straight line menu in duplicate, or the full menu on one side and specialty items on the second side.

Double aisleways would be required between the opposing counters with their width essentially dictated by the total width of the twin hot food counters.

For the free form/random system area sizing is a two-step process. The first step is to determine the capacity of individual serving stations and thus the number of stations required to serve the expected patronage. While a single, long, combination salad and dessert counter might be adequate for the expected patronage, it might be advantageous to provide twin shorter counters simply to divide the incoming traffic. The same reasoning applies to the hot food counter, where, while one long counter may suffice, two shorter counters would better serve the patron.

For carved meat sandwiches, made-to-order cold sandwiches, and grilled items, single counters will suffice; the length of the counters and the number of serving points along them increases as patronage increases. A capable sandwich man can prepare, plate, and garnish one to-order sandwich every 40 seconds. The same timing should be allowed at the sliced meat counter unless the portions are pre-sliced, which will drop the elapsed time to 20 to 25 seconds.

The grilled food stations should be manned by a minimum of two persons at all times, allowing one person to be cooking while the second acts as an order taker and server. The addition of a third person would be in a swing category and he would handle some of the cooking while functioning as an order taker and server.

A single beverage counter is capable of processing 400 to 500 persons an hour. A twin counter will double that number, while the addition of milk and ice cream at the end (in essence, a third location) adds approximately 300 an hour more.

Shown here are two tables. Table at right gives the typical serving capacity of a given length of serving counter. Table below gives a breakdown as to counter allocation, corresponding with the total number of patrons to be served.

FOODSERVICE PROGRAM DEVELOPMENT

The design decisions up to this point form the basis for the development of a realistic foodservice program. It is impossible to consider the design of any project without such a program. This does not mean that you must have a written and published program before design begins or, for that matter, at any time; but simply by making design decisions, you are establishing and defining a foodservice program. And there is real value in having such a program printed and published because then everyone with any responsibility for foodservice facility approval may review the program, amend it if required, and accept the finished product.

It is traumatic for a consultant—and even more so for the operator—to walk into a new facility expecting one set of circum-

TABLE A—TYPICAL STATION CAPACITIES PUBLIC CAFETERIAS

TRAY DISPENSERS—1 for each 250 patrons

COLD FOOD/DESSERT COUNTERS—10 ft. linear display including 20 ft. of overshelf per 600 to 1000 patrons, with a maximum length of 15 ft. to 18 ft.

MADE-TO-ORDER SANDWICHES—One 4 ft. to 6 ft. counter per 150 sandwich orders, with a minimum length 6 ft.

CARVED MEAT COUNTERS—One 6 ft. counter per 150 orders.

GRILLED FOODS COUNTER—One 4 ft. counter per 200 orders, with a minimum length of 6 ft.

HOT FOOD COUNTER—One 10 ft. display counter per 750 total patrons, with a maximum length of 16 ft.

BEVERAGE COUNTER—One 16 ft. to 18 ft. counter per 1000 patrons with a maximum length of 20 ft. to 24 ft. The capacity of the complex can be increased by 500 per meal period with the addition of a separate ice cream and milk dispenser station at the head of the beverage "U".

TABLE B—TYPICAL STATION REQUIREMENTS FOR PUBLIC CAFETERIAS

TOTAL PATRONS PER MEAL

STATION REQUIREMENTS	500	1000	1500	2000	2500	3000	3500	4000	4500	5000
Tray Dispensers (No. of Locations)	2	4	6	8 (2)	10 (2)	12 (2)	16 (3)	18 (3)	20 (3)	22 (3)
Cold Food	1–10 ft.	1–12 ft.	1–16 ft.	2–10 ft	2–12 ft.	2–16 ft.	2–18 ft.	3–15 ft.	3–18 ft.	3–18 ft.
Made-to-Order Sandwich	1–6 ft.	1–6 ft.	2 sta.	2	2	3	3	3	4	4
Hot Carved Sandwich	1–6 ft.	1	1	2	2	2	3	3	3	3
Grilled Food	1–6 ft.	1–6 ft.	2 sta.	3	3	4	4	5	5	6
Hot Food	1–10 ft.	1–14 ft.	1–18 ft.	2–12 ft.	2–14 ft.	2–18 ft.	3–12 ft.	3–15 ft.	3–18 ft.	4–15 ft.
Beverage Counter	1–16 ft.	1–16 ft.	1–20 ft.	2–16 ft.	2–18 ft.	2–24 ft.	3–16 ft.	3–20 ft.	3–24 ft.	4–18 ft.
Cashiers	1	1+1PT	2+1PT	2+2PT	3+1PT	3+2PT	3+3PT	4+3PT	5+3PT	6+3PT

stances only to be faced with a totally different set, simply because the program was not written, and the interpretation by the individuals involved was different. You, therefore, must insist upon the development of a written program. It need not necessarily be extensive, but it should be long enough so that the essentials of service are clearly stated, and hopefully, as a result, clearly understood.

The development of the foodservice program begins with data collection, including the following:

1. Projected number of patrons to be fed
2. Serving Hours
3. Patron Analysis including:
   a. General Economic Structure
   b. Age Group
   c. Ethnic Breakdown
   d. Family Size

These data should be developed for each meal period and day of the week if the patronage is likely to change markedly. As an example of this, consider a cafeteria located in a shopping mall which, itself, is located by an office complex. The lunchtime business would draw heavily from the office facilities, dinner would be mostly shoppers, while weekend business would more probably be heavily family.

Once armed with this basic patron profile, combined with the earlier decisions on menu style, we can begin to investigate the many alternatives in foodservice and servery design. The ethnic, economic, family, and age group profiles now allow us to develop a detailed menu and, further, a hypothetical projection for each menu category. You would then be able to predict, based on your own experience and that of your consultant's, the percentage of patrons selecting each general menu item each meal. This breakdown would include predictions on cold or special order sandwiches; grill, snack, or fast food items; complete hot meals, and various and sundry specialty items. Typical patron entree participation, as experienced in public cafeterias at lunch and dinner, are shown in Table C.

The percentages shown are for a typical shopping center/office oriented facility with a substantial family market. The sandwich popularity at lunch illustrates the trend among today's patrons away from non-hot

TABLE C—TYPICAL ENTREE POPULARITY FOR PUBLIC CAFETERIAS

LUNCH

Hot Entree	40%
Cold Entree (Entree Salads)	5%
Snack Foods (Grilled)	25%
Made-to-Order Sandwiches	
Hot Carved	10%
Cold	15%
No Entree	5%
	100%

DINNER

Hot Entree	60%
Cold Entree (Entree Salads)	2%
Snack Foods (Grilled)	25%
Made-to-Order Sandwiches	
Hot	5%
Cold	3%
No Entree	5%
	100%

food entrees; the dinner percentages reflect the high percentage of snack foods accounted for by younger children in the family market. Still, these percentages are only a guide and must be adjusted for all of the factors listed above. In addition, they should be adjusted seasonally where there will be a large fluctuation in the exchange between hot entrees and cold foods.

Using a straight line or hollow square design practically eliminates the possibility of hot carved and made-to-order cold sandwiches, and has a tendency to limit the variety of snack foods available. Thus, most of the weight given up by these categories would be absorbed by the hot entree category.

SPACE ALLOCATIONS

The space within public cafeterias is divided into three major areas: seating space, servery, and kitchen (including all back-of-the-house areas.) The ratio of these areas depends on the style of serving facility and the method of food production. It will range from a 45/15/40 percent ratio for smaller facilities, to as high as a 60/10/30 percent ratio for much larger facilities. The decrease in relative percentages allocated to the production kitchen supports the theory that you do not need to double your production facilities to double your seating. But when you double the number of people passing through the servery, you do approach a doubling of the required space. The graphs which follow indicate the relationship of square footage allocated to each of the three areas through a range of building sizes.

Table D (below) indicates the effect of increasing dining room size on the square-feet-per-seat computation. Nominally, we assign 15 sq. ft. per seat in preliminary sizing of dining facilities. This allows for aisleways, condiment stands, side stands, planters, etc. You will note from the table that in the smaller seating capacities and square foot areas, the amount required per seat is somewhat larger; as total seating and overall size increase, the square-feet-per-seat figure decreases.

TABLE D—DINING ROOM SIZING FOR PUBLIC CAFETERIAS

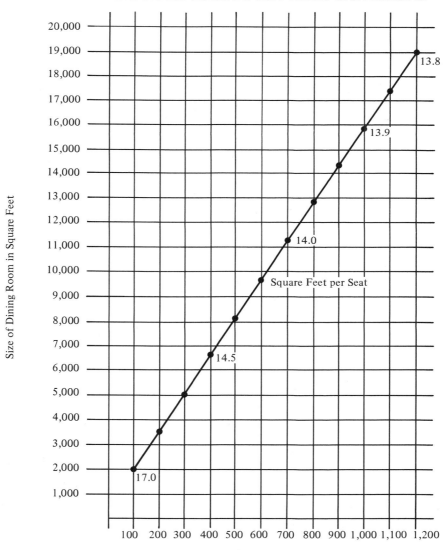

Size of Dining Room in Square Feet

Square Feet per Seat

Peak Number of Patrons Simultaneously in Dining Room
(Charted values include 1.15 multiplier
to allow inefficiency in seating)

Table E (below) indicates the relationship of the servery size to the number of patrons served. Proved industry standards indicate that nominally 20 sq. ft. per person is required within the servery for each patron simultaneously occupying the servery.

Table E illustrates again that when the numbers are low in the servery, the square footage per patron is greater than 20, and that as the number increases the square foot allocation decreases. The computation to arrive at the number of persons accommodated by the servery at one time involves an in-depth analysis of patron eating habits.

Historically, dining patrons prefer the conventional lunch hour, and specifically the period from 11:45 to 12:45. This is particularly true when lunch patronage is substantially from surrounding office buildings, where a scheduled lunch hour in that time period is commonplace. Patrons from the shopping center, on the other hand, are more likely to lunch later since most retail stores are not open until 9:30 or 10, and by noon these early shoppers are still involved. Lunch under these circumstances would tend to peak from 1 to 1:30. Dinner in public cafeterias is normally early, commencing in

TABLE E—SERVERY SIZING FOR PUBLIC CAFETERIAS

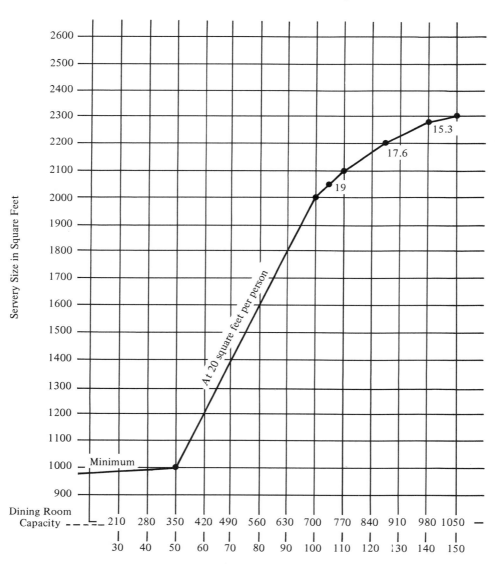

Peak Number of Patrons in Servery Simultaneously

earnest by 5:30, and peaking at 6:15 to 6:30.

Comparing the total patronage expected —and projecting demand of 50 percent of that total patronage during the peak hour—results in the servery population as shown in Table E. Combining the appropriate figures from Table D and Table E will result in a compatible allocation of space between the dining room and the serving area. The kitchen area, which includes all of the rest of the back-of-the-house areas, again is nominally sized at approximately 8 sq. ft. per dining room seat, or between two and three sq. ft. per meal patron.

Table F (below) indicates this relationship between total patrons/total dining room seats and back-of-the-house allocations per patron or seat.

Figure 42 (overleaf) consolidates the earlier tables. The bar chart graphically indicates the ratio between dining room, servery, and kitchen under an increasing patron load and, therefore, an increased total project size. The nominal divisions between what would normally be a straight line cafeteria, what would be a hollow square, and what would best be a random/scatter system shown as a dotted line indicate only an approximation.

TABLE F—TYPICAL SPACE ALLOCATION (BACK-OF-THE-HOUSE) PUBLIC CAFETERIAS

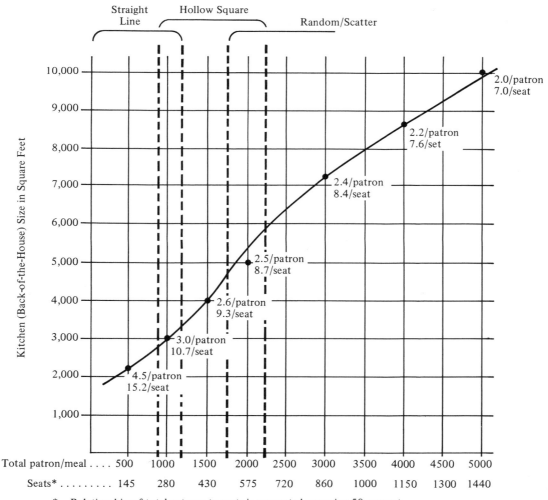

* Relationship of total patrons to seats is computed assuming 50 percent of the total eat in the peak hour, with 2 turnovers per hour.

FIG. 42–COMBINED SPACE ALLOCATION PUBLIC CAFETERIAS

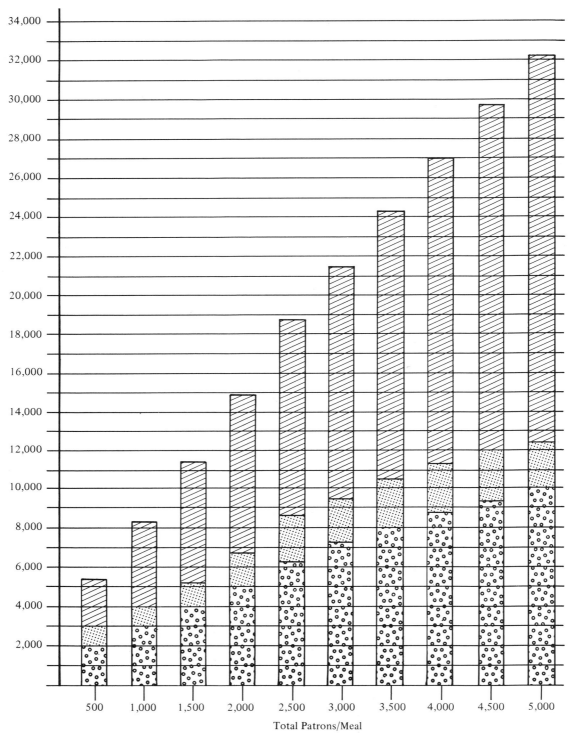

Key

- ⧄ Dining Room
- ⋮ Servery
- ○ Back of the House

DESIGNING FOR FUNCTION

Our design process to this point has allowed us to select the site, develop the food-service program and allocate general space requirements. We are now in the position to begin the process of facility design. The design will be divided into the same three areas established for space allocation as each has its own peculiar requirements.

Back-of-the-House

The arrangement of back-of-the-house spaces involves, most logically, designing from both ends to the middle. Normally two areas of the kitchen are pre-determined in the very early planning stages. These two areas are receiving, and the interface between the kitchen and the serving area (and, to some extent, the warewashing area). Though these are essentially fixed locations this normally does not place undue restraints on the design process.

While we will be designing from both ends toward the middle, our conceptual design process will be to follow the raw food product from receiving to serving.

Receiving

This area includes not only the receiving dock, or some access to the receiving dock, but adequate space for outgoing material. This latter space would include an adequate trash handling or storage facility, space to accommodate vendor items to be returned, such as milk racks, carbonated beverage tanks, bakery and bread racks plus, of course, shipping modules if the facility is commissary supported.

SCHEMATIC ARRANGEMENT AND FLOW

Before undertaking the finite design of the back-of-the-house, you must determine the optimum product flow and the interrelationships of the basic departments. You should begin this task by listing each of the major departments, including:

Receiving	Cold Food Preparation
Storage	Hot Food Preparation
Issue	Utensil Washing
Pre-Preparation	Warewashing

You then proceed to list, in the order of priority, the relationship of each department to each of the other departments. For example, the relationship of receiving to storage is first priority; yet the relationship of receiving to utensil washing would be of the lowest priority. Conversely, the relationship of utensil washing to hot food production would be first priority, while the relationship of utensil washing to issuing would be of the lowest priority.

The result of this exercise will be to establish the optimum relationship of each department to all of the other departments. Graphically, this can be portrayed in a bubble diagram as shown below in Figure 43.

FIG. 43—TYPICAL DESIGN BUBBLE DIAGRAM FOR PUBLIC CAFETERIAS

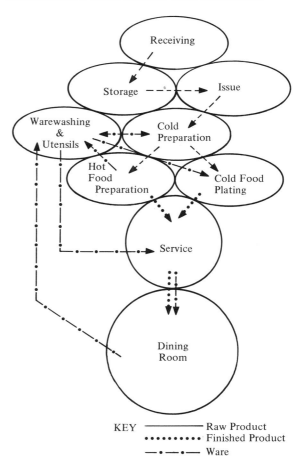

The intent of the bubble diagram is not to determine space allocation, but merely to assist in developing proximities. You may find it necessary to prepare many such diagrams before an acceptable relationship is developed. Note that one end of the bubble diagram is delivery, the input end, while the opposite end is the serving line/dining room for output. Such a diagram will indicate the optimum relationship possible although you may find that under your particular design circumstances it is not obtainable.

Once the relationships are established, you are faced with the task of translating the bubbles into logical operating spaces.

The process of receiving is, to some extent, determined by local delivery conditions. In most metropolitan areas deliveries are at tailgate or dock. In other words, the delivery personnel, whether conventional interstate carrier or the vendor's personnel, will take the goods no further than the receiving dock. If this is the case, then adequate space must be provided on the dock for checking, counting, and weighing.

On the other hand, if you are fortunate enough to have delivery made inside your building, this same checking, weighing, and counting space must be provided within the receiving room. The equipment required for this would include a platform scale, an inspection table and, if an iced product is received, a sink or other repository for the ice. This area should be well lighted to facilitate a thorough, quality inspection and should include at least a shop type desk for receiving personnel to use in recording receipts.

The receiving dock, if under the control of cafeteria personnel, should include additional features such as a hose bib and hose for washing down the area, adequate drainage from the dock and from the truck space adjacent to the dock, CO_2 or dry chemical fire extinguishers for Type B and C fires in case of a vehicle fire, and some method of insect/rodent separation between the dock and the building itself.

Storage

A great deal of discussion has been directed over the years in trying to relate the number of seats and/or patrons to the amount of storage required. Unfortunately, the resulting guidelines are deceptive. Factors that must be considered when assigning storage facilities include:

Frequency of deliveries available for each category of food and supplies.

The effect of commissary deliveries (should that be applicable to the operation).

The style of foodservice production (conventional *vs.* convenience, and the ratio of one to the other).

Despite our earlier cautions concerning rules of thumb, tentative initial allocation of space can begin from this point. If we assume the following conditions:

30 days supply of non-perishables on hand, with deliveries every 2 weeks;

Produce deliveries daily;

Dairy deliveries daily or thrice weekly;

Frozen foods delivery weekly; and

Meats and other perishables delivered twice weekly,

then Table G (p. 157) can serve as the initial allocation of storage space.

Using the same general guidelines, the ratio between room temperature storage and refrigerated storage can be set at 40 percent to 60 percent, respectively. But remember all of the spaces, as well as the allocation of various temperatures within the refrigerated category, must be based on the specific requirements of the project. For instance, if carry-out is a major factor, disposable ware storage must increase, and if fresh fish is used, a fish file or fish storage box must be provided.

Issue/Ingredient Room

An ingredient room is one of the best methods of controlling food costs, inventory, and waste, and for determining precise recipe and portion costs. This room, which encompasses the storage areas, rough preparation, and pre-preparation, as well as issue, thus becomes the major point of control in the operation.

The concept is to control food products from the time of receipt in the facility until they are incorporated into a recipe in the kitchen. Once the food is received rough preparation should take place, including washing and stripping produce, cleaning

TABLE G–TYPICAL STORAGE FACILITY GUIDELINES FOR PUBLIC CAFETERIAS

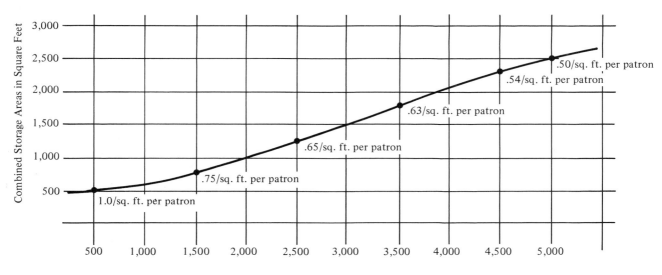

and re-icing fresh fish and chicken, uncrating bulk products, etc. Each day the food production manager or chef reviews the next day's menu and uses his historic references to estimate the number of portions required for each menu item to be served.

He then prepares a requisition, not for ingredients, but in portion numbers for each menu item; *e.g.,* 200 portions of swiss steak, 10 gal. of vegetable soup, 40 portions of lemon meringue pie, etc. This requisition is received in the ingredient room where recipe cards for every menu item are on file. The ingredient room then assembles all of the ingredients necessary for the particular product. The ingredients are weighed, measured, chopped, cut, or otherwise processed to the fullest extent possible in the raw stage, and held together for issue to the appropriate production department. In the case of items that require more than one day's time for production, necessary ingredients are issued at the appropriate time.

This procedure allows absolute control of ingredients, as well as absolute pricing per portion, for all menu items served. Nothing is issued to the production kitchen that is not specifically required for a recipe and so waste and overproduction are eliminated.

The ingredient room would include the previously described storage facilities plus the worktables and sink required to accomplish the pre-preparation tasks. In addition, such specialized items of equipment as slicers, food cutters, vertical cutter/mixer, etc., would be included as would a separate storage refrigerator, referred to as an issue refrigerator. Depending upon the degree of control desired, the issue refrigerator might well open directly into the kitchen and provide the food production manager with access to all of the day's menu requirements without having to physically accept delivery within the kitchen space for items he does not need at the start of the day.

Office space within this area should be provided for the receiving/issue person. This would include space for a desk, file cabinet, and the extensive recipe files. The space allocated to the ingredient function is dictated more by the equipment required than by the number of seats or patrons. A minimal facility will accommodate a small to medium size cafeteria and an increase in space is necessary only to accommodate additional personnel required to complete the tasks assigned and for any additional specialized equipment.

Cold Food Production

The development of the cold food area, and the arrangement of this department within the back-of-the-house scheme is quite critical. Cold food production often provides a preparatory service for hot food production. It also must be immediately adjacent to the ingredient/issue area and have direct access to the cold service areas of the servery, as noted in the conceptual planning section.

Essentially the cold food area consists of preparation and plating tables, plus refrigerated storage for both ingredients and finished plated product. Logically, the storage of raw product should be in the issue refrigerator with the storage of finished, plated product in pass-through refrigerators adjacent to the serving line. Again, the sizing of this area depends upon the menu, the number of employees required to complete the necessary handwork, and the interrelationship between the cold food and hot food preparation areas.

Hot Food Production

Development of the hot food production department follows the same planning procedure as for cold food. Basically, raw products are taken from the issue area and transformed by combining and cooking to the finished products in the hot food serving area. Equipment, depending upon the menu and the amount of convenience foods used, could include roast and/or convection ovens, steam jacketed kettles, steamers (either high pressure, low pressure or atmosphere), fryers, (conventional deep fat or pressure), griddles, tilting braising pans, and possibly broiling equipment (deck type or counter style).

To this basic cooking line, we add preparation tables, sinks, mixers, heated holding equipment, and heated pass-through equipment serving the line. Over the cooking equipment, of course, would be hoods with ventilation and filtering equipment. Note the exception from this equipment list of the commercial range which has all but been eliminated from high volume production kitchens. The menu could, possibly, dictate the requirement for a single range top; if so, it could be added to the production equipment battery.

During the foodservice programming and market analysis stages, a decision would have been made whether to bake in-house or buy from local sources. Desserts, particularly baked products, can be extremely profitable in public cafeterias and the finest available product should be served. Eye appeal is the key merchandising feature you have in a cafeteria and the products must look stupendous. Based on that premise, you must determine whether to make or buy.

Should you decide to bake more than just a limited amount, a separate bakery department should be provided. The bakery would be fed from the ingredient room. With a tight scheduling plan, it could utilize a portion of the hot food production ovens, but it is best to plan a somewhat separate area for the bakery, since this department often starts much before the production kitchen. Bakery equipment would include deck and/or convection ovens, steam jacketed kettle, large and small mixers, dough divider, sheeter, proof cabinet, and an assortment of worktables, sinks, and spice storage bins.

The addition of more sophisticated bakery equipment would be determined by the menu and the availability of qualified personnel to prepare the products. A menu decision might call for offering donuts, croissants, specialty Danish, or any of a number of other delectable items. You, of course, will have to analyze the cost for in-house baking, the quality available in-house *vs.* that from local sources, and the profitability either way.

Whether or not actual baking is done in-house, there must be some provision for the finish baking of certain items. Certainly biscuits and simple batter products, such as muffins, as well as some pies, could be prepared on premise even without a formal bakery.

As we noted in the cold food preparation area, it is difficult to assign a specific square footage to the hot food preparation areas without first reviewing the menu and staffing requirements extensively.

Warewashing

The warewashing department, much as is true of the producing departments, is dependent for its efficiency on a close inter-relationship with other areas of the facility. Warewashing must have good and direct access from the dining area, either by proximity or conveyor, and must also have a direct relationship to the serving area to return the clean dishware and trays. Further, if possible, it should be contiguous with pot and pan washing so that the majority of these utensils can be washed through the dishmachine.

The choice of dishmachines is between the conveyor/rack type, flight type, and circular or carrousel machines. The choice is a matter of both personal preference and the size of the facility. Many large, successful, public cafeterias use circular machines, either with bus person breakdown and direct loading, or in combination with a more conventional soiled dishtable. Equally popular are flight type machines and rack machines with the decision between these two types determined primarily by the capacity required.

The use of a bussing conveyor is advantageous when the warewashing facility is located more than 20 ft. from the dining room space. If, due to space or configuration problems, the warewashing facility has poor accessibility, a bussing conveyor is almost imperative. The only caution here is that conveyors should not be incorporated into the ceiling structure or in under-floor locations unless complete and simple access is provided to the conveyor for the full length of its run. All too often, sophisticated conveyor equipment is allowed to thread its way through a maze of pipes and ducts above a hung ceiling and on the unfortunate occasion of a stoppage access is poor if not impossible.

The loading point of the conveyor should be as centrally located as possible. If necessary, two or more loading points should be provided. Each step a bus person has to take in order to reach the conveyor finds its way to the profit and loss statement as an increased cost of labor.

Sizing warewashing facilities is more simply accomplished. To a great extent, it is determined by the size capacity of the equipment required and the style of equipment chosen. Physically, the circular (carrousel) machines require more space than flight type

machines, but comparing the total amount of loading and drying space available in a circular configuration to that available in a flight type machine, we find the additional space requirement more than repaid in loading and drying capacity.

One advantage of the circular machine is that it can be provided in a myriad of shapes and patterns allowing it to work in spaces not conducive to flight type installation. Because of the requirement for soiled and clean dishtables and the ability to arrange a conventional "U" shaped dishroom, the rack type machines occupy the least amount of space. Their major disadvantage, beyond limited capacity, is the necessity to rack all dishware prior to washing. Flight type and many circular machines have a continuous belt which supports dishware without racks.

SPACE REQUIREMENTS

In each of the preceding departmental descriptions we have made reference to the fact that little exists in the way of square foot guidelines for public cafeterias. However we have, through our experience, developed tentative guidelines which, when undertaking preliminary planning of the back-of-the-house, prove useful.

These guidelines help establish rough parameters for functional areas and allow you to proceed from the bubble diagram to specific space allocation. Once the general allocation (which, again, is far from iron-clad) has been made, the arrangement can be tested; first for product flow, and second for adequacy of the space to accommodate the required equipment.

Product Flow

Again, once the preliminary space allocations have been made, the flow of product from raw to service can be tested. Obviously, the fewer times product flow paths cross, the more efficient the arrangement. Figure 44 (p. 160) shows a typical back-of-the-house arrangement which was derived from the earlier bubble diagram, and is now shown as a test for the product flow.

FIG. 44—TYPICAL PRODUCT FLOW FOR PUBLIC CAFETERIAS

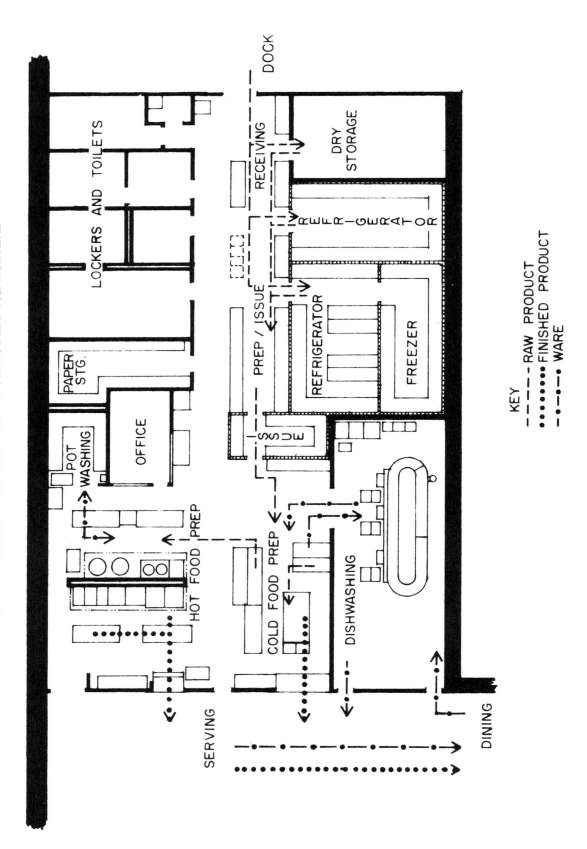

KEY
- - - RAW PRODUCT
• • • • FINISHED PRODUCT
- • - • WARE

SERVERY DESIGN

Even more important than the production kitchen, and certainly more difficult to design efficiently and attractively, is the random/scatter style servery. We established earlier that straight line and hollow square cafeterias follow fairly rigid guidelines and do not pose serious design problems. So, we would like to concentrate here on the much more intricate arrangement of the free form servery.

You will recall we established the overall sizing criteria for the servery based on both total patron counts and also on the number of patrons expected to occupy the servery at one time. In the course of developing the foodservice program, we made a number of significant decisions. First, by selecting the random/scatter cafeteria, we acknowledged that we wished to accept all of our potential customers into the servery without delay, and to provide a more extensive menu than would be feasible with a straight line cafeteria.

Further, we developed approximate ratios indicating the percentage of participation in each of the general menu areas. By this, we mean that we have made a qualitative decision as to how many patrons will order from the grill, how many will eat made-to-order sandwiches, how many will take conventional hot food, how many will have a salad plate or only soup, and how many are just passing through the servery to purchase a single item such as dessert or salad or beverage.

Along with these standard items we should consider specialty items such as soup, hand served desserts, entree salad bowls, etc. These can be treated as individual stations or connected to their related counterparts, as long as there is ease of access for the patron without blocking access to other service points.

And remember, the use of the specialty counter, properly merchandised, not only does a great deal towards improving the whole level of foodservice but has the added advantage of increasing profitability.

In the same way we can size the various serving counters by comparing their ratios to the total number of people in the serving area in a given time, we can also generally determine how many will be at each station,

and therefore determine the number of service points at each which are required to keep any patron waiting an acceptable length of time. We have established, through experience, that the patron should spend no more than five minutes from the time he arrives at the servery until he has passed through the cashier. The breakdown of the servery time is as follows:

Elapsed time (minutes/seconds)	*Activity*
1:00	Tray and utensil selection
	Menu perusal
1:00	Menu decision
	Salad/dessert selection
1:15	Entree/Side Order selection
1:00	Beverage selection
:15	Travel to Cashier
:30	Wait/Pay
Total 5:00	

The next step is to analyze each of these times with an eye to eliminating delays at each point of service. First, be sure there is adequate menu visibility in the vicinity of tray and utensil selection. We cannot over-emphasize the importance of menu and signing at each of the service stations, both to assist the patron in determining his destination and as a secondary merchandising device.

In the tray and utensil area there must be adequate provision for all patrons who arrive within a one-minute period to be accommodated without waiting in line. Patrons must be gotten into the servery and any back-up at the entrance area must be prevented. Once past the tray and silver area you should again provide adequate space to accommodate all of the patrons arriving within a one-minute period. From this area they should be able to observe the servery, consider the menu possibilities, organize their plan of action and, finally, proceed to the first point of pick-up.

A menu selection made at the tray pick-up area might easily be changed once the patron sees the patronage at the various stations. If his initial desire was for a hamburger, but he noted the grill station was experiencing a slight back-up, he might then logically decide to have a sliced roast beef sandwich instead. Therefore, we must provide him space to stand a moment, consider his menu decision, and move on.

Merchandising, and our inborn desire to build check averages, and thus profitability suggest that we locate salads and desserts adjacent to the entry area. A sale at this point might easily be missed were the dessert counter located after the entree counter. Recently we have met opposition to this concept although facts prove time and again that profitability is improved with this arrangement. Our foodservice program has indicated the number of persons expected to patronize the salad and dessert area; we must provide the lineal pick-up area to accommodate this number of people and, in addition, insure that adequate display space has been provided to accommodate the proposed variety.

The basic concept of free flow serving areas is to eliminate tray sliding at pick-up stations. We will tolerate a certain amount of this in the salad and dessert counter since people often desire both. Where salads and desserts are on separate counters we should take steps to insure that the tray slide is not conducive to sliding, but is really a tray rest. This eliminates the tendency of people to act like sheep and line up where there is no need to line up. How difficult it is to convince people who have been lining up for everything all their lives that lining up is neither necessary nor practical in a free flow system.

The individual station sizing is even more critical in the entree areas. Use the program decisions to determine the ratio and the number of grill items *versus* hot and cold sandwiches *versus* hot food entrees, and develop the stations accordingly. Since only one minute has been allowed for entrees, we must be able to accommodate at the three stations all of the persons entering the servery within that minute.

Studies have shown that sandwich ordering, assembly, and service can be accomplished by experienced personnel in 40 seconds. Grill service can also be accommodated in this span of time if the staff is working to a par. To be effective, the par must fluctuate with the peak business. Never

should a grill item be prepared and assembled longer than two minutes before it is presented to the patron and, while the grill man may be able to work six to eight hamburgers ahead during the peak, he may be relegated to working one or two ahead or even to-order during slack periods.

The only reason for putting the grill station within the servery is to provide the patron with the freshest possible product. We, therefore, need to provide a position for both an adequate number of staff and the required number of patrons within the grill area. There is nothing wrong with patrons' standing two or three deep at two or three stations on the grill counter for service. But we must prevent, at all cost, the station appearing overcrowded, or the small line-up in front impeding the flow to other counters.

The hot carved sandwich counter can be set up to slice a selection of meats to order, or to work from a pre-sliced, preportioned inventory. Care must be taken, of course, to present either format in a clean and attractive manner to promote sales.

The hot entree station provides less design problem because service can easily be provided in 20 seconds. There is a tendency to allow more of the straight line concept in the hot food area since dual display of hot entrees is costly, particularly during slower periods. If patron projections are heavy here it would likely dictate the need for more than one counter.

The beverage counter can also be treated as a typical straight line arrangement since often more than one selection will be made. It is not uncommon for a patron to want both water and a cold beverage, or both milk and coffee, and certainly he should be able to select the amount of cream he desires once he has been served coffee by an attendant. Because this must be an attended station, it often works well in combination with hand-dipped ice cream and sundaes.

Dual beverage counters, offering the same selections, are often required to accommodate the peak flow. When this is the case, it is advantageous to position the twin lines back to back so fewer service personnel are required. Again it is imperative that no delay be allowed to develop in the beverage line and adequate space should be provided to allow the patron to by-pass in the line on his way to the cashier. The concept of separate hot and cold beverage lines has been used successfully but care must be taken to split the patronage between these two lines. It may prove that a dual hot line and a single cold line, or vice versa, is in order depending upon the patron, the climate, and so on.

Throughout the sizing and arrangement of the servery it is best to encourage a single direction of flow, and so preclude as much cross traffic and doubling back as possible. The more linear the serving area, the more easily this is accomplished. With a more square space, care must be taken to allow for adequate separation between counters.

The location and number of cashiers are, again, the most important keys in providing uninterrupted patron flow. The patron may be willing to wait a moment to pick up his tray and utensils, or wait a few extra seconds to have his food freshly plated and handed to him, and may even tolerate a short delay in the beverage line, but it is impossible to convince him that he should wait at the cashier's station. The speed and sizing of cashier facilities were discussed earlier; merely note here that space must be provided in logical relationship to the beverage counter and the dining room.

MISCELLANEOUS AREAS

While we have described each of the major production and function areas in the back-of-the-house, there are a number of areas which defy classification, yet must be provided for in some manner. Among these special areas are ice production equipment, management offices, utensil washing, employee lockers and toilets, employee washing facilities, wall space for electrical panels, accommodation for condensing units and carbonated beverage equipment, etc.

One of the most helpful tools in designing any foodservice facility is an equipment checklist. This list, plus another checklist of items most often forgotten, is much too long to include in this chapter. It is, however, available from most universities providing design courses, and from professional foodservice consultants.

SERVERY DECOR

The interior decoration, facade, and graphics for the servery are of equal importance and even, in some cases, more important than the decor of the dining room itself. Merchandising has to be accomplished in the servery and so the attractive display of foods, properly lighted and surrounded by appetite-enhancing colors, is extra insurance toward profitability.

Serveries cannot be stark and be inviting. Hospital white, though depicting cleanliness, is far from conducive to food selection. The servery color must be warm and the stations properly highlighted to attract both the attention and the appetite of the patron. The use of individual service boutiques has proved very successful and has actually made the "shopping" for food an enjoyable part of the dining process.

Of course graphics play an equally significant part in profitability. The efficient and proper direction of patrons, from the menu area to the various service counters, is imperative to attain proper patron counts and to build the check average. While an interior designer can provide an attractive servery and dining room, a graphics consultant is well worth the additional expense.

DINING ROOM DESIGN

Your patrons will, of course, spend more time in your dining room than in any other portion of the facility. You, therefore, cannot allow a superbly conceived servery and the gastronomic delights of your serving counters to be negated by an unimaginative dining room. There is no single rule to follow when choosing dining room decor except that "honesty is the best policy." Don't be phony in the dining room, don't try to be something you are not. Endeavor to magnify the positive features and diminish the negative features, while demonstrating the degree of ambience in which your patrons will be comfortable.

Smaller, divided dining spaces are usually more attractive and conducive to comfortable dining than are large, open expanses. An exception to this might be an especially panoramic view where dividers would encumber the patrons' ability to appreciate the view.

Chairs must be comfortable and tables of adequate size to accommodate persons who wish to eat from their trays, even though we generally expect patrons in public cafeterias to remove food items from the tray, and therefore must provide convenient storage points for these trays as the patron finishes unloading. On the other hand, many people do not object to dining from their trays, and bussing is certainly made easier if at least one tray is left on the table.

The optimum ratio of table sizes is an elusive figure. We have found that a combination of 50 percent tables for four, 40 percent tables for two, and 10 percent available for larger groups of six and eight is generally acceptable. Half of the deuces should be paired so as to be available for either one, two or four. The chairs should be sturdy, should not have protruding rear legs which tend to trip patrons, and should be easily moved to and from the table.

Patron aisles must be of adequate width to allow even the most clumsy to proceed from the cashier to his table without incident. Heavy traffic aisles can be finished with a permanent material such as brick, decorative tiles, etc. The remainder of the dining room should be carpeted in order to provide the necessary accoustic values.

The ceiling should possess as high an accoustical rating as possible. The selection of trays, china, flatware, and napery is all important to the ambience of the project, and should be closely coordinated with both the servery design and the interior scheme for the dining room.

Private Dining

Although private dining rooms are not common to public cafeteria arrangements, the proper selling of such a space can prove most profitable. Entice groups of businessmen to use the cafeteria for luncheon meetings by providing them with their own dining room and you have automatically increased your patronage. Private dining rooms might also be used for conventional waitress service, should you feel that such a venture would be profitable.

SPECIAL FEATURES

There are certain special features which should be included in any public cafeteria design. Among these are provisions for disabled persons. They include ramp access to the front entrance, adequate width for a wheel chair through the serving area, tables designed to accommodate the wheel chair that are not too distant from the entrance, and rest room facilities.

Space should also be provided at the entrance to the serving area to accommodate rolling high chairs so that the young mother planning to eat in the cafeteria has a vehicle to place the baby in while selecting her food and making her way to her table.

SUMMARY OF CAFETERIA DESIGN

Throughout the preceding pages you have been led through the process of cafeteria design, from the initial concept through the production, serving and dining areas. While the appearance of cafeterias may change, over the years, the concepts remain intact.

The most visible change, and one with which we agree wholeheartedly, is the expansion of the menu and the increase of personal service. Economic trends have placed conventional restaurants out of the realm of regular fare for many of the nation's population. With increased disposable income being matched by spiraling inflation, the average working man and woman must find alternate sources to meet their desires to eat out. The obvious solution is the public cafeteria that is located in or adjacent to the shopping center or mall and residential complex.

This trend toward expanding menus has placed the public cafeteria in a more favorable light, and certainly has removed it from the hum-drum atmosphere of years past. Major innovative cafeteria operators, such as Morrison, Marriott, Harry Pope, Blue Boar, Piccadilly, Bishop's and S&W, to mention just a few, are daily improving the image of the public cafeteria and fulfilling the ever-expanding demand to provide quality dining outside the home.

Public Cafeteria

Today's focus in public cafeteria design is on menu expansion and an increase in the personal service provided for patrons. Though disposable income may dwindle, the desire to eat out seems to remain constant. The cafeteria, located on the basis of sound market analysis, and offering popular food, choices at affordable prices, with surroundings and service that are satisfying, holds the key to successful operation.

National Gallery of Art, Washington, D.C., Concourse Cafe/Buffet

This view of the I.M. Pei model (note that roof has been removed that extends over portion behind pillars) shows the sidewalk cafe portion of the National Gallery Cafe/Buffet. (Plan appears on following pages; overall view on page 168.)

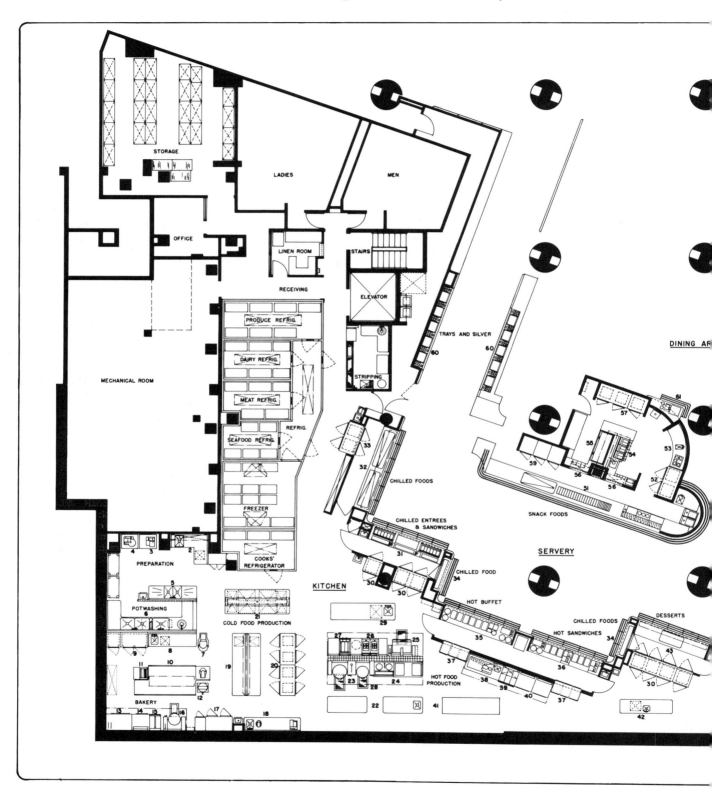

STORAGE

LADIES

MEN

OFFICE

LINEN ROOM

STAIRS

RECEIVING

ELEVATOR

PRODUCE REFRIG.

DAIRY REFRIG.

MEAT REFRIG.

REFRIG.

MECHANICAL ROOM

SEAFOOD REFRIG.

STRIPPING

TRAYS AND SILVER

60

60

DINING AR

57

FREEZER

COOKS' REFRIGERATOR

PREPARATION

4 3 2

5

POTWASHING
6

8

9

7

11 10

12

BAKERY

13 14 15 16 17 18

19

20

COLD FOOD PRODUCTION

21

KITCHEN

29

27 26 25

23 24

22 28

HOT FOOD PRODUCTION

41

CHILLED FOODS

32

33

CHILLED ENTREES
& SANDWICHES

31

30 30

CHILLED FOOD
34

HOT BUFFET

35

SERVERY

HOT SANDWICHES

36

37

38

39

40

37

CHILLED FOODS

34

DESSERTS

43

30

42

SNACK FOODS

51

56 56

55

54

59

53

52

61

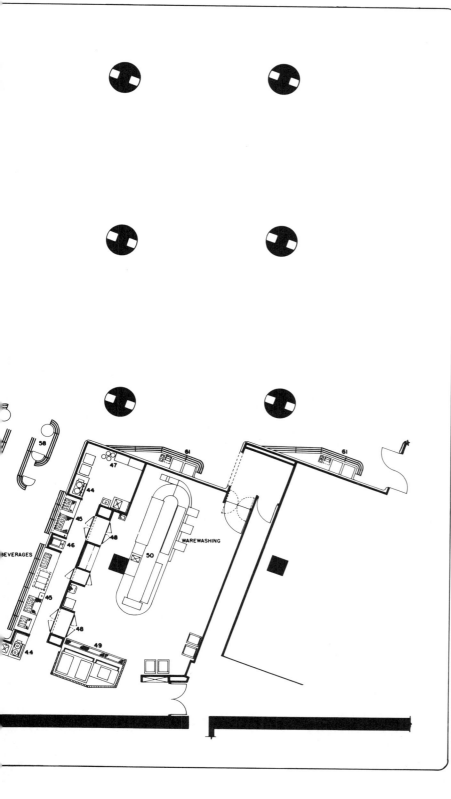

EQUIPMENT SCHEDULE

1. Walk-in Refrigeration
2. Sink
3. Chopper
4. Slicer
5. Preparation Sink
6. Potwashing Sink
7. Mixer
8. Worktable
9. Refrigerator
10. Baker's Table
11. Dough Sheeter
12. Dough Divider
13. Bake Oven
14. Convection Oven
15. Range
16. Kettle
17. Proofing Cabinet
18. Worktable
19. Worktable
20. Roll-in Refrigerator/Freezer
21. Salad Table
22. Worktables
23. Steam Kettle
24. Steam Cooking Assembly
25. Tilting Fry Pan
26. Pressure Fryer
27. Fryer
28. Exhaust Ventilator
29. Worktable
30. Roll-through Refrigerator
31. Charcuterie Counter
32. Salad Counter
33. Roll-through Refrigerator
34. Chilled Food Counter
35. Hot Food Counter
36. Hot Sandwich Counter
37. Food Warmer
38. Bain Marie
39. Range
40. Convection Ovens
41. Heated Table
42. Pastry Table
43. Dessert Counter
44. Coffee Production
45. Beverages—Coffee, milk
46. Shakes
47. Soda Production Equipment
48. Freezers
49. Ice Production and Storage
50. Dishwashing System
51. Beverage Counters
52. Roll-in Freezer
53. Work Counter
54. Fryers
55. Griddle
56. Pass Shelf
57. Refrigerator
58. Cashier Stands
59. Heated/Refrigerated Roll-ins
60. Silver and Tray Counter
61. Water Stations

Designed by: Cini Grissom Associates, Inc.

Overall view above of the I.M. Pei model shows the relationship of the sidewalk cafe in the foreground to the buffet and main dining area behind. (Roof above area beyond sidewalk cafe was removed while model was photographed.) The dining area glows with light and color in a fitting environment for an art gallery. The display at right of both refrigerated and non-refrigerated desserts offers the customer a wide selection.

Above view of the Cafe/Buffet shows the western part of the "buffet" serving area with the fast food line at the right. Pictured below is the carvery at the far left and the hot buffet section. Note lighted sign above which directs patrons quickly.

The hot buffet counter shown above features an additional "sideboard" display for customers to select their entree and supplementary items in the same area.

At right the 4 station cashier area is shown. All the machines are tied into a central data system.

Highland Park Cafeteria

"To cook the best food in the best way we know" was the guideline set for the new food production area when the Highland Park Cafeteria, Dallas was to be replaced with a new building.

A management team provided input for the food facilities consultant and the resulting design has proved itself in meeting production demands for nearly 15,000 meals per week. Planning that met the guidelines set was clearly justified. Food produced in the new facility more than measures up to the quality reputation established during many years of operation at the previous location.

The client wanted a daily menu selection that encompassed:

37 different salads
18 meat or meat-based items
28 vegetables
12 kinds of breadstuffs

Several varieties of each of four types of pies—fruit, custard, icebox, and meringue.

Plus nearly a dozen other desserts, including cakes, cobblers, cookies, and puddings.

Not to mention the appropriate numbers of appetizers, juices, beverages, fruits, and other similar items to round out the fare.

Clearly, reproducing yesterday's menu with today's escalating costs of labor and space—and making the finished operation profitable—represents a neat challenge to a designer. Yet the 50-year-old operation's large number of loyal, devoted, regular customers, all of whom are vociferous in their demands that nothing basic be changed, required it. The concepts of scratch preparation with on-premise cooking and baking were accounted for in the new design.

The food production areas were planned first, using the most spacious and convenient arrangements and layout possible. Around this central point was planned a modern cafeteria serving and dining area, commensurate with the high quality of food and service for which the operation has been known. It has a total seating capacity of 399, 311 at tables, 88 at booths. It is divided into several separate, distinctive settings.

Raw food flow lines are direct to point of use in the kitchen where departments are divided into zones to minimize cross traffic. Finished food moves through separate and ample aisles directly to point of service. Patron and dish flow lines do not interfere with food flow. (See plan, pp. 172–73.)

The zones begin at the dock area which has ample unloading space, as well as facilities for cart and rack washing, plus an enclosed can washer. Stores then move to receiving through large delivery doors with "air curtains" as the only barrier. The aisles are wide, and materials are weighed, counted, and checked-in as received. The buyer's office controls all traffic in and out from this area.

The next area is dry storage and walk-in refrigerators. Dry stores are controlled by the receiving clerk. They are issued on requisition for the daily menu to assure waste and theft control.

Adjacent to the meat walk-in is the butcher shop, equipped to fabricate all cuts of meat, poultry, and fish. Next to

Below: Entrance for "Food-to-Go" is at the rear of the Highland Park Cafeteria with its own parking and landscaped area. The *take-out business is a substantial portion of the cafeteria operation and is steadily increasing in volume.*

the vegetable walk-in is the vegetable preparation area. This area is isolated, and equipment is provided to clean all vegetables prior to storage. Adjoining this is the salad preparation area, with necessary equipment and refrigeration. This is located for direct service to the serving line.

The main cooking area is divided into two zones: vegetable and meat cooking. Both are fully equipped and proximate to holding cabinets and the serving line.

The baker's section is equipped to manufacture quality bread and rolls. Aisle width allows mobile equipment to pass between fixtures easily. The pie preparation area is strategically located. Part of this area is a pass-thru refrigerator to minimize steps in replenishing the line. A pie-cutting table and rack are included to insure that freshly-made pie is also freshly cut and served.

A second pastry area is the cake department. This area is isolated from the kitchen by its location and also by full walls. It is large and fully equipped to manufacture the balance of the desserts that are so important to the menu. It has a large walk-in, with flush sills to permit easy access for mobile racks; the walk-in is shared by the "Food-to-Go" department for storage of telephoned orders.

The dishwashing pantry has a circular, conveyor-type dishmachine. It also contains waste disposing units, a rack storage facility, mobile sinks, a three-compartment sink with a potwasher and heater, and wall racks.

The employee area is on the second floor, and has not only rest rooms and locker space, but a spacious, colorful, quiet dining area. One of the chief assets of the Highland Park Cafeteria is its loyal and faithful personnel; the average employee has been with the company for more than 15 years. The morale of the 125 employees was an important planning component.

Not only does this manifest itself in the exceptional employee facilities, but in such other thoughtful components as spacious aisles for working, fully air conditioned kitchen, and bright lighting and safety devices to reduce hazards and prevent injuries, as well as low noise levels and easy working conditions wherever possible.

Designed by H.G. Rice, FFCS/ISFSC, H.G. Rice & Co. in close cooperation with Mrs. E. Dewey Goodman and Edmund R. Yates, owner/operators

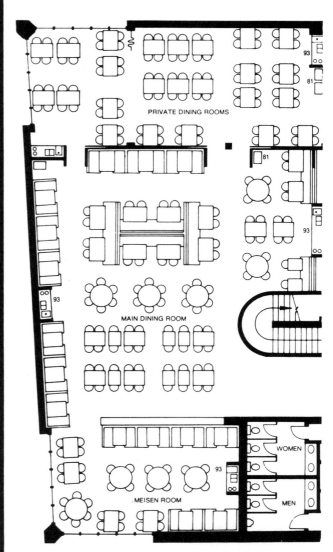

1 Receiving dock
2 Security office
3 Can washing room
4 Maintenance shop
5 Dry store room
6 Walk-in refrigerator
7 Walk-in freezer
8 Beverage refrigerator
9 Fish refrigerator
10 Hand sink
11 Disposer
12 Fish prep tables w/sink
13 Meat saw
14 Vegetable prep tables w/sink
15 Peeler w/stand
16 Produce refrigerator
17 Cook's refrigerator
18 Meat chopper
19 Food cutter
20 Slicer
21 Cook's table w/utensil rack
22 Mixer
23 Racks
24 Cold Bain Marie
25 Hot Bain Marie
26 Steamer
27 Steam-jacketed kettles
28 Tilting fry pan
29 Ranges

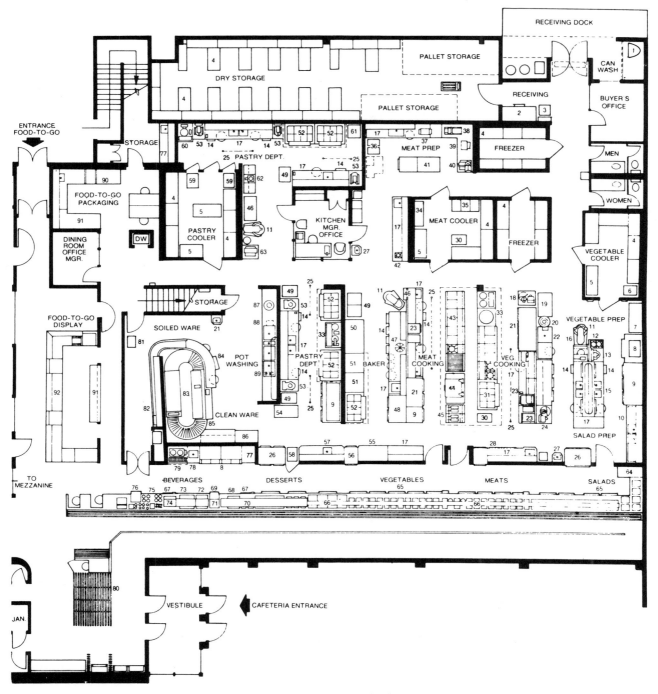

30	Baker's refrigerator & freezer	45	Open top range		able bins	74	Children's seats
31	Baker's stove	46	Char broiler	61	Prep table w/sink	75	Pneumatic tubes to cashier
32	Proof box	47	Fry top range	62	Soiled pot sink w/pump		
33	Baker's work tables	48	Broiler	63	Pot washing machine	76	Wine dispenser
34	Ovens	49	Steamer	64	Pot shelves & racks	77	Service bar area
35	Dough divider	50	Cook's counter w/sink	65	Dishwashing machine	78	Beverage pantries
36	Dough sheeter	51	Hot food wells	66	Soiled dish racks	79	Bar
37	Reach-in refrigerator	52	Microwave oven	67	Portable soak sink	80	Lobby
38	Mixer	53	Portable table w/block	68	Dish carts	81	Check room
39	Employee cafeteria	54	Plate storage	69	Silver sorting area	82	Rest rooms
40	Cafeteria serving counter	55	Assembly counter	70	Rack dollies	83	Stage & dance floor
41	Vending machines	56	Plate dispensers	71	Soak sinks	84	Bussing stations
42	Elevator	57	Food warmer	72	Food supervisor & Chef's office	85	Banquet pantry
43	Manager's office	58	Dispatcher			86	Convertible banquet areas
44	Fryers w/spreaders	59	Oyster bar w/cold pan	73	Soup/salad/dessert pantries		
		60	Breading tables w/port-				

Highland Park Cafeteria continued

Above: Entrance and exit area has alternate cashier stations for serving line patrons. High chair storage is open on both sides. Comfortable seating for waiting patrons is a popular feature.

Below: View of main dining area sh͏ cafeteria serving line at center right lea͏ to curving stairs to mezzanine or to ͏ area. Rare china is displayed in cases extreme right and elsewhere.

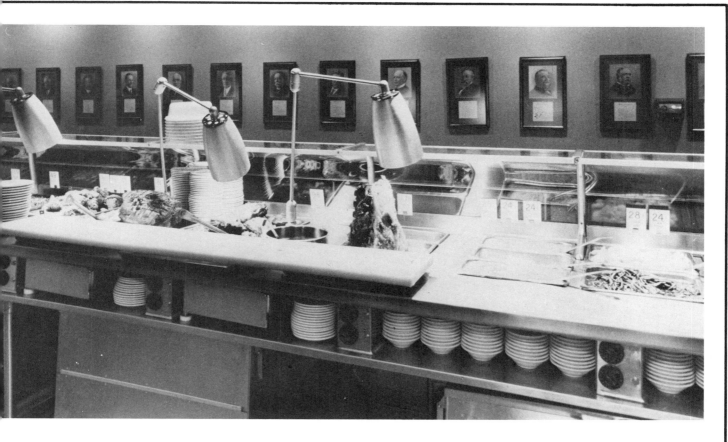

*ve: Work is easier on this line with its inventive use of the
e shelf: heat well controls placed for easy access between
y two wells; "swing-out" scrap pans for fat trimmings under
ing board; under-counter carts and dish carriers, plus provi-
s for easy cleaning.*

*Below: Desserts play a major role in the day's meal for many of
Highland Park Cafeteria's long-time devotees. Dessert display is
part of a master plan to give each concoction full advantage. This
view from the rear side of the counter shows the display super-
structure.*

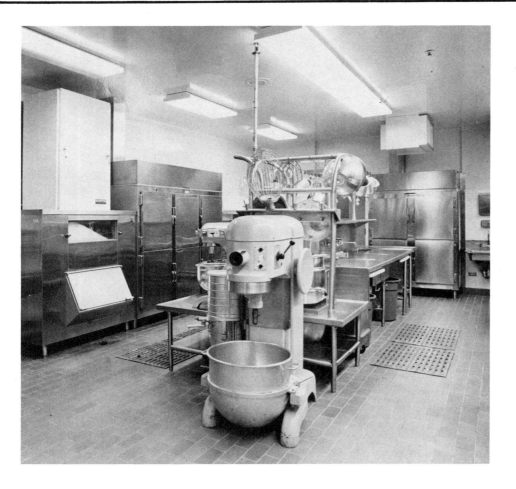

Above left: The salad preparation area, strategically located for supplying the salad area of the serving line, has equipment appropriate to both preparation and service. The flake ice machine at left supplies the salad line cold pan. The steel column over the refrigerators houses remote refrigeration lines running to the compressor room located on the second floor. Sanitation is a key point in the layout of every department; note hand washing facilities at right rear with wrist-handle faucet controls.

Left: Clips on the meat cooler and freezer are used for each department's "Food-to-Go" orders. This is the cook's side of the equipment. Note intercom phone on wall which is one of several located throughout the kitchen for interdepartmental use. Safety considerations were also foremost in planning; the hanging manual fire extinguisher is placed below the housing for the automatic system, the stainless cabinet at the end of the exhaust hood located over the main cooking area.

leveland Clinic Foundation Food Service

signed by: Ron Kooser, Cini
ssom Associates, Inc.

East 90th Street

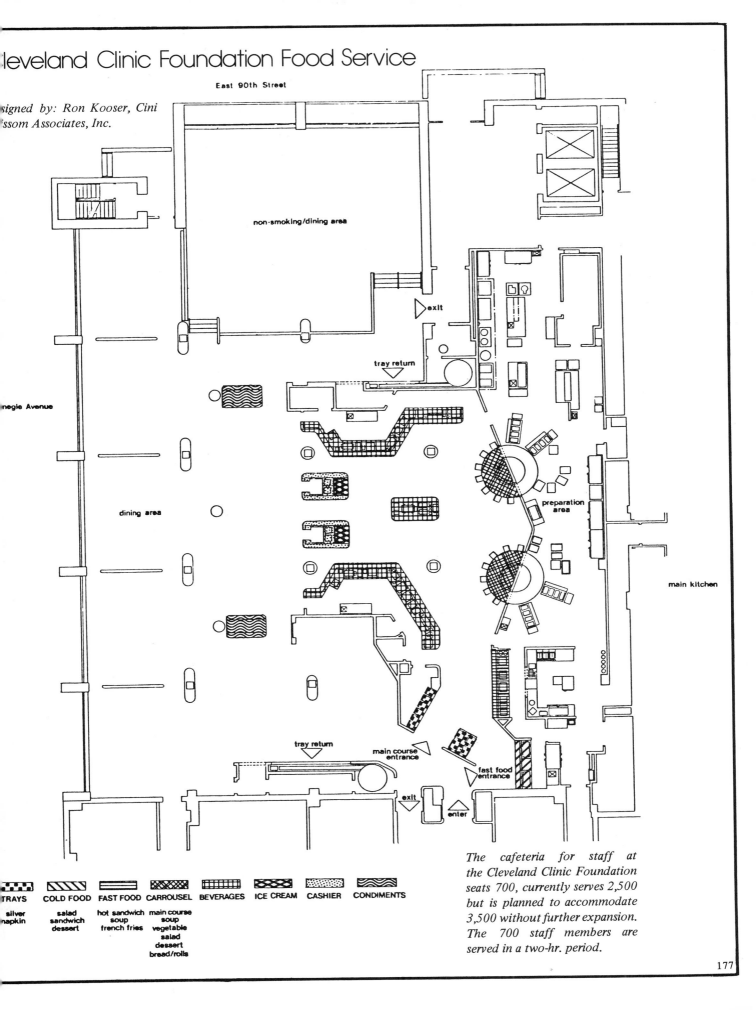

non-smoking/dining area

exit

tray return

negie Avenue

dining area

preparation area

main kitchen

tray return

main course entrance

fast food entrance

exit

enter

TRAYS	COLD FOOD	FAST FOOD	CARROUSEL	BEVERAGES	ICE CREAM	CASHIER	CONDIMENTS
silver napkin	salad sandwich dessert	hot sandwich soup french fries	main course soup vegetable salad dessert bread/rolls				

The cafeteria for staff at the Cleveland Clinic Foundation seats 700, currently serves 2,500 but is planned to accommodate 3,500 without further expansion. The 700 staff members are served in a two-hr. period.

Bishop Buffets, Inc

Is it true that drive-ins, limited menu, family, and specialty operations have obsoleted the traditional cafeteria? You would be hard put to prove it in the face of the performance of Bishop Buffets, Inc.

Headquartered in Cedar Rapids, Iowa, Bishop's has 16 units in major cities in Iowa, Nebraska, and western Illinois. Now past the half-century mark, the company has shown a steady growth rate in volume throughout the years.

In its earlier years, the company located its cafeterias downtown. In more recent years, recognizing the growing importance of easily available parking in attracting customers, it has moved outward, most frequently to shopping centers. Today Bishop's can contract for the size and shape of space it wants; then installs a layout meeting its needs.

The basic design has evolved over the past 20 years. The elements are simple—upgrading of the seating area, both in visual appearance and in furniture and furnishings; a two-line serving area: both L-shaped—one conventional, one a "quick" line with limited items for peak periods; ever increasing emphasis on sanitation; continuous attention to improved, more sophisticated equipment and kitchen area arrangements.

Believing that the word "cafeteria" was often confused by the public with industrial and old-fashioned commercial cafeterias, Bishop's dropped that word from its name and substituted "buffet."

The design premises spring from this philosophy: "The Bishop people address themselves *primarily* to those who eat out for the fun of it, and *secondarily* to the budget-minded. More attention and more investment is put into each customer value to be compatible with the Bishop objective."

"Bishop foodservice—our slogan is For The Fun Of It—finds excellent reception with: (1) young children; (2) young parents with their young children (under teen-age); (3) senior couples with children no longer at home, and (4) the 3-way group: (a) senior couples with (b) their young married children, with (c) their young children."

The plan at right is for the Bishop Buffet in Dubuque, Iowa which averages 8,050 meals per week prepared and served by 45 employees. Typical Bishop feature is a counter positioned near the entrance of the house, making it easy for first-timers to see the starting point and to orient themselves to the arrangement and facilities. A clever arrangement using fixed and removable posts allows a short direct walk to the start of the line at slow times or the building up to a number of loops as crowds gather.

The line ends in the middle of the dining room seating facilities. Thus emerging customers get a clear view of the choice of dining rooms, and travel is minimal for the service girls who carry trays for all customers.

Small cut-out windows in the wall between the serving counter and preparation areas directly behind stimulate close communication. Line and preparation personnel can communicate without leaving the station. The direct view of the customer lineup also permits cooks to provide small batch preparation and aids in production control.

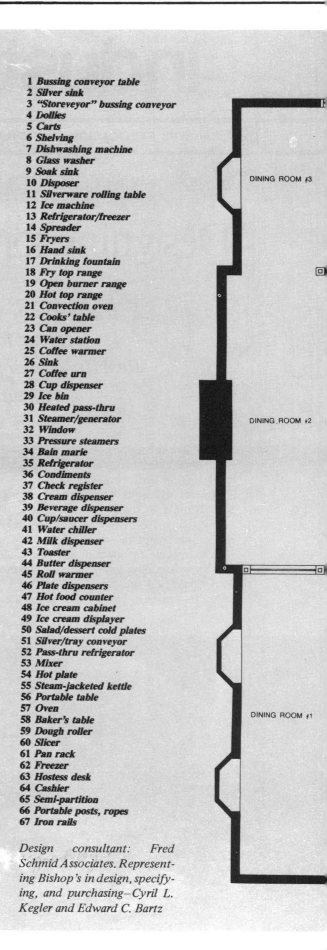

1 Bussing conveyor table
2 Silver sink
3 "Storeveyor" bussing conveyor
4 Dollies
5 Carts
6 Shelving
7 Dishwashing machine
8 Glass washer
9 Soak sink
10 Disposer
11 Silverware rolling table
12 Ice machine
13 Refrigerator/freezer
14 Spreader
15 Fryers
16 Hand sink
17 Drinking fountain
18 Fry top range
19 Open burner range
20 Hot top range
21 Convection oven
22 Cooks' table
23 Can opener
24 Water station
25 Coffee warmer
26 Sink
27 Coffee urn
28 Cup dispenser
29 Ice bin
30 Heated pass-thru
31 Steamer/generator
32 Window
33 Pressure steamers
34 Bain marie
35 Refrigerator
36 Condiments
37 Check register
38 Cream dispenser
39 Beverage dispenser
40 Cup/saucer dispensers
41 Water chiller
42 Milk dispenser
43 Toaster
44 Butter dispenser
45 Roll warmer
46 Plate dispensers
47 Hot food counter
48 Ice cream cabinet
49 Ice cream displayer
50 Salad/dessert cold plates
51 Silver/tray conveyor
52 Pass-thru refrigerator
53 Mixer
54 Hot plate
55 Steam-jacketed kettle
56 Portable table
57 Oven
58 Baker's table
59 Dough roller
60 Slicer
61 Pan rack
62 Freezer
63 Hostess desk
64 Cashier
65 Semi-partition
66 Portable posts, ropes
67 Iron rails

Design consultant: Fred Schmid Associates. Representing Bishop's in design, specifying, and purchasing—Cyril L. Kegler and Edward C. Bartz

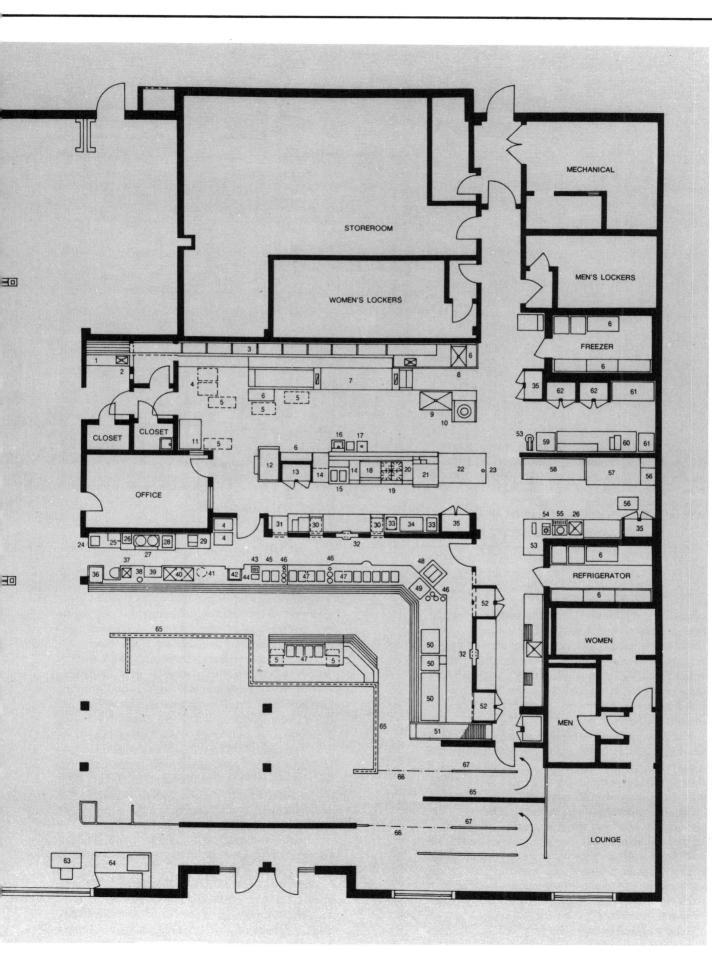

MECHANICAL

STOREROOM

MEN'S LOCKERS

WOMEN'S LOCKERS

FREEZER

CLOSET

CLOSET

OFFICE

REFRIGERATOR

WOMEN

MEN

LOUNGE

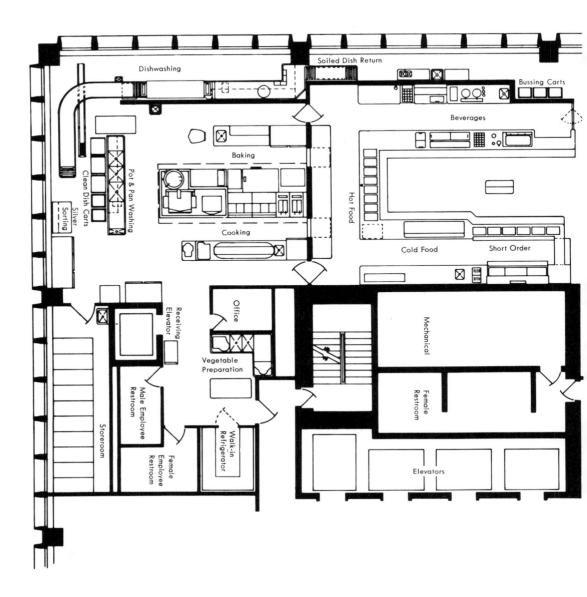

Dishwashing · *Soiled Dish Return* · *Bussing Carts* · *Beverages* · *Baking* · *Clean Dish Carts* · *Pot & Pan Washing* · *Silver* · *Sorting* · *Hot Food* · *Cooking* · *Cold Food* · *Short Order* · *Receiving Elevator* · *Office* · *Mechanical* · *Vegetable Preparation* · *Male Employee Restroom* · *Female Employee Restroom* · *Walk-in Refrigerator* · *Female Restroom* · *Storeroom* · *Elevators*

Pierre Laclede Center Cafeteria

In the past decade few cities have shown the vitality and growth that has marked the "rebirth" of Metropolitan St. Louis, Missouri. Among the most prominent of the new buildings, topped only by the famed Gateway Arch, are the 25- and 23-story structures that comprise Pierre Laclede Center, Clayton, Missouri.

As a part of its services to tenants, the building operators included an eating place on the second floor of one of the two buildings. Besides the normal limitations this location would prescribe,

management added another: all plumbing lines had to be set back at least 5 ft. 8½ in. from outside walls.

The designer/operator has contrived a design plan with many built-in efficiencies. Among others, this cafeteria kitchen is designed to act as the commissary for two other units: The Napoleon Bar, an area inset into the cafeteria dining area, and the Briefeater, a paper-service snack bar located in the adjacent building.

The cafeteria has about 200 seats, runs the longest menu; the Briefeater has a

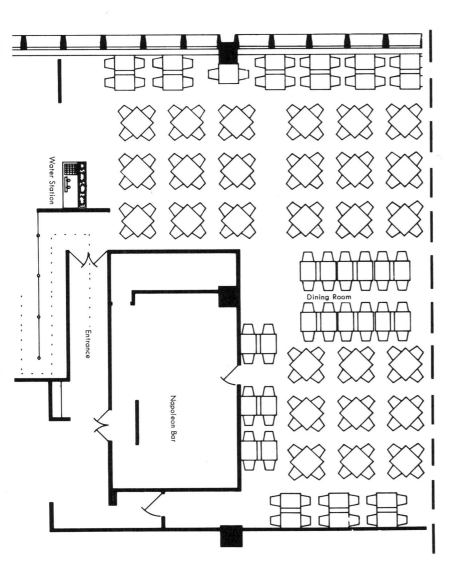

Water Station

Entrance

Napoleon Bar

Dining Room

Designed by: Harry Pope, ISFSC, Pope's Catering Co.

grill for hamburgers, but otherwise offers salads, sandwiches, etc., supplied by the main kitchen. It has a few seats, but much of the business is take-out. The Napoleon has about 30 seats; service is from a hot/cold cart featuring sandwich platters.

The cafeteria and Briefeater are open from 7:30 a.m. to 3 p.m.; the Napoleon from noon to 8 p.m.

Among the operation's design innovations is a device on the server's side of the line that holds plates steady so server can use both hands to place food on plate.

A knife holder has slits in plastic top covering stainless cylinder which keeps knives in safe, yet easy to use, position; holder disassembles easily for cleaning.

At cold beverage station, milk cartons are replenished through lift-off top. Special refrigerated troughs hold butter and ice cream.

Both preparation and serving areas were designed in a "U" shape to save space.

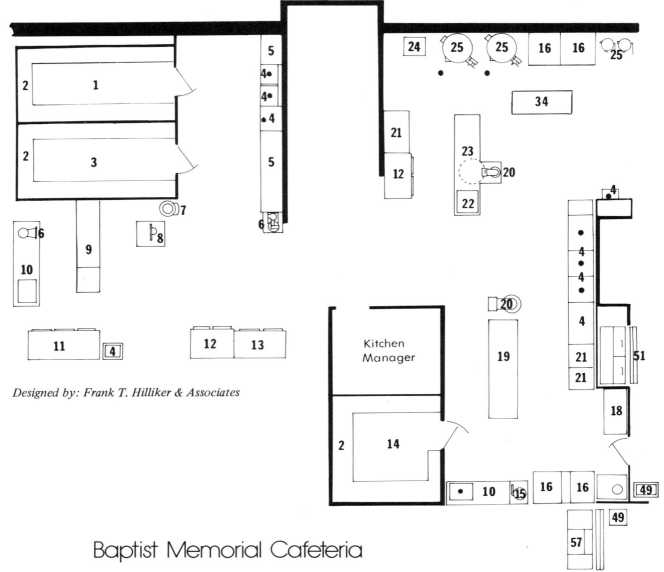

Designed by: Frank T. Hilliker & Associates

Baptist Memorial Cafeteria

Creating an efficient cafeteria facility entirely separate from its patient service is the unusual accomplishment of Baptist Memorial Hospital, Memphis, Tennessee, which is one of the largest privately-owned hospitals in the country.

Baptist Memorial had, a study a few years back indicated, sufficient volume among staff, visitors, and ambulant patients to justify a separate operation from that of patient feeding.

Subsequent remodeling resulted in this new operation. It is of significant size; it is a cafeteria; it has an open square serving section and a dining area with 340 seats. For special events, two meeting rooms can be partitioned off.

Open from 6 a.m. to 8 p.m., it averages nearly 2,300 customers daily, about 400 for breakfast, 1,300 for lunch, and 600 for dinner. There are 51 employees; 19 in preparation, 16 in service, including counter service and cashiers, eight in ware washing; two in cleaning, and six in supervision, including the manager.

The number of seats may seem generous but nearly seven turnovers per seat are required per day. Keeping in mind that meal periods in a hospital context seem to be somewhat circumscribed, it is apparent why two of the principal design criteria for the facility were to minimize labor and to accelerate the service without marring the attractiveness of the eating experience.

Several techniques were used to achieve these goals. One was to place production units near serving counter replenishment points to minimize time and labor. Installation of a soiled ware conveyor near the dining area made self-bussing practical without lowering the tone of the operation.

The success of the design can be attested by the quality and variety of menu offerings in the cafeteria compared to its low check average. Breakfast offers choices of basic egg dishes, three meats, as well as cereals and pastries. Lunch and dinner menus are the same each day but vary somewhat day to day. Each includes five hot entrees, two or three starch items, six to seven vegetables, as well as salads, desserts, breadstuffs.

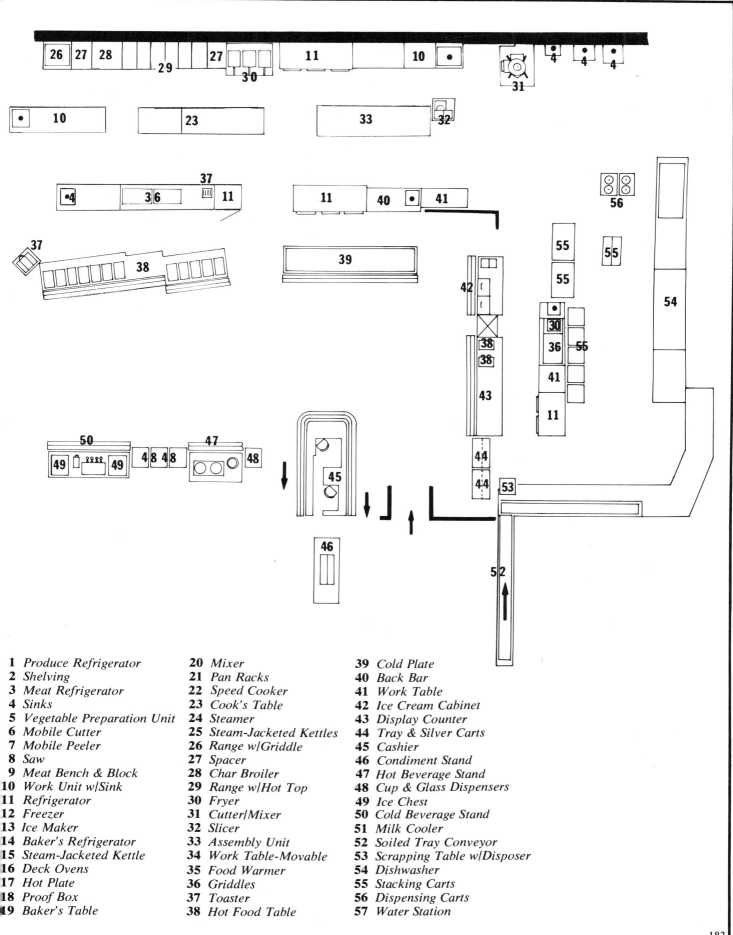

1 Produce Refrigerator
2 Shelving
3 Meat Refrigerator
4 Sinks
5 Vegetable Preparation Unit
6 Mobile Cutter
7 Mobile Peeler
8 Saw
9 Meat Bench & Block
10 Work Unit w/Sink
11 Refrigerator
12 Freezer
13 Ice Maker
14 Baker's Refrigerator
15 Steam-Jacketed Kettle
16 Deck Ovens
17 Hot Plate
18 Proof Box
19 Baker's Table

20 Mixer
21 Pan Racks
22 Speed Cooker
23 Cook's Table
24 Steamer
25 Steam-Jacketed Kettles
26 Range w/Griddle
27 Spacer
28 Char Broiler
29 Range w/Hot Top
30 Fryer
31 Cutter/Mixer
32 Slicer
33 Assembly Unit
34 Work Table-Movable
35 Food Warmer
36 Griddles
37 Toaster
38 Hot Food Table

39 Cold Plate
40 Back Bar
41 Work Table
42 Ice Cream Cabinet
43 Display Counter
44 Tray & Silver Carts
45 Cashier
46 Condiment Stand
47 Hot Beverage Stand
48 Cup & Glass Dispensers
49 Ice Chest
50 Cold Beverage Stand
51 Milk Cooler
52 Soiled Tray Conveyor
53 Scrapping Table w/Disposer
54 Dishwasher
55 Stacking Carts
56 Dispensing Carts
57 Water Station

Hotel/Motel

Jule Wilkinson

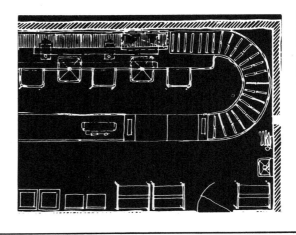

TODAY THE FOODSERVICE operations in a hotel or motor hotel which require the majority of the facility designer's attention are specialty restaurants and coffee shops. Since both types of facilities have been covered in separate chapters (Coffee Shops, *Anatomy of Foodservice Design 1,* pp. 61 to 94 and Specialty Restaurants, this volume, pp. 1 to 70), only basic approaches to new construction are reviewed in this introduction.[1]

A detailed account of a successful program to be used in hotel renovation introduces the section of illustrations which follows. Completing the illustrative material on hotel/motel design are plans from various award-winning facilities.

Among "rules of thumb"[2] suggested by William B. Tabler, architect for many Hilton Hotels, is one well-known to foodservice designers:

The layout . . . especially for the kitchen and dining room accounts for built-in labor costs which are likely to last the life of the building.

Designers recognize that ideally the kitchen should be placed on the same floor as all the hotel/motel dining areas, and preferably with the dining areas located around the kitchen so that food can be produced and served from a single source. However, this cannot be done in many high-rise buildings, especially when land is a major cost. At the New York Hilton, for example, the kitchen and ware washing facilities are located in a central core of the building, extending through six floors and connected by four elevators to each other and to the various restaurants. Continental breakfasts and other room service orders are served from the same elevators.

The core kitchen and ware washing facilities also serve five specialty restaurants and a cocktail lounge. The specialty restaurants include an Italian restaurant, a French restaurant, a Spanish restaurant, a Dutch-style coffee house, an old Bourbon House, and a Near East bar, the Kismet Lounge. Combined with banquet areas, seating capacity is nearly 10,000.

The practice of placing a number of preparation stations side-by-side behind a pick-up counter is used by most commercial kitchens preparing food for a large and complicated menu. The Waldorf-Astoria kitchen, for example, stretches a long distance with station after station placed side-by-side. The waiter enters the kitchen and drops off his order at each station, returning later to pick up the prepared food.

However, Executive Chef Arno Schmidt of the Waldorf-Astoria has evolved a banquet system that permits a banquet for 1,000 to be served in ten minutes using two lines. Parties as large as 6,000 can be served equally speedily at this hotel.

Some kitchens in the larger hotels are immense, the distances walked by the waiters in placing and picking up orders great. Waiters and waitresses in huge American Plan

[1]Much of the material which follows has been excerpted from Donald E. Lundberg, The Hotel and Restaurant Business, (Boston: Cahners Books International, Inc., 1976).
[2]Ibid.

resort hotels before the end of the season develop into potential track stars from the constant running and walking required, and the distances involved.

In most cases, kitchen planning revolves around the amount of space allocated or available for the kitchen. In heart-of-the-city, expensive locations the kitchens are often miniscule, one kitchen employee working almost on the back of another. Surprisingly, small kitchens often turn out to be more efficient than the large ones because of the necessity of planning each work station in detail and the elimination of steps formerly required as foodservice workers moved from station to station, station to storeroom, and within a station. Reducing the size of the menu, in most cases, also improves efficiency.

Where the kitchen is the shape of a square, the kitchen equipment is frequently placed around three walls forming an open square or U. The first station, as the waiter enters the kitchen, is apt to be the dish room; the last station before entering the dining room, the pantry, or coffee and dessert station.

Points of debate in planning a kitchen revolve around whether serving personnel should enter the kitchen, and what they should do if they do enter. Sometimes waiting personnel are scheduled to make salads and toast and do other pantry work. In other operations, management believes the less time the waiting personnel are in the kitchen, the better. In such cases arrangements are made for soiled dishes to be carried into the kitchen via conveyor belt. Another way to move soiled ware is to install a merry-go-round type of dishmachine with part of the rotary rack system extended into the dining room where soiled ware can be directly loaded onto the dishmachine racks.

The answer to the question of how much time waiting personnel should spend in the kitchen is partly determined by the speed of the dining room. If breakfast and lunch are relatively slow, they might be used in the pantry and elsewhere in the kitchen. If there is fast turnover in the dining room, waiting personnel can be more efficiently used there exclusively if they are supported by specialized personnel in the kitchen. A recent trend to buffet breakfast service will affect the number of waiting personnel needed.

To be sure, the number of possible arrangements for a kitchen is so great that two designers would seldom come up with similar plans. Every foodservice designer has a unique approach which is the product of his own observations and experience and which he continues to refine during his career.

The need for the best possible energy management has affected the selection of foodservice equipment in many important ways. Equipment is purchased with particular consideration for the life cycle. Controls are installed which permit energy reduction during the peak load hours when the cost of fuel is highest. For example, ice machines can be purchased that will not be operated during the 5 to 8 p.m. period when there is peak load demand. No hot water need be heated during that period either; instead it can be stored from times when energy cost is less.

Solar Collectors Heat Water

The use of solar collectors to collect heat from the sun and use it in heating the water for hotels and other foodservice was beginning to get serious consideration as early as 1975. Several hotels, especially resort hotels, and motels as well have added collectors which permit a large input of BTUs from the sun and a reduction in the amount of fuel consumed.

For many years it was generally accepted that hotel foodservice was a necessary evil. It was required by hotel guests but was rarely profitable. Two explanations for this are:

Hotelmen were seldom outstanding restaurateurs. The hotel restaurant has traditionally found it difficult to compete with the good restaurant located nearby or one that, even though it is some distance from the hotel, has acquired a culinary reputation. Some restaurant operators say the best location for a restaurant is directly across the street from a major hotel.

Performance in today's hotels and motels no longer supports these arguments. Specialty or theme restaurants now found in many hotels and motels have been much more profitable than the usual dining room and sometimes even do better than coffee shops. In fact, in some of the smaller hotels, the food and beverage operation is the major reason for the existence of the hotel, the rooms being secondary.

The profit potential of specialty restaurants for larger hotels is underscored by the many instances when lobby space has been converted to make room for such restaurants.

The architectural plan for Los Angeles' Century Plaza Hotel inspired a specialty restaurant of great appeal. Designed by Minoru Yamasake, the hotel itself was a landmark in hotel construction in that it created its own environment by including a handsome garden which the lobby and its facilities overlook. Its glass-walled garden restaurant has unique appeal.

In many existing hotels there is a trend to relocate dining room spaces and especially coffee shops so they have direct access to the street. The formal dining room has been out for some time; the specialty room is in. The specialty room is almost always built with access to the street, since patronage from the hotel guests alone will not make it profitable. The cost of transforming dining rooms or other spaces into specialty rooms can be remarkably high.

Space Needed for Foodservice

The Sonesta Hotel has done a number of studies to establish criteria for the allocation of space in a hotel. In foodservice areas they allocate 18 to 20 sq. ft. per seat in a dining room; 15 sq. ft. per seat in a coffee shop; 12 to 15 sq. ft. per seat in banquet facilities. These figures allow 25 to 33 percent of the space for free circulation of service personnel.

These same studies indicate that the kitchen serving a dining room and coffee shop should be about 60 percent of the total area of the dining room and the coffee shop. This indicates that about 10 to 11 sq. ft. should be allowed per seat in these foodservice areas. If there is a coffee shop only, the kitchen should be about 45 percent of the size of the coffee shop serving area, allowing 6¾ sq. ft. per seat. Space allowed for food and beverage storage should be about half that set aside for the kitchen, or about five sq. ft. per seat.

Banquet kitchens, of course, are much smaller; only about one-fifth of the space of the banquet facility is needed for the banquet pantry and only about eight percent of the banquet area is needed for banquet storage.

Often overlooked in planning hotels and motor hotels are the needs of the personnel for eating facilities, lockers, lounge, showers, and similar amenities. Approximately seven sq. ft. should be allotted per guest room in a 100-room property for employee facilities.

In motel planning there must always be room for expansion, up or out. As for square footage, at least 650 sq. ft. are needed per room for a two-story motel; this includes space for the restaurant. Restaurants need between 40 to 60 sq. ft. per person, including parking space and 100 ft. of frontage. One experienced chain with a high rate of success recommends having one parking space for every 2½ seats in the restaurant. Thus, a 100-seat restaurant needs about 40 parking spaces.

Hotel/motel foodservice has become important to successful booking of the package tours which have lately been successfully introduced. Packages including travel, food, and lodging are sold largely by travel agencies. Nearly every large hotel has a marketing department headed by a director of sales, regional salespersons, and often a director of conventions and tours.

The real impact of group business did not hit American hotels until the 1950s. By the late 1960s, most of the large downtown hotels were getting at least 40 percent of their business from conventions and corporate meetings. Some hotels get as much as 90 percent of their business from this sector.

Food Key to Convention Business

Conventioneering means big money to hotels. The average delegate to a national convention makes a considerable investment in lodging, food, car rental, and entertainment. What makes conventioning even more interesting to hotelmen is that conventions can often be scheduled to fill low occupancy periods, weekends, and off-seasons. Once a convention has checked in, most of the guests take most of their meals in the hotel.

This avenue of profit has resulted in ever greater emphasis on the importance of foodservice in the total effort to expand the hotel/motel profit potential.   Ed. Note

Hotel/motel foodservice facilities that score today are specialty restaurants and coffee shops whether plans are for new construction or renovation. Using input tested in successful renovation of over-age hotel foodservice facilities assures that plan is suited to market and space and that new unit will operate at a profit.

Sheraton-Boston Hotel

Rehabilitation assignments constitute less than ten percent of a professional foodservice consultant's projects since foodservice planners have historically been associated with new kitchens in new buildings. Our present economy has discouraged new construction, and many foodservice consultants are feeling the effects of this depressed market. Rehabilitation of existing foodservice installations opens up a brand new market.

The consulting field at this time should concentrate its efforts on developing and educating this market to the urgent need of professional help since renovation in varying degrees is needed in over 90 percent of the kitchens in schools, hospitals, and restaurants, in addition to hotels. In fact, the majority of foodservice installations over ten years

old require some planning and equipment evaluation.

Rehabilitation is an investment that will pay foodservice operators high dividends in utility, labor, insurance, maintenance, and, oftentimes, in reduced costs for space. Feasibility studies consistently indicate that rehabilitation investments pay for themselves in less than two years and after that continue to add to profits.

Rehabilitation also presents an opportunity to upgrade sanitation standards. One may ask, "What is sanitation worth?" The answer may well be "What is an outbreak of food poisoning worth?"

As this account of the process shows, as applied to the Sheraton Boston Hotel dining room, rehabilitation planning is initiated in the field rather than on

the drafting board. Existing electric loads, mechanical routings, exhaust capacities, equipment accessibility, layout, and construction characteristics must be analyzed at the site and put in balance with well-defined operating criteria.

This analysis is like "panning for gold"—an unused duct chase could be converted to a revenue-producing area. A change in prime cooking fuels can achieve greater efficiency. Resurfacing a floor area can prevent accidents. New equipment placements can improve service and controls; the potential for profitable discoveries is unlimited.

At the Sheraton Boston Hotel, the reconstruction had to be completed within 30 days. Good planning and excellent contractor participation brought it about as scheduled.

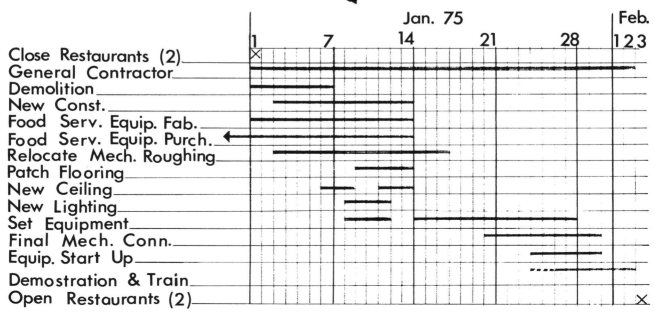

1 MONTH REHAB. SCHED.
MISSION IMPOSSIBLE

FIG. 45—OPERATIONAL CRITERIA CHECKLIST FOR HOTEL KITCHEN REHABILITATION

Project _____ Date _____

_____ Job No. _____

Copy _____

_____

Food and/or Beverage Rooms

type	no. seats service	menu information
A.		
B.		
C.		
D.		
E.		
F.		
G.		

1.	Butcher Shop	yes ☐	no ☐
2.	Bake Shop	yes ☐	no ☐
3.	Pastry Shop	yes ☐	no ☐
4.	Room Service	yes ☐	no ☐
5.	Employee Cafeteria	yes ☐	no ☐
6.	Need for Food Checker	yes ☐	no ☐
7.	Kitchen Service Bar (liquor)	yes ☐	no ☐
8.	Chef's Office	yes ☐	no ☐
9.	Silver Burnishing	yes ☐	no ☐
10.	Special Provisions ? (sea food)	yes ☐	no ☐
11.	Dairy Products—available	yes ☐	no ☐
12.	Draft Beer Dispensing	yes ☐	no ☐
13.	Wine Service	yes ☐	no ☐
14.	Ice Cream	make ☐	buy ☐
15.	Ice Capacities	cubes _____ #	flakes _____ #

16. Attach Market Food Survey (if available)

17. Food Deliveries   good ☐   fair ☐   poor ☐

18. Any Special Liquor Restrictions   yes ☐   no ☐
    - Comment _____

19. Attach Info on Labor Market (if available)

20. Public Area Cooking/Prep.   yes ☐   no ☐
    - Specify Type _____

21. Convenience Foods - use -   yes ☐   no ☐
    - comment _____

Remarks:

_____

FIG. 46—MECHANICAL CRITERIA CHECKLIST FOR HOTEL KITCHEN REHABILITATION

Project _____ Date _____

_____ Job No. _____

_____

Copy _____

_____

No.	Item			

1. Prime Cooking Fuel   Gas ☐   Electric ☐
2. Electric ____/____ volts ____ phase _____ cycle _____
3. Gas   yes ☐   no ☐   type _____
4. Steam   yes ☐   no ☐   pressure _____
5. Cooling Tower   yes ☐   no ☐
6. Refrigeration   air cooled ☐   water cooled ☐
7. Hot Water temperature ____°F or ____°C
8. Comments on any unusual mechanical characteristics _____

_____

9. Fire Extng. Equip. Co^2 ☐   steam ☐   dry chemicals ☐
10. Garbage Disposals   yes ☐   no ☐
11. Garbage Refrigerator   yes ☐   no ☐
12. Incinerator   yes ☐   no ☐
13. Compactor   yes ☐   no ☐
14. Bottles   store ☐   crush ☐   dispose ☐
15. Construction of walls _____ Clg. _____ Flr. _____
16. Ceiling Ht. ____ feet ____ inches
17. Elevator Size ___ wide ____ depth
18. Approving local authorities _____

_____

19. Architect _____ Phone _____
     Address _____
20. Engineer _____ Phone _____
     Address _____
21. General Status of Project on Date of This Questionnaire _____

_____

Remarks

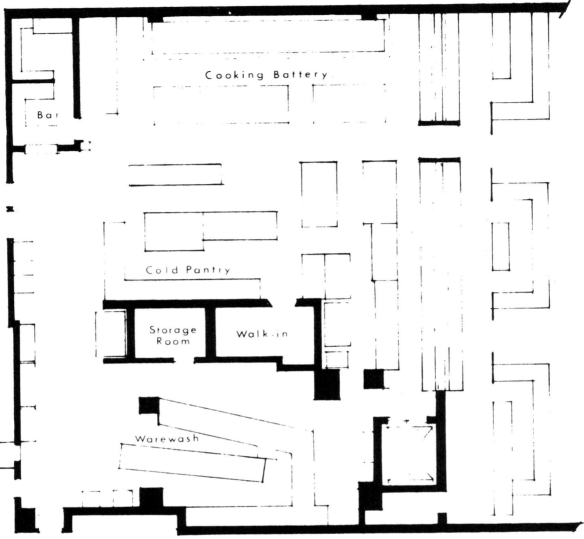

Sheraton-Boston Hotel continued

Ten years might seem a short life for an average kitchen installation, but when the area is serving a million and a half meals annually, the foodservice equipment sees a lot of wear. This explains why the Sheraton-Boston Hotel completely renovated its second floor kitchen which serves both the 180-seat Falstaff Room, an Old English chop and steak house, and the 250-seat Pavilion coffee shop. The emphasis in design for the new kitchen was on more modern equipment and more efficient service.

Energy conservation controls and improved safeguards against fire and air pollution were other factors that made the new installation advantageous. A 50 percent increase in guest rooms resulting from the addition of a new tower would also soon require more than the 4,500 meals a day averaged previously in the two installations.

The modernization of the hotel's original kitchens and service pantries was planned to improve dining service, sanitation, maintenance, fuel conservation, employees' environment, and safety.

In the renovated kitchen the equipment layout was planned with both production and food pick-up circulation as a keynote to the design. Customers in the Pavilion can readily see one piece of new equipment—a glass door pass-thru refrigerator. Besides being good merchandising, the display refrigerator permits pre-plating of desserts and salads.

Guests cannot see, but will appreciate because it prevents air pollution, the new high-velocity cooking exhaust system, which eliminates the necessity of washing and replacing filters. The exhaust hood is sprayed with a detergent internally, and dangerous grease is washed out of the exhaust with a minimal use of

water—a push-button washdown that is a maximum safeguard against fire.

The cooking battery is designed with a new short order station and has been expanded to include microwave and convection oven equipment. A walkway has been provided behind the cooking battery to allow access for cleaning.

The warewashing facilities have been completely renewed with an automatic conveyorized system. Parts of the system include food refuse disposer flushing, silver soaking, sorting areas, and automatic detergent injectors.

One of the simplest of the energy conservation innovations in the kitchen installation was the invention of the Sheraton-Boston's chief engineer. The battery of heat lamps has an individual micro-switch turn-on for each lamp; whenever a plate is set on a stainless steel arm under the lamp, it flicks on.

AFTER REHABILITATION

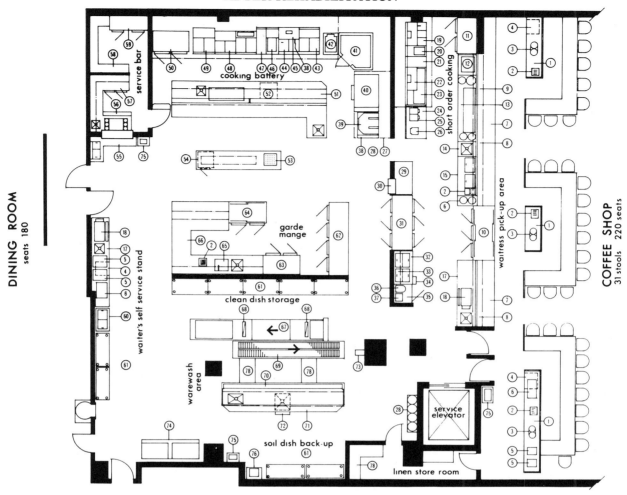

Designed by: Group One, Inc.

DESIGN CRITERIA

Improve Traffic Pattern to Warewash

Provide Short Order for Coffee Shop

Rehabilitate Portion of Existing Equipment

Provide New Equipment Only

Provide New Water Wash Exhaust Equipment

Install Corner Guards

Patch Walls and Floors

New Lighting and Ceilings

New Disposal System

New Warewashing Equipment

New Fire Protection System

Up Grade All Service Stations

Open Up Area, Remove Obstructing Partitions

Provide New Access Doors from Coffee Shop

All New Mechanical Systems and Controls

EQUIPMENT LIST

1. Waitress Serv. Std.
2. Toasters
3. Coffee Warmers
4. Roll Warmers
5. Beverage Disp.
6. Milk Disp.
7. Waitress Sto. Counters
8. Waitress Pass Shelves
9. Heat Lamps
10. Pass Thru Refrig.
11. Refrig.
12. Microwave Oven
13. Steam Table
14. Sink
15. Sandwich Unit
16. Portable Self-leveling Dispensers
17. Utility Counter
18. Coffee Urns
19. Range
20. Fryer
21. Portable Spreader
22. Salamander Broiler
23. Griddle
24. Work Table
25. Waffle Maker
26. Sandwich Press
27. Exhaust Ventilators
28. Fire Protection System
29. Work Table
30. Pass Shelf
31. Pass Thru Refrig.
32. Ice Cream Cab.
33. Syrup Rail
34. Scoop Sink
35. Freezer
36. Frappe Mixer
37. Hot Syrup Disp.
38. Water Filler
39. Braising Pan
40. Convection Oven
41. Corner Refrig.
42. Steamer
43. Range
44. Range
45. Salamander Broilers
46. Fryer
47. Portable Spreader
48. Ranges
49. Broiler
50. Refrigerator
51. Chef's Table
52. Refrigerator
53. Make-Up Table
54. Refrigerator
55. Waitress Liquor Make
56. Cocktail Station
57. Refrigerator
58. Storage Shelving
59. Refrigerator
60. Ice Carts
61. Portable Trucks
62. Refrigerator
63. Freezer
64. Pass Thru Refrig.
65. Slicer
66. Cold Service Disp. Center
67. Dish-washing Mach.
68. Exhaust Ducts
69. Feed Back Conveyor
70. Garbage Trough
71. Soil Dish Table
72. Silver Soak Sink
73. Hose Reel
74. Ice Machines
75. Hand Sinks
76. Janitor's Sink
77. Shelving
78. Sliding Bridges

MODERNIZED SHORT ORDER PANTRY

Arrow on plan at right points to pass-thru refrigerator in full view of Pavilion patrons at the Sheraton Boston Hotel. It merchandises salad and dessert specialties and also permits pre-plating of these items, for holding under optimal sanitation conditions. The pass-thrus are pictured above from the kitchen side showing a portable self-leveling plate dispenser positioned to speed the replacement of the pass-thru's contents. Note warewashing changes on facing page.

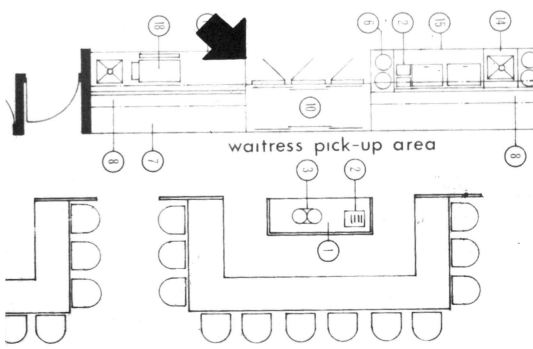

waitress pick-up area

NEW WAREWASHING

Conveyorized

Sorting

Scrapping

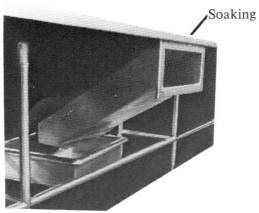

Soaking

Dearborn Inn

The Dearborn Inn, Greenfield Village, serves 8500 meals per week from its recently remodeled kitchen. The Inn carries out the Early American theme of the restoration which is adjacent to it. Dining areas, including banquet rooms, can seat 900.

EQUIPMENT LIST

1. Pot Sinks
2. Disposer
3. Soiled Pot Rack
4. Clean Pot Rack
5. Vegetable Peeler
6. Vegetable Prep. Sinks
7. Disposer
8. Mobile Cutter Stand
9. Food Cutter (Existing)
10. Mobile Slicer Stand
11. Slicer (Existing)
12. Cutting Board Top Table
13. Mixer Attachment Rack
14. Mobile Work Tables
15. 60-qt. Mixer
16. Open No.
17. Hand Sink
18. Crushed Ice Machine
19. Salad Plating Table w/Ice Pan
20. Mobile Plate Dispenser
21. Waitress Pick-Up Counter
22. Undercounter Refrigerator
23. Salad Dressing Pans
24. Pass-Thru Refrigerator
25. Refrigerator (Existing)
26. Dessert Refrigerator (Existing)
27. Refrigerated Cold Pan
28. Open No.
29. Open No.
30. Open No.
31. Freezer
32. Refrigerator
33. Refrigerator
34. Refrigerated Fish File
35. Broiler (Double)
36. Work Table w/Sink
37. Convection Oven (Two-Deck)
38. Special Floor Drain
39. Tilting Braising Pan
40. Kettle Stand
41. 20-qt. Kettles
42. Undercounter Food Warmer
43. Work Table
44. 40-gal. Kettles
45. Work Table
46. Kettle Filler Stanchion
47. Utility Supply Raceway
48. Exhaust Hood
49. Fry Top Range
50. Salamander Broiler
51. Hot Top Range w/Oven
52. Undercounter Refrigerator
53. Hot Food Wells
54. Open No.
55. Undercounter Refrigerator
56. Open No.
57. Deep Fat Fryer
58. Bain-Marie
59. Spreader
60. Steamer (3-Deck) w/Generator
61. Undercounter Freezer
62. High Pressure Steamer
63. Banquet Carts (Existing)
64. Soup Wells
65. Soup Cup Dispenser
66. Heated Plate Cabinet
67. Heat Lamps
68. Plate Cover Dispensers
69. Hot Food Pick-Up Table
70. Bar Cash Register (Existing)
71. Pot Hanger Racks (Not Shown)
72. Refrigerated Garnish Stand
73. Glass Dispenser
74. Beverage Stand
75. Milk Dispenser (By Owner)
76. Iced Tea Dispenser (By Owner)
77. Portable Ice Bin
78. Open No.
79. Coffee Urn
80. Roll Warmer
81. Plate Dispensers
82. Dipperwell
83. Ice Cream Freezer (By Owner)
84. Milk Shake Machine
85. Open No.
86. Bus Box Racks
87. Dishmachine (Existing)
88. Disposer
89. Bus Box Rests (Removable)
90. Soak Sink (Portable)
91. Open No.
92. Open No.
93. Open No.
94. Open No.
95. Open No.
96. Open No.
97. Open No.
98. Open No.
99. Trash Can Washer (Existing)
100. Compactor (By Owner)
101. Open No.
102. Roll-In Refrigerator
103. Cooling Rack
104. Proofing Box
105. Exhaust Hood
106. Oven w/Steam Injection
107. Baker's Stove (Existing)
108. Special Floor Drain
109. 20-gal. Kettle (Existing)
110. Sink
111. Work Table
112. Baker's Table
113. Ingredient Bins
114. Mixer (20-qt.) Existing
115. Freezer
116. Roll Cutter
117. 80-qt. Mixer (Existing)

Designed by: Ron Kooser, Cini Grissom Associates, Inc.

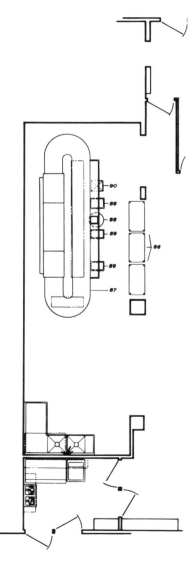

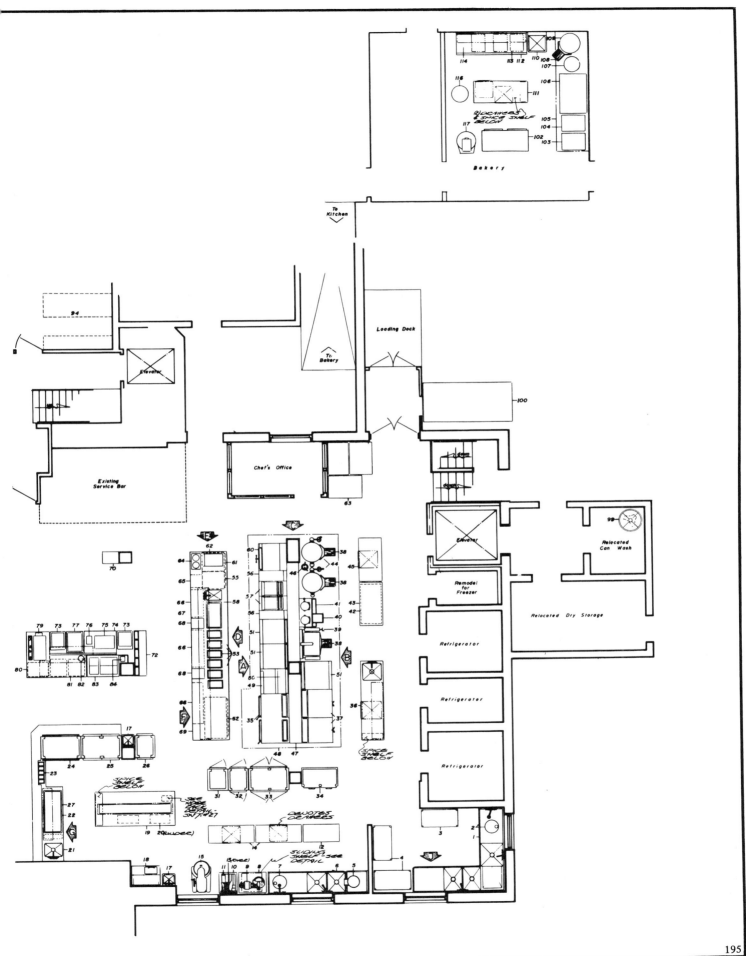

Stouffer's Denver Inn

Stouffer's Denver Inn, located adjacent to the airport, is noted for the high breakfast volume in its 380-seat dining room. There are additional banquet facilities for 550. It is a total franchise operated by Aircoa.

Designed by: Ron Kooser, Cini Grissom Associates, Inc.

EQUIPMENT LIST

1. Roll Warmers
2. Bread, Rolls Counter
3. Bread Plate Dispenser
4. Soup Bowl Dispenser
5. Heated Soup Wells
6. Drainer Trough
7. Milk Dispenser
8. Counter
9. Glass Dispenser
10. Open No.
11. Open No.
12. Iced Tea Dispenser
13. Ice Bin
14. Beverage Counter
15. Water Glass Filler
16. Juice Dispenser
17. Cup and Saucer Dispenser
18. Open No.
19. Coffee Counter
20. Open No.
21. Open No.
22. Drip Trough
23. Coffee Urn
24. Refrigerator
25. Service Counter
26. Heat Lamp
27. Entree Plate Dispenser
28. Heated Food Wells
29. Plate Dispenser
30. Open No.
31. Open No.
32. Bain-Marie
33. Open No.
34. Salad Dressing Pans
35. Overcounter Refrigerator
36. Refrigerated Cold Pan
37. Cutting Board
38. Toaster
39. Refrigerated Sandwich Pans
40. Open No.
41. Heat Lamp
42. Microwave Oven
43. Ice Cream Cabinet
44. Dipperwell
45. Dessert Table
46. Refrigerator

47. Steam Cooker, Stand, and Generator
48. Spreader
49. Deep Fat Fryers
50. Open No.
51. Open No.
52. Combination Cook Top Range
53. Exhaust Hood
54. Fry Top Range
55. Charbroiler
56. Open.No.
57. Broiler
58. Tilting Fry Pan
59. Drainer Trough
60. Open No.
61. Mobile Racks
62. Mobile Work Table
63. Exhaust Hood
64. Mobile Convection Ovens
65. 20-qt. Kettles
66. 40-gal. Kettles
67. Work Table w/Sink
68. 3-Compt. Steamer & Generator
69. 60-qt. Mixer
70. Open No.
71. Open No.
72. Slicer
73. Portable Stand
74. 20-qt. Mixer
75. Food Cutter
76. Work Table
77. Stand
78. Disposer
79. Dishmachine
80. Open No.
81. Open No.
82. Booster Heater
83. Hose Station
84. Silver Sorting Table
85. Dishroom Shelving
86. Disposer
87. Pot Sinks
88. Pot Racks
89. Pot Sink Heater
90. Open No.
91. Vegetable Disposer

92. Vegetable Prep. Table
93. Open No.
94. Open No.
95. Open No.
96. Work Table w/Sink
97. Cube/Flaked Ice Bin
98. Flaked Ice Maker
99. Cube Ice Maker
100. Banquet Carts
101. Exhaust Hood
102. Plate Dispenser
103. Set-Up Table
104. Work Tables (Mobile)
105. Hand Sinks
106. Vegetable Cooler
107. Refrigerator Shelving
108. Mobile Racks
109. Refrigeration System
110. Open No.
111. Open No.
112. Storeroom Shelving
113. Pallets
114. Liquor Storage Shelving
115. Linen Storage Shelving
116. Receiving Scales
117. Time Clock
118. Open No.
119. Freezer
120. Room Service Carts
121. Mop Sink
122. Pallets
123. Freezer
124. Refrigeration System
125. Meat Cooler
126. Refrigerator Shelving
127. Refrigeration System
128. Beer Cooler
129. Refrigeration System
130. Cashier Stand
131. Room Service Desk
132. Office Furniture
133. Fire Protection Systems
134. Room Floor Ice Machines (Not Shown)

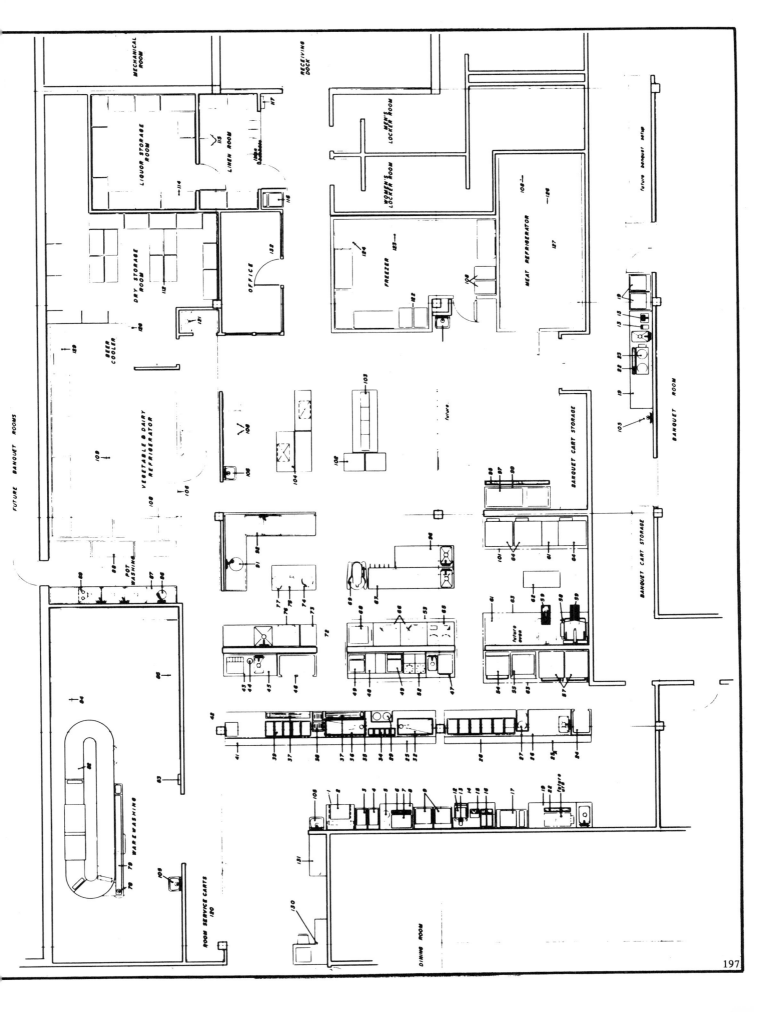

197

The Marriott Inn, Blacksburg, Va.

Designed by: Cini Grissom Associates, Inc.

EQUIPMENT LIST

1. Mop Sink
2. Receiving Table
3. Scale
4. Walk-in Refrigerator/Freezer
5. Refrigerator Refrigeration System
6. Freezer Refrigeration System
7. Mobile Shelf Units
8. Mobile Tray Racks
9. Storeroom Shelf Units
10. Woven Wire Partition
11. Floor Grate
12. Cube Ice Machine
13. Ice Bin
14. Flake Ice Machine
15. Flexible Hose Glass Filler
16. Mobile Cart
17. Mobile Glass Dispenser
18. Mobile Heated Server
19. Equipment Table with Sink
20. Dunnage Shelving
21. Coffee Maker
22. Banquet Plating Table
23. Slicer
24. Mobile Equipment Table
25. Mobile Bin
26. Worktable with Sink & Shelf Over
27. Disposer
28. Two Compartment Sink & Worktable w/Shelf
29. Twenty Quart Mixer
30. Hand Sink
31. Worktable with Sink & Shelf
32. Two Compartment Steamer
33. Even Heat Top Range
34. Equipment Table
35. Fryer
36. Convection Oven
37. Deck Oven
38. Exhaust Ventilator
39. Exhaust Ventilator
40. Fat Filter
41. Reach-in Refrigerator
42. Reach-in Refrigerator/Freezer
43. Broiler
44. Equipment Table
45. Fryers
46. Microwave Oven
47. Griddle with Oven
48. Salamander
49. Heat Top Range with Oven
50. Equipment Table
51. High Pressure Steamer & Generator
52. Waffle Baker
53. Sandwich Grill
54. Hand Sink
55. Ice Cream Cabinet with Sink & Dipper Well
56. Overshelf
57. Shake Mixer
58. Reach-in Refrigerator
59. Pass-Through Refrigerator
60. Toaster
61. Hot and Cold Food Pick-up Counter
62. Carbon Dioxide Tanks
63. Soda Factory
64. Mobile Ice Bin
65. Overshelf
66. Tea Dispenser
67. Soda Dispenser
68. Pot Rack (Ceiling Mounted)
69. Overshelf
70. Beverage Counter
71. Butter Dispenser
72. Conveyor Toaster
73. Reach-in Refrigerator
74. Dual Temperature Refrigerator
75. Cashier Counter
76. Soiled Dish Table
77. Water Cooler
78. Pot Washing Unit
79. Pot Washing Sink
80. Mobile Pot Rack
81. Overshelf
82. Silver Burnisher
83. Mobile Dish Cart
84. Clean Dish Table
85. Rack Dolly
86. Booster Heater
87. Hose Station
88. Silver Soak Sink
89. Exhaust Duct Riser
90. Dishwashing Machine
91. Pre-rinse Spray Nozzle
92. Disposer
93. Linen Cabinets
94. Bar
95. Beer Storage Refrigerator
96. Sinks, Drainboard, & Cocktail Station
97. Soap Dispenser
98. Glass Froster
99. Cash Register
100. Drink Mixer
101. Blender
102. Portable Ice Bin

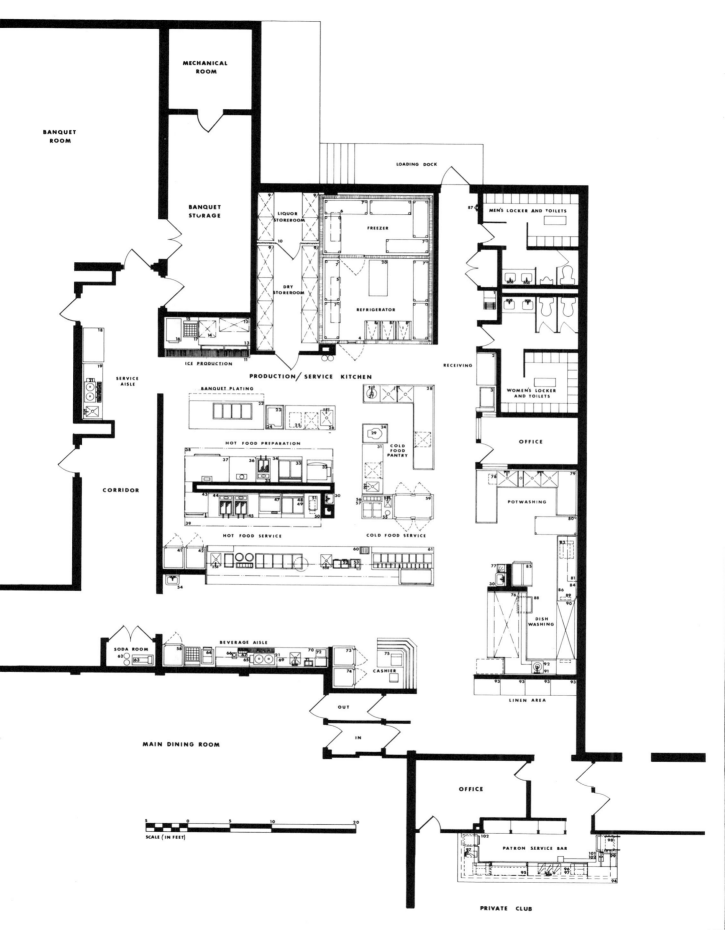

MECHANICAL
ROOM

BANQUET
ROOM

BANQUET
STORAGE

LIQUOR
STOREROOM

DRY
STOREROOM

LOADING DOCK

FREEZER

REFRIGERATOR

MEN'S LOCKER AND TOILETS

WOMEN'S LOCKER
AND TOILETS

OFFICE

ICE PRODUCTION

RECEIVING

SERVICE
AISLE

PRODUCTION / SERVICE KITCHEN

CORRIDOR

BANQUET PLATING

HOT FOOD PREPARATION

COLD
FOOD
PANTRY

POTWASHING

HOT FOOD SERVICE

COLD FOOD SERVICE

DISH
WASHING

SODA ROOM

BEVERAGE AISLE

CASHIER

LINEN AREA

MAIN DINING ROOM

OUT

IN

OFFICE

SCALE (IN FEET)

PATRON SERVICE BAR

PRIVATE CLUB

The Holiday Inn, Bethesda, Md.

EQUIPMENT LIST

1. Hot Food Counter
2. Microwave Oven
3. Refrigerator
4. Freezer
5. Sink
6. Plate Dispensers
7. Toaster
8. Cold Food Counter
9. Cutting Boards
10. Refrigerator
11. Ice Cream Cabinet
12. Worktable
13. Dipperwell
14. Ventilator
15. Broiler
16. Spreader
17. Fryer
18. Spreader
19. Salamander
20. Ranges
21. Refrigerator
22. Tilting Fry Pan
23. Kettle
24. Steamer
25. Range
26. Convection Oven
27. Bake Oven
28. Shellfish Preparation
29. Hand Lavatory
30. Mobile Table
31. Slicer
32. Mixer
33. Vegetable Cutter
34. Worktable
35. Preparation Sink
36. Disposer
37. Walk-In Refrigerator/ Freezer
38. Refrigeration Systems
39. Refrigerator Shelving
40. Mobile Racks
41. Mixer
42. Utensil Rack
43. Proof Box
44. Worktable
45. Utility Sink
46. Pot Washing Sink
47. Clean Pot Rack
48. Clean Dishtable
49. Silver Burnisher
50. Booster Heater
51. Dishmachine
52. Soiled Dish Table
53. Disposer
54. Beverage Table
55. Coffee Urn
56. Cup and Saucer Dispenser
57. Glass Dispenser
58. Ice Bin
59. Iced Tea Dispenser
60. Soup Station
61. Roll Warmer
62. Overshelf Unit
63. Plating Tables
64. Ice Machines
65. Ice Bin
66. Soda System
67. Storage Shelves
68. Wine Refrigerator
69. Shelving Units
70. Refrigeration Systems
71. Soiled Dish Table
72. Dishmachine
73. Clean Dish Table
74. Refrigerator
75. Ventilator
76. Range
77. Oven
78. Broiler
79. Worktable
80. Walk-In Refrigerator
81. Shelving Units
82. Refrigeration System
83. Slicer
84. Mobile Table
85. Service Counter
86. Pot Washing Sink
87. Work Table
88. Ice Bin
89. Service Tables
90. Bar Top
91. Underbar Equipment
92. Ice Chest
93. Liquor Storage Units
94. Refrigerator
95. Cash Register

Designed by: Cini Grissom Associates, Inc.

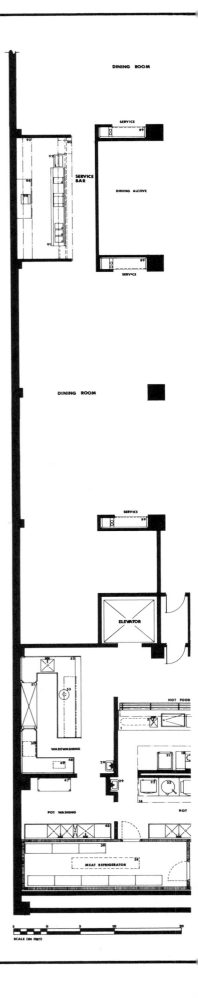

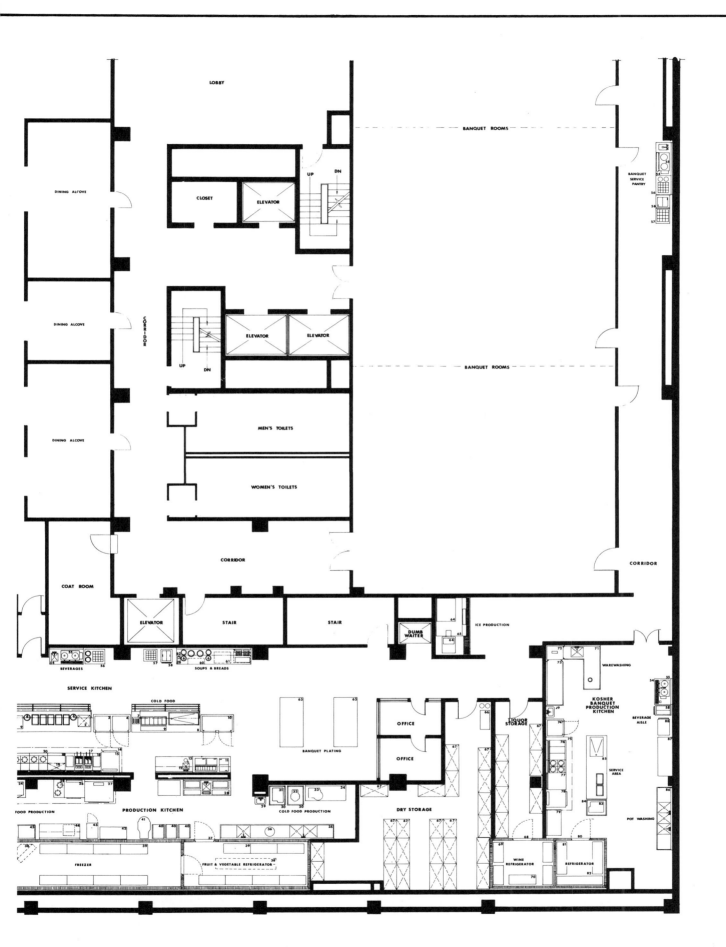

LOBBY

BANQUET ROOMS

DINING ALCOVE

CLOSET

ELEVATOR

UP   DN

BANQUET SERVICE PANTRY

56
58
57

DINING ALCOVE

CORRIDOR

ELEVATOR   ELEVATOR

UP   DN

BANQUET ROOMS

DINING ALCOVE

MEN'S TOILETS

WOMEN'S TOILETS

CORRIDOR

CORRIDOR

COAT ROOM

ELEVATOR

STAIR

STAIR

DUMB WAITER

64

ICE PRODUCTION

65

64

BEVERAGES

56

57   58

SOUPS & BREADS

WAREWASHING

72   71

73

74

KOSHER BANQUET PRODUCTION KITCHEN

54

BEVERAGE AISLE

58

88

SERVICE KITCHEN

COLD FOOD

63

63

OFFICE

LIQUOR STORAGE

67   75

76

SERVICE AREA

65

87

BANQUET PLATING

OFFICE

66

FOOD PRODUCTION

PRODUCTION KITCHEN

COLD FOOD PRODUCTION

34

67

67

DRY STORAGE

84

83

79

86

POT WASHING

FREEZER

41

40   40   40

37

39

39

FRUIT & VEGETABLE REFRIGERATOR

67   67   67

68

69

WINE REFRIGERATOR

70

80

81

REFRIGERATOR

82

201

Popponesset Inn New Seabury, Mass.

This hotel restaurant located in New Seabury, Massachusetts, a resort area, serves 3,675 meals per week. It has 176 seats.

All equipment was designed to accommodate unification of pan sizes which simplifies food handling, storage, and dispensing.

This is a remodeled kitchen so the cooking battery was designed around structural columns.

The pastry shop was planned to produce goods for other restaurants beside this one.

Labor-saving design includes a unique waitress check rack that runs the entire length of the pass-thru shelf; it has ball bearing grippers that eliminate need for wire check hooks; the underbar "designed for action" has beverage cooler, ice machine, glass washing machine, hot water booster, and carbonated beverage dispensers.

Designed by: Charles Wood, Group One Inc.

EQUIPMENT LIST

1. Cold storage rooms
2. Refrigeration systems
3. Soiled dish conveyor
4. Bridge
5. Waste disposer
6. Soiled dish table
7. Tray dispenser
8. Table
9. Booster heater
10. Sink heater
11. Dish machine
12. Pot rack
13. Table
14. Pot sink
15. Waste disposer
16. Cold storage shelving
17. Racks
18. Dry storage shelving
19. Glass rack dollied
20. Table
21. Table
22. Mixer
23. Waste disposer
24. Table
25. Table
26. Heat Lamps
27. Table
28. Slicer Stand
29. Dish cart
30. Table
31. Table
32. Reach-in refrigerator
33. Bowl and Stand
34. Table
35. Table
36. Mixer
37. Reach-In refrigerator
38. Ice-cream cabinet
39. Silva cart
40. Water station Saver dispenser
41. Coffee maker
42. Tea dispenser
43. Coffee Warmer
44. Roll Warmer
45. Roll-In refrigerator
46. Reach-In refrigerator

Appendix

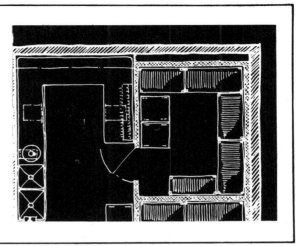

'DON'T FORGET' TIPS FOR FACILITY PLANNING DESIGN

This checklist of planning details can help eliminate problems from oversights or errors.

By Paul R. Broten

Adequate food facilities planning involves thousands of details. These details cannot be neglected if the facility is to be truly successful.

In order to reduce the high costs of construction loans by reducing construction time, many specifications and drawings are often slashed to the barest minimum, or even sacrificed completely. Unfortunately, details that are out of sight can easily become out of mind.

The following checklist of design reminders has been developed over the past 20 years in an effort to eliminate some of the mistakes or errors of omission which occur so frequently in today's new projects.

ARCHITECTURAL ITEMS

Parking
□ Guests·
□ Employees: Any likelihood of change in public transit capabilities in near future?
□ Service help (telephone, refrigerator repair, catering trucks, courtesy vehicles, etc.).

Receiving
□ Is dock adequate? Correct height? Hydraulic dock levelers? Bumpers?
□ Timekeeper or gate guard? Visibility for ingress & egress of all employees and service personnel. Time clock punch-in/punch-out visibility. Easy access to personnel office or hiring office.

□ Linear access to elevators? Can trucks, etc. go in easily without sharp turns required by corridors, aisles, etc.?
□ Queuing and turn around area for delivery trucks.
□ Compactor feed and discharge area adequate with minimal interference to incoming traffic flow.
□ Are dock ingress/egress doors at least 60″ wide double doors? Swing in direction not to impede traffic?
□ 24-hour lighting and all-year weather protection.
□ Is area sufficiently remote from guest entrance to minimize noise, insect, and odor problems often attendant at receiving activities?

Guest/Customer Entrances
□ Aesthetics, appearance: day/night; winter/summer. What is the guest's "first impression?"
□ Any temporary parking for discharge of guests? Car hops? Doorman station? Taxi call? Weather and wind protection? Ease of opening doors?
□ Exterior menu display. Illuminated? Other notices? Any community, civic or other bulletin board notices? Where?
□ Credit card and trade association decals: where mounted? Good visibility? Jeopardize exterior decor in any way?
□ Queuing and waiting spaces adequate? Easy access to lounges, beverage service, restrooms, phones?

Provision for future expansion of facilities? Master plan?

GENERAL KITCHEN ITEMS FREQUENTLY OMITTED

□ Fire extinguishing provisions: Steam or CO_2 in ducts. Sprinklers. CO_2 extinguisher stations (space for same) throughout kitchen.
□ Steam jacketed kettles and coffee urns to bear tag showing factory test according to ASME and local codes.
□ Ladder for coffee re-pour (or similar provision if not automatic re-pour).
□ Ice making and storage.
□ Thermometers on or in refrigerators.
□ Rack return in dishwashing pantry.
□ Portable tables and/or sinks for use with attachments for large mixing machines.
□ Overhead utensil and pot storage racks.
□ Steamer basket storage adjacent to vegetable preparation stations (possibly portable).
□ Cutlery storage for chef's knives (locked).
□ Cutlery sharpening equipment and space.
□ Duckboards or vinyl matting (link type).
□ Storage for attachments adjacent to mixing machines.
□ Tape music in kitchen areas? Monitor for P.A. system(s) desired?
□ Water filters (if required), with locations for same.
□ Gas cock in bake shop for Baked Alaska, etc.
□ Hose connection in dish pantry and garbage raking and can areas.

☐ Water stations (flexible hose pot filler or similar) by ranges, steam jacketed kettles, mixers, etc.

☐ Steam hose by garbage can washer. Steam outlet for hose by ranges, fryers, etc. for cleaning. Duct cleaning?

☐ Key cabinet (locked) in chef's or steward's office for refrigerators, storeroom, bar storage keys. Master key system?

☐ Portable insulated containers. Other catering equipment?

☐ Any carry-out or catering service? Storage for disposables of all types?

☐ Vending machines and space for same. Including cigarettes, newspapers, stamps, etc., as well as normal food and beverage type. Cigar and cigarette storage humidor?

☐ Any legs on equipment? Supplied as accessories?

☐ Chase for remote refrigeration lines supplied inside garde manger and similar counters? Adequate in size?

☐ Flower storage for functions?

☐ Cash register, checking and credit card machines, etc., location (especially in bars, guest areas). Comply with local regulations for guest visibility?

☐ Rinse injector, detergent dispensers on dish machines. Who supplies, installs, etc? Provision made for same? Especially if remote from machine area. (Plumbing, electrical)?

☐ Extra spare parts ordered plus necessary overages for future replacement items (e.g., light fixtures [lenses or globes], tiles, carpets, draperies, etc., especially items which may become obsolete patterns, etc.).

☐ Equipment has union, UL, and NSF labels?

☐ Are sufficient books of line cuts (installation drawings) being supplied for use by all trades? Specified?

☐ Can openers located, specified? Portable?

☐ Padlocks for refrigerators to be master-keyed?

☐ Napkin steamer desired?

☐ Bottle breaking and cull disposal.

☐ Can iced tea and iced coffee service be handled year around? Space sufficient?

☐ Are tray sizes modulated for economy and interchangeability in trucks, refrigerators, elevators, dumbwaiters, shelving?

☐ Cutting boards, 2″ sectional maple or NSF approved. In consumables *or* in equipment specifications (not omitted in both)?

☐ Scales: Receiving scales (more than one type required)? Portion scales required for slicer, etc.? Adequate protection so carts don't strike and damage vertical elements? Membrane waterproofing below floor level scales?

☐ Storage space provided near dishwashing dispenser area for detergents, rinse injection materials, cleaning, soaking compounds?

☐ Will wine racks accept odd-sized bottles (e.g., Mateus, Lancer, Jeroboams, etc.)?

☐ Where do waiters/waitresses station themselves in non-busy periods? Station visibility? Secondary chore requirements on station, etc.

Operational Provisions

☐ Space for remote condensing units for refrigerators provided?

☐ Any raised bases for condensing units?

☐ Space for remote carbonator for soda fountain? CO_2 bottle storage adjacent?

☐ High chair or junior chair storage (closet)? Cushions or raised seats for conventional chairs. How cleaned?

☐ Table storage (banquets, etc.)?

☐ Adequate parking within service spaces for portable equipment (hand trucks, etc.)?

☐ Are hand trucks, dollies (including room service equipment), etc. in kitchen equipment contract. Adequate inventory called for?

☐ Any portable bars? Where stored?

☐ Portable equipment storage. Temporary: in use where? Long term: How cleaned? Where?

☐ Tray stand (portable) storage space?

☐ Janitor closet? Sink, mops, brooms, snow shovels, tiki torches, etc.

☐ Any equipment on raised bases (masonry, tile, etc.)? Has base diagram been provided?

☐ Any drip pans or curbs? Stock kettles. Steamers. Potato peeler. Ice making machine.

☐ Vertical traffic: dumbwaiters; elevators; escalators; subveyors; chutes for trash, garbage, linen, bottle breaking.

☐ Terminate in what space? Near receiving (shipping)? Near incinerator/trash room? Directly into compactor? Any raking or sorting desired? Space where? Linen sorting area? Access to elevator if necessary.

☐ Have ramps been eliminated wherever possible? If not possible to eliminate, is grade the minimum possible? (Should not exceed 3/4″ vertical for each foot horizontal.)

☐ Exterior signs, roof and/or road signs, flag poles?

☐ Garbage refrigerator, raking table, can wash, etc.?

☐ Incinerator? Comply with codes? Compactor perhaps better? Portable compactors?

☐ Dumpster or trash container park area required? Suitably camouflaged?

☐ First aid kits? Where located?

☐ Inside releases for walk-in refrigerators.

☐ Fly and insect control: fans; screens; insecticide dispensers; electronic/electric grids, lights.

☐ Kosher or special dietary areas or limitations. Extra china and flatware storage and inventories provided?

☐ Catering or carry-out storage.

☐ Phone booths located.

☐ Any vending machines (cigarettes, etc.)? Located? Electrical outlet specified? Adequate "shopping space" in front of machines? Space for waste receptacles. Adequate air conditioning or ventilation?

☐ Wheel chair ramps adjacent to conventional stairs for non-ambulatory guests?

☐ Waste can locations and specs for public spaces (even if no food in area) to help avoid "litter bugs"?

☐ Book match storage. Fireproof locker?

☐ Bingo prize storage.

☐ Any display, trolley table, side cooking? Aisle space adequate for traffic, carts, and trolley waiter?

☐ Refrigerated wine storage also used as display, merchandising? Adjacent to dining area entry?

☐ Are corridors free of protrusions (drinking fountains, fixtures, thermostats, etc.) to avoid collision by trucks or maid carts? Wall cladding?

☐ Clip-on ash trays for function/meeting room chairs.

EMPLOYEE FACILITIES

☐ Time clock and clock card racks.

☐ Eating facilities for employees: Cafeteria? Cook's table in kitchen?

☐ Locker facilities.

☐ Toilet or shower facilities adjacent to kitchen.

☐ Drinking fountains.

☐ Phone booths.

☐ Smoking area; recreation or off-duty area?

☐ Any segregated facilities?

☐ Storage (locked) for utensils or tools.

☐ Vending machines.

☐ Any dormitory or staff housing required? Now? Possible future?

☐ Security check station?

☐ Access to personnel office or hiring function, uniform issue.

☐ Transportation to/from work location. Any late shift problems?

UNION RESTRICTIONS AFFECTING DESIGN

☐ What waiter self-service allowed by locals? Coffee? Ice cream? Other beverage?

☐ Waiter bussing allowed? If so, presorting at soiled dish table, etc.?

☐ Can bartenders use glass washers? Sterilizers?

CODE RESTRICTIONS

☐ Compliance clause in specs?

☐ Allow chemical glass sterilizers?

☐ Garbage disposals allowed?

☐ Restrictions on incinerators? Compactors?

☐ Any hour restrictions on deliveries and pick-ups?

☐ Local liquor code permit sales at all times planned? License application adequately in advance of opening? More than one required? Any special "expediting" required?

SPECIFICATIONS FOR KITCHEN EQUIPMENT

Do specifications include who:

☐ Supplies item?

☐ Delivers to what point?

☐ Unloads truck?

☐ Handles inside building?

☐ Uncrates and sets in place?

☐ Makes final utility connections?

☐ Charges, adjusts, and places in operation (dish machines, refrigeration, revolving ovens, etc.)?

☐ Disposes of crating—removal from premises?

☐ Supplies accessories: plumbing brass and trim; hood lights and vapor proof covers; refrigerator lights; steam table pans, etc.; mixer bowls, attachments, etc.; shelving?

UTILITIES, MECHANICAL AND ELECTRICAL ITEMS

Ventilation

☐ Fan control point in kitchen (pilot lights to show when fan is running).

☐ Exhaust hoods, or down draft exhaust cowls (in addition to normal range and oven hoods) over: dish machine; pot washing; bains marie, stock kettles, steamers, silver washing; napkin steamer.

☐ Filters in hoods all same size (inventory simplification).

☐ Extra filters ordered (or specified) to install while one set being cleaned.

☐ Duct cleanouts: provided.

☐ Access doors in ducts.

☐ Access panels in hung ceilings to reach duct access doors.

☐ Drip line from dish machine exhaust duct to drain condensed moisture.

☐ Fire dampers required/desired in ducts?

☐ Be sure fans turned on after long shutdown (winter, etc.) before doing cleaning, setting up dining room, etc., to avoid dirt being distributed in cleaned rooms.

☐ Is hood gutter to be used for plaster ground for skirt or soffit?

☐ Are ducts to be painted and/or insulated? So specified?

☐ Is chef's office (or secretary's, steward's, room service order office, etc.) to be air conditioned? Specially ventilated?

☐ Any "air door" (air screen) at receiving entrance for insect prevention while permanent doors open during receiving?

☐ Screens on windows specified?

Electrical

☐ Any 440 or other unusual voltage equipment? If so, is 110 volt or low voltage provided or required for starting, holding, solenoids, controls, etc., in system? This applies particularly to dish machines, refrigeration, etc.

☐ Telephones located properly? Any intercom system?

☐ Does all equipment come with internal wiring and junction box mounted externally? If not, what arrangements required with electrician? Union problems?

☐ Convenience outlets (or junction box) adjacent to: coffee makers or urns for timers and/or pumps; freezer doors for heater strip (defrost); refrigerators (walk-in and reach-in) for lights and fans even if remote compressors; hoods; steamers for timers; dining room tables for table lamps; illuminated signs (including exit signs).

☐ Lights for hoods and walk-in refrigerators (vaporproof?).

☐ Any emergency lighting required or desired?

☐ Dimmers on dining, lounge or function area lights?

☐ Telephone jacks in dining areas? Elsewhere? Is there any place convenient for a guest who does not wish to talk in presence of other guests?

☐ Lighting specified for bar work board; bar cash register (so as not to detract from lounge decor); any bar front (guest side) accent lighting?

☐ A tape music system? Specified? Provided for in decorating scheme? Juke box or coin operated music required? Remote speakers and selector stations wiring shown? Paging system? Amusement machines?

☐ Illuminated signs for elevator foyers and/or elevator cabs?

☐ Taxi "call" light at doorman station.

Steam

☐ To ovens?

☐ Blow out lines *before* final connection of steam thermostats to avoid clogging of protective strainers.

☐ To hoods for fire protection? Quick lever opening valves? Properly trapped to avoid condensate accumulation before valve?

☐ For duct cleaning? To be installed in ducts?

Plumbing

☐ Floor drains adjacent to refrigerators and portable compactor stations. Other general purpose F.D.'s or floor sinks.

☐ Indirect wastes from steam tables, bains marie, etc., if desired and/or required by code.

☐ Is line to soda fountain from carbonator specified as stainless steel?

☐ Any pneumatic tubes (or carrierless [airmatic] pneumatic tubes) to be considered for kitchen orders and/or checks?

☐ Soap dispensers in rest rooms. (Is concealed tank and piping in plumbing specifications?) Discharge not directly over lavatory fittings (offset).

☐ Space for ash trays by urinals. Desired?

☐ Space for towel holders and waste receptacles. Specified?

☐ Water softeners and/or filters required?

☐ Juvenile size and level fixtures desired?

☐ Lighting adequate for mirror, sanitary areas.

☐ Plumbing facilities for handicapped guests.

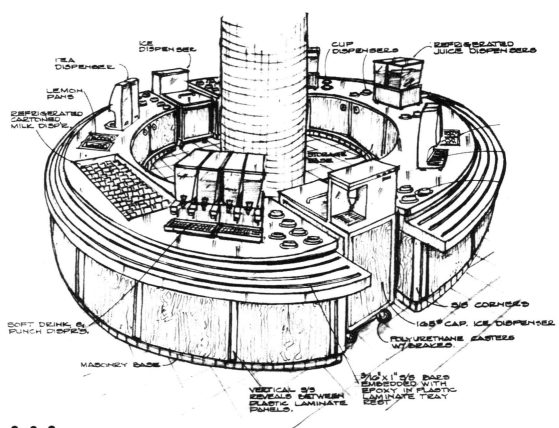

Selling...
with Pencil & Paper

by **H. G. Rice**

Simple to do, perspective sketches insure customer understanding, save designer time.

As with any design group, my associates and I are anxious to incorporate into our planning the thinking, and considerable talents, of the operators and dietitians in charge of the facilities we are designing. They, after all, will have the responsibility of using these facilities long after we, and other planners have gone.

But, by definition, these are skilled foodservice production and merchandising people. Not surprisingly, most of those we have worked with cannot easily read plans, and have trouble understanding elevations.

To overcome this common problem in communication, we have developed this "free hand" sketch method of presenting our prelimi-

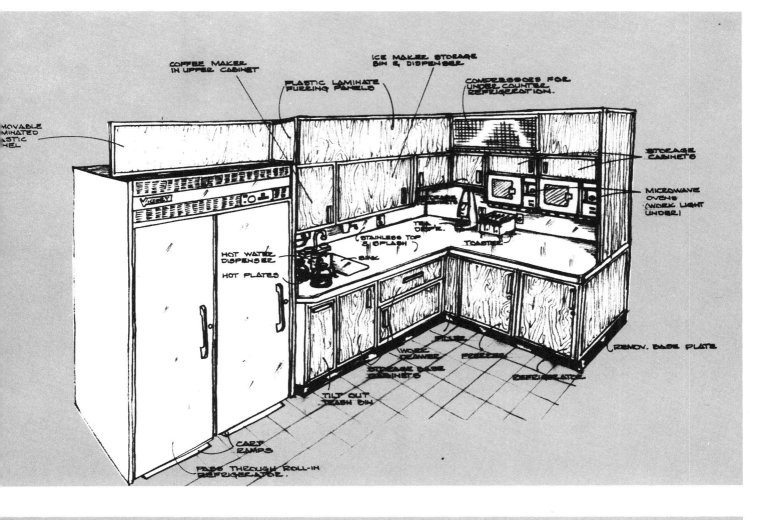

MOVABLE
LAMINATED
PLASTIC
PANEL

COFFEE MAKER
IN UPPER CABINET

PLASTIC LAMINATE
FURRING PANELS

ICE MAKER STORAGE
BIN & DISPENSER

COMPRESSORS FOR
UNDER COUNTER
REFRIGERATION.

STORAGE
CABINETS

MICROWAVE
OVENS
(WORK LIGHT
UNDER)

HOT WATER
DISPENSER

HOT PLATES

STAINLESS TOP
& SPLASH

TEA DIAPE.

TOASTER

SINK

WORK
CLEANER

FILLER

FREEZER

REMOV. BASE PLATE

STORAGE BASE
CABINETS

REFRIGERATOR

TILT OUT
TRASH BIN

CART
RAMPS

PASS THROUGH ROLL-IN
REFRIGERATOR.

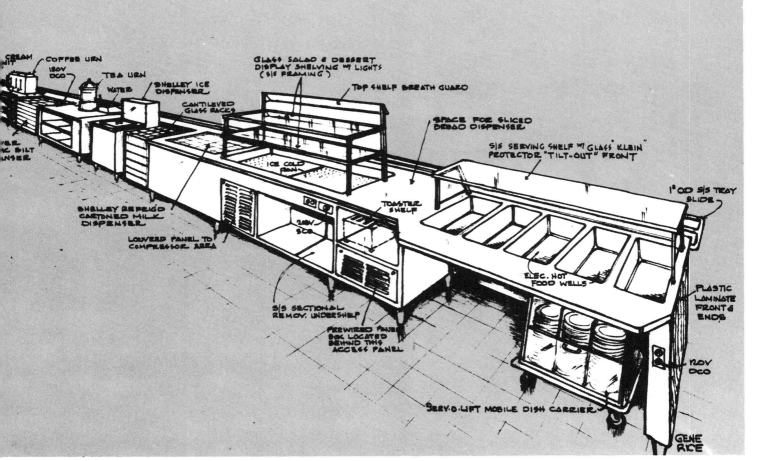

CREAM
UNIT

COFFEE URN

130V
DCO

TEA URN

WATER

SHELLEY ICE
DISPENSER

CANTILEVED
GLASS RACKS

GLASS SALAD & DESSERT
DISPLAY SHELVING W/ LIGHTS
(S/S FRAMING)

TOP SHELF BREATH GUARD

SPACE FOR SLICED
BREAD DISPENSER

S/S SERVING SHELF W/ GLASS "KLEIN"
PROTECTOR "TILT-OUT" FRONT

MILK
BILT
DENSER

ICE COLD
PAN

1" OD S/S TRAY
SLIDE

SHELLEY REFRIGD
CARTONED MILK
DISPENSER

LOUVERED PANEL TO
COMPRESSOR AREA

230V
SCO

TOASTER
SHELF

ELEC. HOT
FOOD WELLS

PLASTIC
LAMINATE
FRONT &
ENDS

S/S SECTIONAL
REMOV. UNDERSHELF

PREWIRED PANEL
BOX LOCATED
BEHIND THIS
ACCESS PANEL

120V
DCO

SERV-O-LIFT MOBILE DISH CARRIER

GENE
RICE

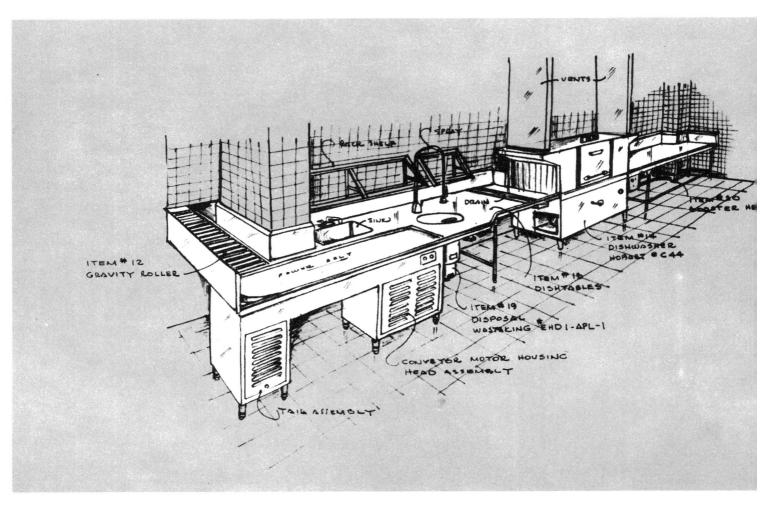

ITEM #12
GRAVITY ROLLER

POWER BELT

TAIL ASSEMBLY

CONVEYOR MOTOR HOUSING
HEAD ASSEMBLY

ITEM #19
DISPOSAL
WASTEKING EHD1-APL-1

SINK

DRAIN

BACK SHELF

SPRAY

VENTS

ITEM #18
DISHTABLES

ITEM #14
DISHWASHER
HOBART #C44

ITEM #20
BOOSTER HEATER

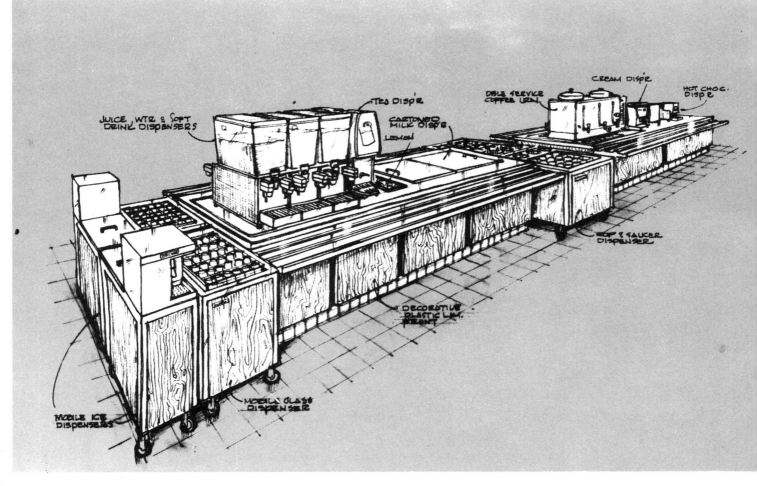

JUICE, WTR & SOFT
DRINK DISPENSERS

TEA DISP'R

CARTONED
MILK DISP'R

LEMON

TABLE SERVICE
COFFEE URN

CREAM DISP'R

HOT CHOC.
DISP'R

CUP & SAUCER
DISPENSER

DECORATIVE
PLASTIC LAM.
FRONT

MOBILE GLASS
DISPENSER

MOBILE ICE
DISPENSERS

Selling ...

nary concepts. To make these perfectly clear, the sketch sheet number is keyed to our plan with an arrow indicating the direction in which the view was taken.

By having these sketches available at preliminary design meetings, we find that everyone present can participate to a great degree, without any need for hesitancy. Because of this, significant progress can be made in finalizing plans ahead of schedule.

To the dietitian or operator, and their staffs, the sketches clearly indicate the proposed work stations and other arrangements, making it possible for them to freely comment and/or criticize. On the spot they can add or delete such items as drawers, overhead shelves, cabinets with doors, and the like, to suit their particular requirements.

Visually, they come to realize how the individual buy-out and custom items work and fit together. We thus avoid that dreadful moment that can come when the equipment is delivered and set in place, and the client takes the first look and says: "Oh! I didn't know it was going to look like that!"

A further advantage is early agreement. The food facility consultant utilizing this sketching method can introduce various system concepts into the early planning stages and get immediate "yes" or "no" answers from the client on those concepts; this allows him to proceed immediately. Too often, with plans alone, the client needs time to review and digest them slowly before committing himself to an answer.

We find making these sketches to be a simple matter. We use a pad of 12″ x 18″ tracing paper with a simple two-point perspective grid under the sheet we are working on,

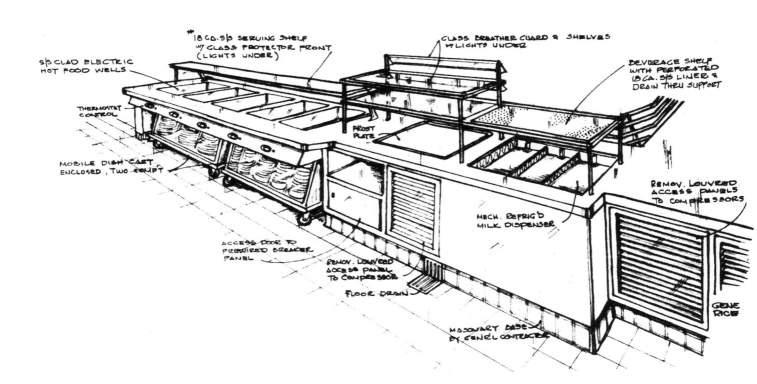

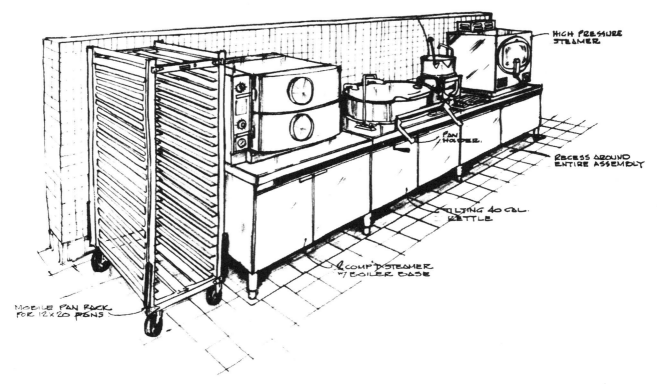

HIGH PRESSURE STEAMER

RECESS AROUND ENTIRE ASSEMBLY

PAN HOLDER.

TILTING 40 GAL. KETTLE

COMP'T STEAMER W/ BOILER BASE

MOBILE PAN RACK FOR 12 x 20 PANS

and just sketch away.

Our clients really like the presentations made in this way, and we very often get their complete approval at the first plan presentation, so again time is saved over conventional methods of presentation.

Further, the associate in our office who is to do the final contract documents (mechanicals, electricals, etc.) knows exactly what is contemplated. Here — in our "in-house" production time — we again realize substantial time savings.

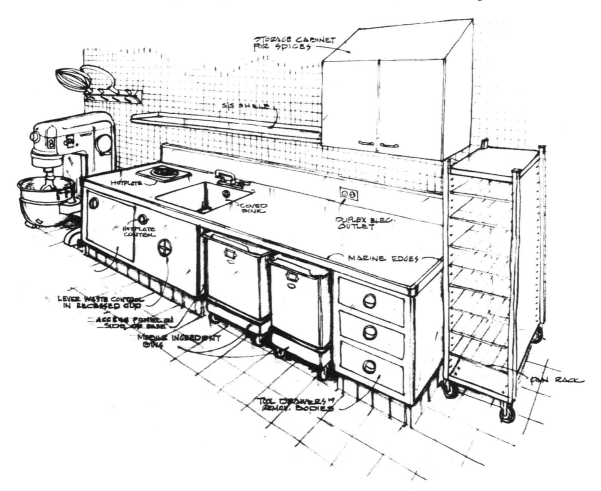

STORAGE CABINET FOR SPICES

S/S SHELF

HOTPLATE

COVED SINK

DUPLEX ELEC. OUTLET

MARINE EDGES

HOTPLATE CONTROL

PAN RACK

LEVER WASTE CONTROL IN RECESSED CUP

ACCESS PANEL AT SIDE OF BASE

MOBILE INGREDIENT BINS

TOOL DRAWERS W/ REMOV. BODIES

INDEX